HISTORY OF INDIA : SOCIAL AND ECONOMIC

HISTORY OF INDIA : SOCIAL AND ECONOMIC

R.N. Dhar

CYBER TECH PUBLICATIONS
4264/3, Ansari Road, Daryaganj, New Delhi-110002 (India)
Ph.: 011-23244078, 011-43559448 Fax: 011-23280028
E-Mail: cyberpublicationsdelhi@yahoo.com
Website: www.cybertechpublications.com

HISTORY OF INDIA : SOCIAL AND ECONOMIC

R.N. Dhar

First Edition 2010

Published by :

G.S. Rawat for **Cyber Tech Publications**
4264/3, Ansari Road, Daryaganj, New Delhi-110002 (India)
Ph.: 011-23244078, 011-43559448 Fax: 011-23280028
E-Mail: cyberpublicationsdelhi@yahoo.com
Website: www.cybertechpublications.com

Printed at: Asian Offset Printers, Delhi-53

Preface

The economic system of any country is geared to satisfy the unlimited wants of its people, using scarce resources, through organized group behaviour. Hence, human behaviour plays an important role in determining economic activity. Human behaviour in turn is influenced to a great extent by social institutions. Hence, the economic history of a people is obviously an aspect of their social history, and cannot be fully comprehended without reference to it. It is interwoven with the structure and norms of the social institutions of a country, and economic developments both influence and in turn are influenced by the social institutions. In short, economic development has both social causes and consequences.

Ancient and Medieval Characteristics: Though ancient India had a significant urban population, much of India's population resided in villages, whose economy was largely isolated and self-sustaining. Agriculture was the predominant occupation of the populace and satisfied a village's food requirements besides providing raw materials for hand based industries like textile, food processing and crafts. Besides farmers, other classes of people were barbers, carpenters, doctors (Ayurvedic practitioners), goldsmiths, weavers, etc.

Religion: Religion, especially Hinduism, played an influential role in shaping economic activities. The Indian caste system castes and sub-castes, despite its social fallbacks, functioned much like medieval European guilds, ensuring division of labour and provided for training of apprentices. The caste system restricted people from changing one's occupation and aspiring to an upper caste's lifestyle. Thus, a barber could not become a goldsmith and even a highly skilled carpenter could not aspire to the lifestyle or privileges enjoyed by a

Kshatriya. Kshatriya person of a warrior class. This barrier to mobility on labour restricted economic prosperity to a few castes.

Pilgrimage towns like Allahabad, Benares, Nasik, Puri, Orissa Puri, etc., mostly centred around rivers, developed into centres of trade and commerce. Religious functions, festivals and the practice of taking a pilgrimage resulted in a flourishing "pilgrimage economy"

The two social institutions on the basis of which Indian society has been organized since ancient times, are the Hindu Joint Family and the Cast System. Many scholars have put the blame for India's economic backwardness on the shoulders of these two institutions. However, a detailed analysis of their characteristics and the changes in them through the ages will reveal that these institutions have not determined economic growth, but have certainly influenced its form tempo.

—Author

CONTENTS

Preface

1. Introduction 1
2. Society and Religion 41
3. Culture and the Society 87
4. Caste and Class in Indian Society 124
5. The Economy of India 151
6. The Role of Government in the Economy 159
7. Agriculture and its Role in Economic Development 197
8. Government and Politics 222
9. The Social Setup and Politics 249

Bibliography 277

Index 279

1

INTRODUCTION

India's "great cycle of history," as Professor Hugh Tinker put it, entails repeating themes that continue to add complexity and diversity to the cultural matrix. Throughout its history, India has undergone innumerable episodes involving military conquests and integration, cultural infusion and assimilation, political unification and fragmentation, religious toleration and conflict, and communal harmony and violence. A few other regions in the world also can claim such a vast and differentiated historical experience, but Indian civilization seems to have endured the trials of time the longest. India has proven its remarkable resilience and its innate ability to reconcile opposing elements from many indigenous and foreign cultures. Unlike the West, where modern political developments and industrialization have created a more secular worldview with redefined roles and values for individuals and families, India remains largely a traditional society, in which change seems only superficial. Although India is the world's largest democracy and the seventh-most industrialized country in the world, the underpinnings of India's civilization stem primarily from its own social structure, religious beliefs, philosophical outlook, and cultural values. The continuity of those time-honed traditional ways of life has provided unique and fascinating patterns in the tapestry of contemporary Indian civilization.

The earliest imprints of human activities in India go back to the Paleolithic Age, roughly between 400,000 and 200,000 B.C. Stone implements and cave paintings from this period have been discovered in many parts of the South Asia. Evidence of domestication of animals, the adoption of agriculture, permanent village settlements, and wheel-turned pottery dating from the middle of the sixth millennium B.C. has been found in the foothills of Sindh and Baluchistan (or Balochistan in current Pakistani usage), both in present-day Pakistan. One of the first great civilizations—with a writing system, urban centers, and a diversified social and economic system—appeared around 3,000 B.C. along the Indus River valley in Punjab and Sindh. It covered more than 800,000 square kilometers, from the borders of Baluchistan to the deserts of Rajasthan, from the Himalayan foothills to the southern tip of Gujarat. The remnants of two major cities—Mohenjo-daro and Harappa—reveal remarkable engineering feats of uniform urban planning and carefully executed layout, water supply, and drainage. Excavations at these sites and later archaeological digs at about seventy other locations in India and Pakistan provide a composite picture of what is now generally known as Harappan culture (2500-1600 B.C.).

The major cities contained a few large buildings including a citadel, a large bath—perhaps for personal and communal ablution—differentiated living quarters, flat-roofed brick houses, and fortified administrative or religious centers enclosing meeting halls and granaries. Essentially a city culture, Harappan life was supported by extensive agricultural production and by commerce, which included trade with Sumer in southern Mesopotamia (modern Iraq). The people made tools and weapons from copper and bronze but not iron. Cotton was woven and dyed for clothing; wheat, rice, and a variety of vegetables and fruits were cultivated; and a number of animals, including the humped bull, were domesticated. Harappan culture was conservative and remained relatively unchanged for centuries; whenever cities were rebuilt after periodic flooding, the new level of construction closely followed the previous pattern. Although stability, regularity, and conservatism seem to have been the hallmarks of this people, it is unclear who wielded authority, whether an aristocratic, priestly, or commercial minority.

By far the most exquisite but most obscure Harappan artifacts unearthed to date are steatite seals found in abundance at Mohenjo-daro. These small, flat, and mostly square objects with human or animal motifs provide the most accurate picture there is of Harappan life. They also have inscriptions generally thought to be in the Harappan script, which has eluded scholarly attempts at deciphering it. Debate abounds as to whether the script represents numbers or an alphabet, and, if an alphabet, whether it is proto-Dravidian or proto-Sanskrit.

The possible reasons for the decline of Harappan civilization have long troubled scholars. Invaders from central and western Asia are considered by some historians to have been the "destroyers" of Harappan cities, but this view is open to reinterpretation. More plausible explanations are recurrent floods caused by tectonic earth movement, soil salinity, and desertification. A series of migrations by Indo-European-speaking seminomads took place during the second millennium B.C. Known as Aryans, these preliterate pastoralists spoke an early form of Sanskrit, which has close philological similarities to other Indo-European languages, such as Avestan in Iran and ancient Greek and Latin. The term *Aryan* meant pure and implied the invaders' conscious attempts at retaining their tribal identity and roots while maintaining a social distance from earlier inhabitants.

Although archaeology has not yielded proof of the identity of the Aryans, the evolution and spread of their culture across the Indo-Gangetic Plain is generally undisputed. Modern knowledge of the early stages of this process rests on a body of sacred texts: the four Vedas (collections of hymns, prayers, and liturgy), the Brahmanas and the Upanishads (commentaries on Vedic rituals and philosophical treatises), and the Puranas (traditional mythic-historical works). The sanctity accorded to these texts and the manner of their preservation over several millennia—by an unbroken oral tradition—make them part of the living Hindu tradition.

These sacred texts offer guidance in piecing together Aryan beliefs and activities. The Aryans were a pantheistic people, following their tribal chieftain or raja, engaging in wars with each other or with other alien ethnic groups, and slowly becoming settled agriculturalists with consolidated territories and differentiated occupations. Their skills in using horse-drawn chariots and their knowledge of astronomy and mathematics gave them a military and technological advantage that led others to accept their social customs and religious beliefs. By around 1,000 B.C., Aryan culture had spread over most of India north of the Vindhya Range and in the process assimilated much from other cultures that preceded it.

The Aryans brought with them a new language, a new pantheon of anthropomorphic gods, a patrilineal and patriarchal family system, and a new social order, built on the religious and philosophical rationales of *varnashramadharma.* Although precise translation into English is difficult, the concept *varnashramadharma* , the bedrock of Indian traditional social organization, is built on three fundamental notions: *varna* (originally, "color," but later taken to mean social class), *ashrama* (stages of life such as youth, family life, detachment from the material world, and renunciation), and dharma (duty, righteousness, or sacred cosmic law). The underlying belief is that present happiness and future salvation are contingent upon one's ethical or moral conduct; therefore, both society and individuals are expected to pursue a diverse but righteous path deemed appropriate for everyone based on one's birth, age, and station in life. The original three-tiered society—Brahman (priest; .), Kshatriya (warrior), and Vaishya (commoner)—eventually expanded into four in order to absorb the subjugated people—Shudra (servant)—or even five, when the outcaste peoples are considered.

The basic unit of Aryan society was the extended and patriarchal family. A cluster of related families constituted a village, while several villages formed a tribal unit. Child marriage, as practiced in later eras, was uncommon, but the partners' involvement in the selection of a mate and dowry and bride-price were customary. The birth of a son was welcome because he could later tend the herds, bring honor in battle, offer sacrifices to the gods, and inherit property and pass on the family name. Monogamy was widely accepted although polygamy was not unknown, and even polyandry is mentioned in later writings. Ritual suicide of widows was expected at a husband's death, and this might have been the beginning of the practice known as sati in later centuries, when the widow actually burnt herself on her husband's funeral pyre.

Permanent settlements and agriculture led to trade and other occupational differentiation. As lands along the Ganga (or Ganges) were cleared, the river became a trade route, the numerous settlements on its banks acting as markets. Trade was restricted initially to local areas, and barter was an essential component of trade, cattle being the unit of value in large-scale transactions, which further limited the geographical reach of the trader. Custom was law, and kings and chief priests were the arbiters, perhaps advised by certain elders of the community. An Aryan raja, or king, was primarily a military leader, who took a share from the booty after successful cattle raids or battles. Although the rajas had managed to assert their authority, they scrupulously avoided conflicts with priests as a group, whose knowledge and austere religious life surpassed others in the community, and the rajas compromised their own interests with those of the priests.

From their original settlements in the Punjab region, the Aryans gradually began to penetrate eastward, clearing dense forests and establishing "tribal" settlements along the Ganga and Yamuna (Jamuna) plains between 1500 and ca. 800 B.C. By around 500 B.C., most of northern India was inhabited and had been brought under cultivation, facilitating the increasing knowledge of the use of iron implements, including ox-drawn plows, and spurred by the growing population that provided voluntary and forced labor. As riverine and inland trade flourished, many towns along the Ganga became centers of trade, culture, and luxurious living. Increasing population and surplus production provided the bases for the emergence of independent states with fluid territorial boundaries over which disputes frequently arose.

The rudimentary administrative system headed by tribal chieftains was transformed by a number of regional republics or hereditary monarchies that devised ways to appropriate revenue and to conscript labor for expanding the areas of settlement and agriculture farther east and south, beyond the Narmada River. These emergent states collected revenue through officials, maintained armies, and built new cities and highways. By 600 B.C., sixteen such territorial powers—including the Magadha, Kosala, Kuru, and Gandhara—stretched across the North India plains from modern-day Afghanistan to Bangladesh. The right of a king to his throne, no matter how it was gained, was usually legitimized through elaborate sacrifice rituals and genealogies concocted by priests who ascribed to the king divine or superhuman origins.

The victory of good over evil is epitomized in the epic *Ramayana* (The Travels of Rama, or Ram in the preferred modern form), while another epic, *Mahabharata* (Great Battle of the Descendants of Bharata), spells out the concept of dharma and duty. More than 2,500 years later, Mohandas Karamchand (Mahatma) Gandhi, the father of modern India, used these concepts in the fight for independence. The *Mahabharata* records the feud between Aryan cousins that culminated in an epic battle in which both gods and mortals from many lands allegedly fought to the death, and the *Ramayana* recounts the kidnapping of Sita, Rama's wife, by Ravana, a demonic king of Lanka (Sri Lanka), her rescue by her husband (aided by his animal allies), and Rama's coronation, leading to a period of prosperity and justice. In the late twentieth century, these epics remain dear to the hearts of Hindus and are commonly read and enacted in many settings. In the 1980s and 1990s, Ram's story has been exploited by Hindu militants and politicians to gain power, and the much disputed Ramjanmabhumi, the birth site of Ram, has become an extremely sensitive communal issue, potentially pitting Hindu majority against Muslim minority.

THE MAURYAN EMPIRE

By the end of the sixth century B.C., India's northwest was integrated into the Persian Achaemenid Empire and became one of its satrapies. This integration marked the beginning of administrative contacts between Central Asia and India. Although Indian accounts to a large extent ignored Alexander the Great's Indus campaign in 326 B.C., Greek writers recorded their impressions of the general conditions prevailing in South Asia during this period. Thus, the year 326 B.C. provides the first clear and historically verifiable date in Indian history. A two-way cultural fusion between several Indo-Greek elements—especially in art, architecture, and coinage—occurred in the next several hundred years. North India's political landscape was transformed by the emergence of Magadha in the eastern Indo-Gangetic Plain. In 322 B.C., Magadha, under the rule of Chandragupta Maurya, began to assert its hegemony over neighboring areas. Chandragupta, who ruled from 324 to 301 B.C., was the architect of the first Indian imperial power—the Mauryan Empire (326-184 B.C.)—whose capital was Pataliputra, near modern-day Patna, in Bihar.

Situated on rich alluvial soil and near mineral deposits, especially iron, Magadha was at the center of bustling commerce and trade. The capital was a city of magnificent palaces, temples, a university, a library, gardens, and parks, as reported by Megasthenes, the third-century B.C. Greek historian and ambassador to the Mauryan court. Legend states that Chandragupta's success was due in large measure to his adviser Kautilya, the Brahman author of the *Arthashastra* (Science of Material Gain), a textbook that outlined governmental administration and political strategy. There was a highly centralized and hierarchical government with a large staff, which regulated tax collection, trade and commerce, industrial arts, mining, vital statistics, welfare of foreigners, maintenance of public places including markets and temples, and prostitutes. A large standing army and a well-developed espionage system were maintained. The empire was divided into provinces, districts, and villages governed by a host of centrally appointed local officials, who replicated the functions of the central administration.

Ashoka, grandson of Chandragupta, ruled from 269 to 232 B.C. and was one of India's most illustrious rulers. Ashoka's inscriptions chiseled on rocks and stone pillars located at strategic locations throughout his empire—such as Lampaka (Laghman in modern Afghanistan), Mahastan (in modern Bangladesh), and Brahmagiri (in Karnataka)—constitute the second set of datable historical records. According to some of the inscriptions, in the aftermath of the carnage resulting from his campaign against the powerful kingdom of Kalinga (modern Orissa), Ashoka renounced bloodshed and pursued a policy of nonviolence or ahimsa, espousing a theory of rule by righteousness. His toleration for different religious beliefs and languages reflected the realities of India's regional pluralism although he personally seems to have followed Buddhism. Early Buddhist stories assert that he convened a Buddhist council at his capital, regularly undertook tours within his realm, and sent Buddhist missionary ambassadors to Sri Lanka.

Contacts established with the Hellenistic world during the reign of Ashoka's predecessors served him well. He sent diplomatic-cum-religious missions to the rulers of Syria, Macedonia, and Epirus, who learned about India's religious traditions, especially Buddhism. India's northwest retained many Persian cultural elements, which might explain Ashoka's rock inscriptions—such inscriptions were commonly associated with Persian rulers. Ashoka's Greek and Aramaic inscriptions found in Kandahar in Afghanistan may also reveal his desire to maintain ties with people outside of India.

After the disintegration of the Mauryan Empire in the second century B.C., South Asia became a collage of regional powers with overlapping boundaries. India's unguarded northwestern border again attracted a series of invaders between 200 B.C. and A.D. 300. As the Aryans had done, the invaders became "Indianized" in the process of their conquest and settlement. Also, this period witnessed remarkable intellectual and artistic achievements inspired by cultural diffusion and syncretism. The Indo-Greeks, or the Bactrians, of the northwest contributed to the development of numismatics; they were followed by another group, the Shakas (or Scythians), from the steppes of Central Asia, who settled in western India. Still other nomadic people, the Yuezhi, who were forced out of the Inner Asian steppes of Mongolia, drove the Shakas out of northwestern

India and established the Kushana Kingdom (first century B.C.-third century A.D.). The Kushana Kingdom controlled parts of Afghanistan and Iran, and in India the realm stretched from Purushapura (modern Peshawar, Pakistan) in the northwest, to Varanasi (Uttar Pradesh) in the east, and to Sanchi (Madhya Pradesh) in the south. For a short period, the kingdom reached still farther east, to Pataliputra. The Kushana Kingdom was the crucible of trade among the Indian, Persian, Chinese, and Roman empires and controlled a critical part of the legendary Silk Road. Kanishka, who reigned for two decades starting around A.D. 78, was the most noteworthy Kushana ruler. He converted to Buddhism and convened a great Buddhist council in Kashmir. The Kushanas were patrons of Gandharan art, a synthesis between Greek and Indian styles, and Sanskrit literature. They initiated a new era called Shaka in A.D. 78, and their calendar, which was formally recognized by India for civil purposes starting on March 22, 1957, is still in use.

THE DECCAN AND THE SOUTH

During the Kushana Dynasty, an indigenous power, the Satavahana Kingdom (first century B.C.-third century A.D.), rose in the Deccan in southern India. The Satavahana, or Andhra, Kingdom was considerably influenced by the Mauryan political model, although power was decentralized in the hands of local chieftains, who used the symbols of Vedic religion and upheld the *varnashramadharma.* The rulers, however, were eclectic and patronized Buddhist monuments, such as those in Ellora (Maharashtra) and Amaravati (Andhra Pradesh). Thus, the Deccan served as a bridge through which politics, trade, and religious ideas could spread from the north to the south.

Farther south were three ancient Tamil kingdoms—Chera (on the west), Chola (on the east), and Paṅdya (in the south)—frequently involved in internecine warfare to gain regional supremacy. They are mentioned in Greek and Ashokan sources as lying at the fringes of the Mauryan Empire. A corpus of ancient Tamil literature, known as Sangam (academy) works, including *Tolkappiam* , a manual of

Tamil grammar by Tolkappiyar, provides much useful information about their social life from 300 B.C. to A.D. 200. There is clear evidence of encroachment by Aryan traditions from the north into a predominantly indigenous Dravidian culture in transition.

Dravidian social order was based on different ecoregions rather than on the Aryan *varna* paradigm, although the Brahmans had a high status at a very early stage. Segments of society were characterized by matriarchy and matrilineal succession—which survived well into the nineteenth century—cross-cousin marriage, and strong regional identity. Tribal chieftains emerged as "kings" just as people moved from pastoralism toward agriculture, sustained by irrigation based on rivers, small-scale tanks (as man-made ponds are called in India) and wells, and brisk maritime trade with Rome and Southeast Asia.

Discoveries of Roman gold coins in various sites attest to extensive South Indian links with the outside world. As with Pataliputra in the northeast and Taxila in the northwest (in modern Pakistan), the city of Madurai, the Pandyan capital (in modern Tamil Nadu), was the center of intellectual and literary activities. Poets and bards assembled there under royal patronage at successive concourses and composed anthologies of poems, most of which have been lost. By the end of the first century B.C., South Asia was crisscrossed by overland trade routes, which facilitated the movements of Buddhist and Jain missionaries and other travelers and opened the area to a synthesis of many cultures.

GUPTA AND HARSHA

The Classical Age refers to the period when most of North India was reunited under the Gupta Empire (ca. A.D. 320-550). Because of the relative peace, law and order, and extensive cultural achievements during this period, it has been described as a "golden age" that crystallized the elements of what is generally known as Hindu culture with all its variety, contradiction, and synthesis. The golden age was confined to the north, and the classical patterns began to spread south only after the Gupta Empire had vanished from the historical scene. The military exploits of the first three rulers—Chandragupta I (ca. 319-335), Samudragupta (ca. 335-376), and Chandragupta II (ca. 376-415)—brought all of North India under their leadership. From Pataliputra, their capital, they sought to retain political preeminence as much by pragmatism and judicious marriage alliances as by military strength. Despite their self-conferred titles, their overlordship was threatened and by 500 ultimately ruined by the Hunas (a branch of the White Huns emanating from Central Asia), who were yet another group in the long succession of ethnically and culturally different outsiders drawn into India and then woven into the hybrid Indian fabric.

Under Harsha Vardhana (or Harsha, r. 606-47), North India was reunited briefly, but neither the Guptas nor Harsha controlled a centralized state, and their administrative styles rested on the collaboration of regional and local officials for administering their rule rather than on centrally appointed personnel. The Gupta period marked a watershed of Indian culture: the Guptas performed Vedic sacrifices to legitimize their rule, but they also patronized Buddhism, which continued to provide an alternative to Brahmanical orthodoxy.

The most significant achievements of this period, however, were in religion, education, mathematics, art, and Sanskrit literature and drama. The religion that later developed into modern Hinduism witnessed a crystallization of its components: major sectarian deities, image worship, devotionalism, and the importance of the temple. Education included grammar, composition, logic, metaphysics, mathematics, medicine, and astronomy. These subjects became highly specialized and reached an advanced level. The Indian numeral system—sometimes erroneously attributed to the Arabs, who took it from India to Europe where it replaced the Roman system—and the decimal system are Indian inventions of this period. Aryabhatta's expositions on astronomy in 499, moreover, gave calculations of the solar year and the shape and movement of astral bodies with remarkable accuracy. In medicine, Charaka and Sushruta wrote about a fully evolved system, resembling those of Hippocrates and Galen in Greece. Although progress in physiology and biology was hindered by religious injunctions against contact with dead bodies, which discouraged dissection and anatomy, Indian physicians excelled in pharmacopoeia, caesarean section, bone setting, and skin grafting.

THE SOUTHERN RIVALS

When Gupta disintegration was complete, the classical patterns of civilization continued to thrive not only in the middle Ganga Valley and the kingdoms that emerged on the heels of Gupta demise but also in the Deccan and in South India, which acquired a more prominent place in history. In fact, from the mid-seventh to the mid-thirteenth centuries, regionalism was the dominant theme of political or dynastic history of South Asia. Three features, as political scientist Radha Champakalakshmi has noted, commonly characterize the sociopolitical realities of this period. First, the spread of Brahmanical religions was a two-way process of Sanskritization of local cults and localization of Brahmanical social order. Second was the ascendancy of the Brahman priestly and landowning groups that later dominated regional institutions and political developments. Third, because of the seesawing of numerous dynasties that had a remarkable ability to survive perennial military attacks, regional kingdoms faced frequent defeats but seldom total annihilation.

Peninsular India was involved in an eighth-century tripartite power struggle among the Chalukyas (556-757) of Vatapi, the Pallavas (300-888) of Kanchipuram, and the Pandyas (seventh through the tenth centuries) of Madurai. The Chalukya rulers were overthrown by their subordinates, the Rashtrakutas, who ruled from 753 to 973. Although both the Pallava and Pandya kingdoms were enemies, the real struggle for political domination was between the Pallava and Chalukya realms.

Despite interregional conflicts, local autonomy was preserved to a far greater degree in the south where it had prevailed for centuries. The absence of a highly centralized government was associated with a corresponding local autonomy in the administration of villages and districts. Extensive and well-documented overland and maritime trade flourished with the Arabs on the west coast and with Southeast Asia. Trade facilitated cultural diffusion in Southeast

Asia, where local elites selectively but willingly adopted Indian art, architecture, literature, and social customs.

The interdynastic rivalry and seasonal raids into each other's territory notwithstanding, the rulers in the Deccan and South India patronized all three religions—Buddhism, Hinduism, and Jainism. The religions vied with each other for royal favor, expressed in land grants but more importantly in the creation of monumental temples, which remain architectural wonders. The cave temples of Elephanta Island (near Bombay, or Mumbai in Marathi), Ajanta, and Ellora (in Maharashtra), and structural temples of Kanchipuram (in Tamil Nadu) are enduring legacies of otherwise warring regional rulers. By the mid-seventh century, Buddhism and Jainism began to decline as sectarian Hindu devotional cults of Shiva and Vishnu vigorously competed for popular support.

Although Sanskrit was the language of learning and theology in South India, as it was in the north, the growth of the *bhakti* (devotional) movements enhanced the crystallization of vernacular literature in all four major Dravidian languages: Tamil, Telugu, Malayalam, and Kannada; they often borrowed themes and vocabulary from Sanskrit but preserved much local cultural lore. Examples of Tamil literature include two major poems, *Cilappatikaram* (The Jewelled Anklet) and *Manimekalai* (The Jewelled Belt); the body of devotional literature of Shaivism and Vaishnavism—Hindu devotional movements; and the reworking of the *Ramayana* by Kamban in the twelfth century. A nationwide cultural synthesis had taken place with a minimum of common characteristics in the various regions of South Asia, but the process of cultural infusion and assimilation would continue to shape and influence India's history through the centuries.

THE COMING OF ISLAM

Islam was propagated by the Prophet Muhammad during the early seventh century in the deserts of Arabia. Less than a century after its inception, Islam's presence was felt throughout the Middle East, North Africa, Spain, Iran, and Central Asia. Arab military forces conquered the Indus Delta region in Sindh in 711 and established an Indo-Muslim state there. Sindh became an Islamic outpost where Arabs established trade links with the Middle East and were later joined by teachers or sufis , but Arab influence was hardly felt in the rest of South Asia. By the end of the tenth century, dramatic changes took place when the Central Asian Turkic tribes accepted both the message and mission of Islam. These warlike people first began to move into Afghanistan and Iran and later into India through the northwest. Mahmud of Ghazni (971-1030), who was also known as the "Sword of Islam," mounted seventeen plundering expeditions between 997 and 1027 into North India, annexing Punjab as his eastern province. The invaders' effective use of the crossbow while at a gallop gave them a decisive advantage over their Indian opponents, the Rajputs. Mahmud's conquest of Punjab foretold ominous consequences for the rest of India, but the Rajputs appear to have been both unprepared and unwilling to change their military tactics, which ultimately collapsed in the face of the swift and punitive cavalry of the Afghans and Turkic peoples.

In the thirteenth century, Shams-ud-Din Iletmish (or Iltutmish; r. 1211-36), a former slave-warrior, established a Turkic kingdom in Delhi, which enabled future sultans to push in every direction; within the next 100 years, the Delhi Sultanate extended its sway east to Bengal and south to the Deccan, while the sultanate itself experienced repeated threats from the northwest and internal revolts from displeased, independent-minded nobles. The sultanate was in constant flux as five dynasties rose and fell: Mamluk or Slave (1206-90), Khalji (1290-1320), Tughluq (1320-1413), Sayyid (1414-51), and Lodi (1451-1526). The Khalji Dynasty under Ala-ud-Din (r. 1296-1315) succeeded in bringing most of South India under its control for a time, although conquered areas broke away quickly. Power in Delhi was often gained by violence—nineteen of the thirty-five sultans were assassinated—and was legitimized by reward for tribal loyalty. Factional rivalries and court intrigues were as numerous as they were treacherous; territories controlled by the sultan expanded and shrank depending on his personality and fortunes.

Both the Quran and sharia (Islamic law) provided the basis for enforcing Islamic administration over the independent Hindu rulers, but the sultanate made only fitful progress in the beginning, when many campaigns were undertaken for plunder and temporary reduction of fortresses. The effective rule of a sultan depended largely on his ability to control the strategic places that dominated the military highways and trade routes, extract the annual land tax, and maintain personal authority over military and provincial governors. Sultan Ala-ud-Din made an attempt to reassess, systematize, and unify land revenues and urban taxes and to institute a highly centralized system of administration over his realm, but his efforts were abortive. Although agriculture in North India improved as a result of new canal construction and irrigation methods, including what came to be known as the Persian wheel, prolonged political instability and parasitic methods of tax collection brutalized the peasantry. Yet trade and a market economy, encouraged by the free-spending habits of the aristocracy, acquired new impetus both inland and overseas. Experts in metalwork, stonework, and textile manufacture responded to the new patronage with enthusiasm.

SOUTHERN DYNASTIES

The sultans' failure to hold securely the Deccan and South India resulted in the rise of competing southern dynasties: the Muslim Bahmani Sultanate (1347-1527) and the Hindu Vijayanagar Empire (1336-1565). Zafar Khan, a former provincial governor under the Tughluqs, revolted against his Turkic overlord and proclaimed himself sultan, taking the title Ala-ud-Din Bahman Shah in 1347. The Bahmani Sultanate, located in the northern Deccan, lasted for almost two centuries, until it fragmented into five smaller states in 1527. The Bahmani Sultanate adopted the patterns established by the Delhi overlords in tax collection and administration, but its downfall was caused in large measure by the competition and hatred between *deccani* (domiciled Muslim immigrants and local converts) and *paradesi* (foreigners or officials in temporary service). The Bahmani Sultanate initiated a process of cultural synthesis visible in Hyderabad, where cultural flowering is still expressed in vigorous schools of *deccani* architecture and painting.

Founded in 1336, the empire of Vijayanagar (named for its capital Vijayanagar, "City of Victory," in present-day Karnataka) expanded rapidly toward Madurai in the south and Goa in the west and exerted intermittent control over the east coast and the extreme southwest. Vijayanagar rulers closely followed Chola precedents, especially in collecting agricultural and trade revenues, in giving encouragement to commercial guilds, and in honoring temples with lavish endowments. Added revenue needed for waging war against the Bahmani sultans was raised by introducing a set of taxes on commercial enterprises, professions, and industries. Political rivalry between the Bahmani and the Vijayanagar rulers involved control over the Krishna-Tunghabadhra river basin, which shifted hands depending on whose military was superior at any given time. The Vijayanagar rulers' capacity for gaining victory over their enemies was contingent on ensuring a constant supply of horses—initially through Arab traders but later through the Portuguese—and maintaining internal roads and communication networks. Merchant guilds enjoyed a wide sphere of operation and were able to offset the power of landlords and Brahmans in court politics. Commerce and shipping eventually passed largely into the hands of foreigners, and special facilities and tax concessions were provided for them by the ruler. Arabs and Portuguese competed for influence and control of west coast ports, and, in 1510, Goa passed into Portuguese possession.

The city of Vijayanagar itself contained numerous temples with rich ornamentation, especially the gateways, and a cluster of shrines for the deities. Most prominent among the temples was the one dedicated to Virupaksha, a manifestation of Shiva, the patron-deity of the Vijayanagar rulers. Temples continued to be the nuclei of diverse cultural and intellectual activities, but these activities were based more on tradition than on contemporary political realities. (However, the first Vijayanagar ruler—Harihara I—was a Hindu who converted to Islam and then reconverted to Hinduism for political expediency.) The temples sponsored no intellectual exchange with Islamic theologians because Muslims were generally assigned to an "impure" status and were thus excluded from entering temples. When the five rulers of what was once the Bahmani Sultanate combined their forces and attacked Vijayanagar in 1565, the empire crumbled at the Battle of Talikot.

THE MUGHALS

In the early sixteenth century, descendants of the Mongol, Turkish, Iranian, and Afghan invaders of South Asia—the Mughals—invaded India under the leadership of Zahir-ud-Din Babur. Babur was the great-grandson of Timur Lenk (Timur the Lame, from which the Western name Tamerlane is derived), who had invaded India and plundered Delhi in 1398 and then led a short-lived empire based in Samarkand (in modern-day Uzbekistan) that united Persian-based Mongols (Babur's maternal ancestors) and other West Asian peoples. Babur was driven from Samarkand and initially established his rule in Kabul in 1504; he later became the first Mughal ruler (1526-30). His determination was to expand eastward into Punjab, where he had made a number of forays. Then an invitation from an opportunistic Afghan chief in Punjab brought him to the very heart of the Delhi Sultanate, ruled by Ibrahim Lodi (1517-26). Babur, a seasoned military commander, entered India in 1526 with his well-trained veteran army of 12,000 to meet the sultan's huge but unwieldy and disunited force of more than 100,000 men. Babur defeated the Lodi sultan decisively at Panipat (in modern-day Haryana, about ninety kilometers north of Delhi). Employing gun carts, moveable artillery, and superior cavalry tactics, Babur achieved a resounding victory. A year later, he decisively defeated a Rajput confederacy led by Rana Sangha. In 1529 Babur routed the joint forces of Afghans and the sultan of Bengal but died in 1530 before he could consolidate his military gains. He left behind as legacies his memoirs (*Babur Namah*), several beautiful gardens in Kabul, Lahore, and Agra, and descendants who would fulfill his dream of establishing an empire in Hindustan.

When Babur died, his son Humayun (1530-56), also a soldier, inherited a difficult task. He was pressed from all sides by a reassertion of Afghan claims to the Delhi throne, by disputes over his own succession, and by the Afghan-Rajput march into Delhi in 1540. He fled to Persia, where he spent nearly ten years as an embarrassed guest at the Safavid court. In 1545 he gained a foothold in Kabul, reasserted his Indian claim, defeated Sher Khan Sur, the most powerful Afghan ruler, and took control of Delhi in 1555.

Humayun's untimely death in 1556 left the task of further imperial conquest and consolidation to his thirteen-year-old son, Jalal-ud-Din Akbar (r. 1556-1605). Following a decisive military victory at the Second Battle of Panipat in 1556, the regent Bayram Khan pursued a vigorous policy of expansion on Akbar's behalf. As soon as Akbar came of age, he began to free himself from the influences of overbearing ministers, court factions, and harem intrigues, and demonstrated his own capacity for judgment and leadership. A "workaholic" who seldom slept more than three hours a night, he personally oversaw the implementation of his administrative policies, which were to form the backbone of the Mughal Empire for more than 200 years. He continued to conquer, annex, and consolidate a far-flung territory bounded by Kabul in the northwest, Kashmir in the north, Bengal in the east, and beyond the Narmada River in the south—an area comparable in size to the Mauryan territory some 1,800 years earlier.

Akbar built a walled capital called Fatehpur Sikri (Fatehpur means Fortress of Victory) near Agra, starting in 1571. Palaces for each of Akbar's senior queens, a huge artificial lake, and sumptuous water-filled courtyards were built there. The city, however, proved short-lived, perhaps because the water supply was insufficient or of poor quality, or, as some historians believe, Akbar had to attend to the northwest areas of his empire and simply moved his capital for political reasons. Whatever the reason, in 1585 the capital was relocated to Lahore and in 1599 to Agra.

Akbar adopted two distinct but effective approaches in administering a large territory and incorporating various ethnic groups into the service of his realm. In 1580 he obtained local revenue statistics for the previous decade in order to understand details of productivity and price fluctuation of different crops. Aided by Todar Mal, a Rajput king, Akbar issued a revenue schedule that the peasantry could tolerate while providing maximum profit for the state. Revenue demands, fixed according to local conventions of cultivation and quality of soil, ranged from one-third to one-half of the crop and were paid in cash. Akbar relied heavily on land-holding zamindars. They used their considerable local knowledge and influence to collect revenue and to transfer it to the treasury, keeping a portion in return for services rendered. Within his administrative system, the warrior aristocracy (*mansabdars*) held ranks (*mansabs*) expressed in numbers of troops, and indicating pay, armed contingents, and obligations. The warrior aristocracy was generally paid from revenues of nonhereditary and transferrable *jagirs* (revenue villages).

An astute ruler who genuinely appreciated the challenges of administering so vast an empire, Akbar introduced a policy of reconciliation and assimilation of Hindus (including Maryam al-Zamani, the Hindu Rajput mother of his son and heir, Jahangir), who represented the majority of the population. He recruited and rewarded Hindu chiefs with the highest ranks in government; encouraged intermarriages between Mughal and Rajput aristocracy; allowed new temples to be built; personally participated in celebrating Hindu festivals such as Dipavali, or Diwali, the festival of lights; and abolished the *jizya* (poll tax) imposed on non-Muslims. Akbar came up with his own theory of "rulership as a divine illumination," enshrined in his new religion Din-i-Ilahi (Divine Faith), incorporating the principle of acceptance of all religions and sects. He encouraged widow marriage, discouraged child marriage, outlawed the practice of sati, and persuaded Delhi merchants to set up special market days for women, who otherwise were secluded at home. By the end of Akbar's reign, the Mughal Empire extended throughout most of India north of the Godavari River. The exceptions were Gondwana in central India, which paid tribute to the Mughals, and Assam, in the northeast.

Mughal rule under Jahangir (1605-27) and Shah Jahan (1628-58) was noted for political stability, brisk economic activity, beautiful paintings, and monumental buildings. Jahangir married the Persian princess whom he renamed Nur Jahan (Light of the World), who emerged as the most powerful individual in the court besides the emperor. As a result, Persian poets, artists, scholars, and officers—including her own family members—lured by the Mughal court's brilliance and luxury, found asylum in India. The number of unproductive, time-serving officers mushroomed, as did corruption, while the excessive Persian representation upset the delicate balance of impartiality at the court. Jahangir liked Hindu festivals but promoted mass conversion to Islam; he persecuted the followers of Jainism and even executed Guru Arjun Das, the fifth saint-teacher of the Sikhs. Nur Jahan's abortive schemes to secure the throne for the prince of her choice led Shah Jahan to rebel in 1622. In that same year, the Persians took over Kandahar in southern Afghanistan, an event that struck a serious blow to Mughal prestige.

Between 1636 and 1646, Shah Jahan sent Mughal armies to conquer the Deccan and the northwest beyond the Khyber Pass. Even though they demonstrated Mughal military strength, these campaigns consumed the imperial treasury. As the state became a huge military machine, whose nobles and their contingents multiplied almost fourfold, so did its demands for more revenue from the peasantry. Political unification and maintenance of law and order over wide areas encouraged the emergence of large centers of commerce and crafts—such as Lahore, Delhi, Agra, and Ahmadabad—linked by roads and waterways to distant places and ports. The world-famous Taj Mahal was built in Agra during Shah Jahan's reign as a tomb for his beloved wife, Mumtaz Mahal. It symbolizes both Mughal artistic achievement and excessive financial expenditures when resources were shrinking. The economic position of peasants and artisans did not improve because the administration failed to produce any lasting change in the existing social structure. There was no incentive for the revenue officials, whose concerns primarily were personal or familial gain, to generate resources independent of dominant Hindu zamindars and village leaders, whose self-interest and local dominance prevented them from handing over the full amount of revenue to the imperial treasury. In their ever-greater dependence on land revenue, the Mughals unwittingly nurtured forces that eventually led to the break-up of their empire.

The last of the great Mughals was Aurangzeb (r. 1658-1707), who seized the throne by killing all his brothers and imprisoning his own father. During his fifty-year reign, the empire reached its utmost physical limit but also witnessed the unmistakable symptoms of decline. The bureaucracy had grown bloated and excessively corrupt, and the huge and unwieldy army demonstrated outdated weaponry and tactics. Aurangzeb was not the ruler to restore the dynasty's declining fortunes or glory. Awe-inspiring but lacking in the charisma needed to attract outstanding lieutenants, he was driven to extend Mughal rule over most of South Asia and to reestablish Islamic orthodoxy by adopting a reactionary attitude toward those Muslims whom he had suspected of compromising their faith.

Aurangzeb was involved in a series of protracted wars—against the Pathans in Afghanistan, the sultans of Bijapur and Golkonda in the Deccan, and the Marathas in Maharashtra. Peasant uprisings and revolts by local leaders became all too common, as did the conniving of the nobles to preserve their own status at the expense of a steadily weakening empire. The increasing association of his government with Islam further drove a wedge between the ruler and his Hindu subjects.

Aurangzeb forbade the building of new temples, destroyed a number of them, and reimposed the *jizya*. A puritan and a censor of morals, he banned music at court, abolished ceremonies, and persecuted the Sikhs in Punjab. These measures alienated so many that even before he died challenges for power had already begun to escalate. Contenders for the Mughal throne fought each other, and the short-lived reigns of Aurangzeb's successors were strife-filled. The Mughal Empire experienced dramatic reverses as regional governors broke away and founded independent kingdoms. The

Mughals had to make peace with Maratha rebels, and Persian and Afghan armies invaded Delhi, carrying away many treasures, including the Peacock Throne in 1739.

THE MARATHAS

The tale of the Marathas' rise to power and their eventual fall contains all the elements of a thriller: adventure, intrigue, and romanticism. Maratha chieftains were originally in the service of Bijapur sultans in the western Deccan, which was under siege by the Mughals. Shivaji Bhonsle (1627-80), a tenacious and fierce fighter recognized as the "father of the Maratha nation," took advantage of this conflict and carved out his own principality near Pune, which later became the Maratha capital. Adopting guerrilla tactics, he waylaid caravans in order to sustain and expand his army, which soon had money, arms, and horses. Shivaji led a series of successful assaults in the 1660s against Mughal strongholds, including the major port of Surat. In 1674 he assumed the title of "Lord of the Universe" at his elaborate coronation, which signaled his determination to challenge the Mughal forces as well as to reestablish a Hindu kingdom in Maharashtra, the land of his origin. Shivaji's battle cries were *swaraj* (translated variously as freedom, self-rule, independence), *swadharma* (religious freedom), and *goraksha* (cow protection). Aurangzeb relentlessly pursued Shivaji's successors between 1681 and 1705 but eventually retreated to the north as his treasury became depleted and as thousands of lives had been lost either on the battlefield or to natural calamities. In 1717 a Mughal emissary signed a treaty with the Marathas confirming their claims to rule in the Deccan in return for acknowledging the fictional Mughal suzerainty and remission of annual taxes. Yet the Marathas soon captured Malwa from Mughal control and later moved east into Orrisa and Bengal; southern India also came under their domain. Recognition of their political power finally came when the Mughal emperor invited them to act as auxiliaries in the internal affairs of the empire and still later to help the emperor in driving the Afghans out of Punjab.

The Marathas, despite their military prowess and leadership, were not equipped to administer the state or to undertake socioeconomic reform. Pursuing a policy characterized by plunder and indiscriminate raids, they antagonized the peasants. They were primarily suited for stirring the Maharashtrian regional pride rather than for attracting loyalty to an all-India confederacy. They were left virtually alone before the invading Afghan forces, headed by Ahmad Shah Abdali (later called Ahmad Shah Durrani), who routed them on the blood-drenched battlefield at Panipat in 1761. The shock of defeat hastened the break-up of their loosely knit confederacy into five independent states and extinguished the hope of Maratha dominance in India.

THE SIKHS

The Afghan defeat of the Maratha armies accelerated the breakaway of Punjab from Delhi and helped the founding of Sikh overlordship in the northwest. Rooted in the *bhakti* movements that developed in the second century B.C. but swept across North India during the fifteenth and sixteenth centuries, the Sikh religion appealed to the hard-working peasants. The Sikh *khalsa* (army of the pure) rose up against the economic and political repressions in Punjab toward the end of Aurangzeb's rule. Guerrilla fighters took advantage of the political instability created by the Persian and Afghan onslaught against Delhi, enriching themselves and expanding territorial control. By the 1770s, Sikh hegemony extended from the Indus in the west to the Yamuna in the east, from Multan in the south to Jammu in the north. But the Sikhs, like the Marathas, were a loose, disunited, and quarrelsome conglomerate of twelve kin-groups. It took Ranjit Singh (1780-1839), an individual with modernizing vision and leadership, to achieve supremacy over the other kin-groups and establish his kingdom in which Sikhs, Hindus, and Muslims lived together in comparative equality and increasing prosperity. Ranjit Singh employed European officers and introduced strict military discipline into his army before expanding into Afghanistan, Kashmir, and Ladakh.

THE COMING OF THE EUROPEANS

The quest for wealth and power brought Europeans to Indian shores in 1498 when Vasco da Gama, the Portuguese voyager, arrived in Calicut (modern Kozhikode, Kerala) on the west coast. In their search for spices and Christian converts, the Portuguese challenged Arab supremacy in the Indian Ocean, and, with their galleons fitted with powerful cannons, set up a network of strategic trading posts along the Arabian Sea and the Persian Gulf. In 1510 the Portuguese took over the enclave of Goa, which became the center of their commercial and political power in India and which they controlled for nearly four and a half centuries.

Economic competition among the European nations led to the founding of commercial companies in England (the East India Company, founded in 1600) and in the Netherlands (Verenigde Oost-Indische Compagnie—the United East India Company, founded in 1602), whose primary aim was to capture the spice trade by breaking the Portuguese monopoly in Asia. Although the Dutch, with a large supply of capital and support from their government, preempted and ultimately excluded the British from the heartland of spices in the East Indies (modern-day Indonesia), both companies managed to establish trading "factories" (actually warehouses) along the Indian coast. The Dutch, for example, used various ports on the Coromandel Coast in South India, especially Pulicat (about twenty kilometers north of Madras), as major sources for slaves for their plantations in the East Indies and for cotton cloth as early as 1609. (The English, however, established their first factory at what today is known as Madras only in 1639.) Indian rulers enthusiastically accommodated the newcomers in hopes of pitting them against the Portuguese. In 1619 Jahangir granted them permission to trade in his territories at Surat (in Gujarat) on the west coast and Hughli (in West Bengal) in the east. These and other locations on the peninsula became centers of international trade in spices, cotton, sugar, raw silk, saltpeter, calico, and indigo.

English company agents became familiar with Indian customs and languages, including Persian, the unifying official language under the Mughals. In many ways, the English agents of that period lived like Indians, intermarried willingly, and a large number of them never returned to their home country. The knowledge of India thus acquired and the mutual ties forged with Indian trading groups gave the English a competitive edge over other Europeans. The French commercial interest—Compagnie des Indes Orientales (East India Company, founded in 1664)—came late, but the French also established themselves in India, emulating the precedents set by their competitors as they founded their enclave at Pondicherry (Puduchcheri) on the Coramandel Coast.

In 1717 the Mughal emperor, Farrukh-siyar (r. 1713-19), gave the British—who by then had already established themselves in the south and the west—a grant of thirty-eight villages near Calcutta, acknowledging their importance to the continuity of international trade in the Bengal economy. As did the Dutch and the French, the British brought silver bullion and copper to pay for transactions, helping the smooth functioning of the Mughal revenue system and increasing the benefits to local artisans and traders. The fortified warehouses of the British brought extraterritorial status, which enabled them to administer their own civil and criminal laws and offered numerous employment opportunities as well as asylum to foreigners and Indians. The British factories successfully competed with their rivals as their size and population grew. The original clusters of fishing villages (Madras and Calcutta) or series of islands (Bombay) became headquarters of the British administrative zones, or presidencies as they generally came to be known. The factories and their immediate environs, known as the White-town, represented the actual and symbolic preeminence of the British—in terms of their political power—as well as their cultural values and social practices; meanwhile, their Indian collaborators lived in the Black-town, separated from the factories by several kilometers.

The British company employed sepoys—European-trained and European-led Indian soldiers—to protect its trade, but local rulers sought their services to settle scores in regional power struggles. South India witnessed the first open confrontation between the

British and the French, whose forces were led by Robert Clive and François Dupleix, respectively. Both companies desired to place their own candidate as the nawab, or ruler, of Arcot, the area around Madras. At the end of a protracted struggle between 1744 and 1763, when the Peace of Paris was signed, the British gained an upper hand over the French and installed their man in power, supporting him further with arms and lending large sums as well. The French and the British also backed different factions in the succession struggle for Mughal viceroyalty in Bengal, but Clive intervened successfully and defeated Nawab Siraj-ud-daula in the Battle of Plassey (Palashi, about 150 kilometers north of Calcutta) in 1757. Clive found help from a combination of vested interests that opposed the existing nawab: disgruntled soldiers, landholders, and influential merchants whose commercial profits were closely linked to British fortunes. Later, Clive defeated the Mughal forces at Buxar (Baksar, west of Patna in Bihar) in 1765, and the Mughal emperor (Shah Alam, r. 1759-1806) conferred on the company administrative rights over Bengal, Bihar, and Orissa, a region of roughly 25 million people with an annual revenue of 40 million rupees (for current value of the rupee). The imperial grant virtually established the company as a sovereign power, and Clive became the first British governor of Bengal. Besides the presence of the Portuguese, Dutch, British, and French, there were two lesser but noteworthy colonial groups. Danish entrepreneurs established themselves at several ports on the Malabar and Coromandel coasts, in the vicinity of Calcutta and inland at Patna between 1695 and 1740. Austrian enterprises were set up in the 1720s on the vicinity of Surat in modern-day southeastern Gujarat. As with the other non-British enterprises, the Danish and Austrian enclaves were taken over by the British between 1765 and 1815.

THE BRITISH EMPIRE IN INDIA

Company Rule, 1757-1857

A multiplicity of motives underlay the British penetration into India: commerce, security, and a purported moral uplift of the people. The "expansive force" of private and company trade eventually led to the conquest or annexation of territories in which spices, cotton, and opium were produced. British investors ventured into the unfamiliar interior landscape in search of opportunities that promised substantial profits. British economic penetration was aided by Indian collaborators, such as the bankers and merchants who controlled intricate credit networks. British rule in India would have been a frustrated or half-realized dream had not Indian counterparts provided connections between rural and urban centers. External threats, both real and imagined, such as the Napoleonic Wars (1796-1815) and Russian expansion toward Afghanistan (in the 1830s), as well as the desire for internal stability, led to the annexation of more territory in India. Political analysts in Britain wavered initially as they were uncertain of the costs or the advantages in undertaking wars in India, but by the 1810s, as the territorial aggrandizement eventually paid off, opinion in London welcomed the absorption of new areas. Occasionally the British Parliament witnessed heated debates against expansion, but arguments justifying military operations for security reasons always won over even the most vehement critics.

The British soon forgot their own rivalry with the Portuguese and the French and permitted them to stay in their coastal enclaves, which they kept even after independence in 1947. The British, however, continued to expand vigorously well into the 1850s. A number of aggressive governors-general undertook relentless campaigns against several Hindu and Muslim rulers. Among them were Richard Colley Wellesley (1798-1805), William Pitt Amherst (1823-28), George Eden (1836-42), Edward Law (1842-44), and James Andrew Brown Ramsay (1848-56; also known as the Marquess of Dalhousie). Despite desperate efforts at salvaging their tottering power and keeping the British at bay, many Hindu and Muslim rulers lost their territories: Mysore (1799, but later restored), the Maratha Confederacy (1818), and Punjab (1849). The British success in large measure was the result not only of their superiority in tactics and weapons but also of their ingenious relations with Indian rulers through the "subsidiary alliance" system, introduced in the early nineteenth century. Many rulers bartered away their real responsibilities by agreeing to uphold British paramountcy in India, while they retained a fictional sovereignty under the rubric of Pax Britannica. Later, Dalhousie espoused the "doctrine of lapse" and annexed outright the estates of deceased princes of Satara (1848), Udaipur (1852), Jhansi (1853), Tanjore (1853), Nagpur (1854), and Oudh (1856).

European perceptions of India, and those of the British especially, shifted from unequivocal appreciation to sweeping condemnation of India's past achievements and customs. Imbued with an ethnocentric sense of superiority, British intellectuals, including Christian missionaries, spearheaded a movement that sought to bring Western intellectual and technological innovations to Indians. Interpretations of the causes of India's cultural and spiritual "backwardness" varied, as did the solutions. Many argued that it was Europe's mission to civilize India and hold it as a trust until Indians proved themselves competent for self-rule.

The immediate consequence of this sense of superiority was to open India to more aggressive missionary activity. The contributions of three missionaries based in Serampore (a Danish enclave in Bengal)—William Carey, Joshua Marshman, and William Ward—remained unequaled and have provided inspiration for future generations of their successors. The missionaries translated the Bible into the vernaculars, taught company officials local languages, and, after 1813, gained permission to proselytize in the company's territories. Although the actual number of converts remained negligible, except in rare instances when entire groups embraced Christianity, such as the Nayars in the south or the Nagas in the northeast, the missionary impact on India through publishing, schools, orphanages, vocational institutions, dispensaries, and hospitals was unmistakable.

The British Parliament enacted a series of laws, among which the Regulating Act of 1773 stood first, to curb the company traders' unrestrained commercial activities and to bring about some order in territories under company control. Limiting the company charter to periods of twenty years, subject to review upon renewal, the 1773 act gave the British government supervisory rights over the Bengal, Bombay, and Madras presidencies. Bengal was given preeminence over the rest because of its enormous commercial vitality and because it was the seat of British power in India (at Calcutta), whose governor was elevated to the new position of governor-general. Warren Hastings was the first incumbent (1773-85). The India Act of 1784, sometimes described as the "half-loaf system," as it sought to mediate between Parliament and the company directors, enhanced Parliament's control by establishing the Board of Control, whose members were selected from the cabinet. The Charter Act of 1813 recognized British moral responsibility by introducing just and humane laws in India, foreshadowing future social legislation, and outlawing a number of traditional practices such as sati and *thagi* (or thugee, robbery coupled with ritual murder).

As governor-general from 1786 to 1793, Charles Cornwallis (the Marquis of Cornwallis), professionalized, bureaucratized, and Europeanized the company's administration. He also outlawed private trade by company employees, separated the commercial and administrative functions, and remunerated company servants with generous graduated salaries. Because revenue collection became the company's most essential administrative function, Cornwallis made a compact with Bengali zamindars, who were perceived as the Indian counterparts to the British landed gentry. The Permanent Settlement system, also known as the zamindari system, fixed taxes in perpetuity in return for ownership of large estates; but the state was excluded from agricultural expansion, which came under the purview of the zamindars. In Madras and Bombay, however, the *ryotwari* (peasant) settlement system was set in motion, in which peasant cultivators had to pay annual taxes directly to the government.

Neither the zamindari nor the *ryotwari* systems proved effective in the long run because India was integrated into an international economic and pricing system over which it had no control, while increasing numbers of people subsisted on agriculture for lack of other employment. Millions of people involved in the heavily taxed

Indian textile industry also lost their markets, as they were unable to compete successfully with cheaper textiles produced in Lancashire's mills from Indian raw materials.

Beginning with the Mayor's Court, established in 1727 for civil litigation in Bombay, Calcutta, and Madras, justice in the interior came under the company's jurisdiction. In 1772 an elaborate judicial system, known as *adalat* , established civil and criminal jurisdictions along with a complex set of codes or rules of procedure and evidence. Both Hindu pandits and Muslim *qazis* (sharia court judges) were recruited to aid the presiding judges in interpreting their customary laws, but in other instances, British common and statutory laws became applicable. In extraordinary situations where none of these systems was applicable, the judges were enjoined to adjudicate on the basis of "justice, equity, and good conscience." The legal profession provided numerous opportunities for educated and talented Indians who were unable to secure positions in the company, and, as a result, Indian lawyers later dominated nationalist politics and reform movements.

Education for the most part was left to the charge of Indians or to private agents who imparted instruction in the vernaculars. But in 1813, the British became convinced of their "duty" to awaken the Indians from intellectual slumber by exposing them to British literary traditions, earmarking a paltry sum for the cause. Controversy between two groups of Europeans—the "Orientalists" and "Anglicists"—over how the money was to be spent prevented them from formulating any consistent policy until 1835 when William Cavendish Bentinck, the governor-general from 1828 to 1835, finally broke the impasse by resolving to introduce the English language as the medium of instruction. English replaced Persian in public administration and education.

The company's education policies in the 1830s tended to reinforce existing lines of socioeconomic division in society rather than bringing general liberation from ignorance and superstition. Whereas the Hindu English-educated minority spearheaded many social and religious reforms either in direct response to government policies or in reaction to them, Muslims as a group initially failed to do so, a position they endeavored to reverse. Western-educated Hindu elites sought to rid Hinduism of its much criticized social evils: idolatry, the caste system, child marriage, and sati. Religious and social activist Ram Mohan Roy (1772-1833), who founded the Brahmo Samaj (Society of Brahma) in 1828, displayed a readiness to synthesize themes taken from Christianity, Deism, and Indian monism, while other individuals in Bombay and Madras initiated literary and debating societies that gave them a forum for open discourse. The exemplary educational attainments and skillful use of the press by these early reformers enhanced the possibility of effecting broad reforms without compromising societal values or religious practices.

The 1850s witnessed the introduction of the three "engines of social improvement" that heightened the British illusion of permanence in India. They were the railroads, the telegraph, and the uniform postal service, inaugurated during the tenure of Dalhousie as governor-general. The first railroad lines were built in 1850 from Howrah (Haora, across the Hughli River from Calcutta) inland to the coalfields at Raniganj, Bihar, a distance of 240 kilometers. In 1851 the first electric telegraph line was laid in Bengal and soon linked Agra, Bombay, Calcutta, Lahore, Varanasi, and other cities. The three different presidency or regional postal systems merged in 1854 to facilitate uniform methods of communication at an all-India level. With uniform postal rates for letters and newspapers—one-half anna and one anna, respectively (sixteen annas equalled one rupee)—communication between the rural and the metropolitan areas became easier and faster. The increased ease of communication and the opening of highways and waterways accelerated the movement of troops, the transportation of raw materials and goods to and from the interior, and the exchange of commercial information.

The railroads did not break down the social or cultural distances between various groups but tended to create new categories in travel. Separate compartments in the trains were reserved exclusively for the ruling class, separating the educated and wealthy from ordinary people. Similarly, when the Sepoy Rebellion was quelled in 1858, a British official exclaimed that "the telegraph saved India." He envisaged, of course, that British interests in India would continue indefinitely.

THE BRITISH RAJ, 1858-1947

Sepoy Rebellion, 1857-59

On May 10, 1857, Indian soldiers of the British Indian Army, drawn mostly from Muslim units from Bengal, mutinied in Meerut, a cantonment eighty kilometers northeast of Delhi. The rebels marched to Delhi to offer their services to the Mughal emperor, and soon much of north and central India was plunged into a year-long insurrection against the British.

The uprising, which seriously threatened British rule in India, has been called many names by historians, including the Sepoy Rebellion, the Great Mutiny, and the Revolt of 1857; many people in South Asia, however, prefer to call it India's first war of independence. Undoubtedly, it was the culmination of mounting Indian resentment toward British economic and social policies over many decades. Until the rebellion, the British had succeeded in suppressing numerous riots and "tribal" wars or in accommodating them through concessions, but two events triggered the violent explosion of wrath in 1857. First, was the annexation in 1856 of Oudh, a wealthy princely state that generated huge revenue and represented a vestige of Mughal authority. The second was the British blunder in using cartridges for the Lee-Enfield rifle that were allegedly greased with animal fat, which was offensive to the religious beliefs of Muslim and Hindu sepoys. The rebellion soon engulfed much of North India, including Oudh and various areas once under the control of Maratha princes. Isolated mutinies also occurred at military posts in the center of the subcontinent. Initially, the rebels, although divided and uncoordinated, gained the upper hand, while the unprepared British were terrified, and even paralyzed, without replacements for the casualties. The civil war inflicted havoc on both

Indians and British as each vented its fury on the other; each community suffered humiliation and triumph in battle as well, although the final outcome was victory for the British. The last major sepoy rebels surrendered on June 21, 1858, at Gwalior (Madhya Pradesh), one of the principal centers of the revolt. A final battle was fought at Sirwa Pass on May 21, 1859, and the defeated rebels fled into Nepal.

The spontaneous and widespread rebellion later fired the imagination of the nationalists who would debate the most effective method of protest against British rule. For them, the rebellion represented the first Indian attempt at gaining independence. This interpretation, however, is open to serious question.

After the Sepoy Rebellion

The civil war was a major turning point in the history of modern India. In May 1858, the British exiled Emperor Bahadur Shah II (r. 1837-57) to Burma, thus formally liquidating the Mughal Empire. At the same time, they abolished the British East India Company and replaced it with direct rule under the British crown. In proclaiming the new direct-rule policy to "the Princes, Chiefs, and Peoples of India," Queen Victoria (who was given the title Empress of India in 1877) promised equal treatment under British law, but Indian mistrust of British rule had become a legacy of the 1857 rebellion. Many existing economic and revenue policies remained virtually unchanged in the post-1857 period, but several administrative modifications were introduced, beginning with the creation in London of a cabinet post, the secretary of state for India. The governor-general (called viceroy when acting as the direct representative of the British crown), headquartered in Calcutta, ran the administration in India, assisted by executive and legislative councils. Beneath the governor-general were the provincial governors, who held power over the district officials, who formed the lower rungs of the Indian Civil Service. For decades the Indian Civil Service was the exclusive preserve of the British-born, as were the superior ranks in such other professions as law and medicine. The British administrators were imbued with a sense of duty in ruling India and were rewarded with good salaries, high status, and opportunities for promotion. Not until the 1910s did the British reluctantly permit a few Indians into their cadre as the number of English-educated Indians rose steadily.

The viceroy announced in 1858 that the government would honor former treaties with princely states and renounced the "doctrine of lapse," whereby the East India Company had annexed territories of rulers who died without male heirs. About 40 percent of Indian territory and between 20 and 25 percent of the population remained under the control of 562 princes notable for their religious (Islamic, Sikh, Hindu, and other) and ethnic diversity. Their propensity for pomp and ceremony became proverbial, while their domains, varying in size and wealth, lagged behind sociopolitical transformations that took place elsewhere in British-controlled India.

A more thorough reorganization was effected in the constitution of army and government finances. Shocked by the extent of solidarity among Indian soldiers during the rebellion, the government separated the army into the three presidencies.

British attitudes toward Indians shifted from relative openness to insularity and xenophobia, even against those with comparable background and achievement as well as loyalty. British families and their servants lived in cantonments at a distance from Indian settlements. Private clubs where the British gathered for social interaction became symbols of exclusivity and snobbery that refused to disappear decades after the British had left India. In 1883 the government of India attempted to remove race barriers in criminal jurisdictions by introducing a bill empowering Indian judges to adjudicate offenses committed by Europeans. Public protests and editorials in the British press, however, forced the viceroy, George Robinson, Marquis of Ripon (who served from 1880 to 1884), to capitulate and modify the bill drastically. The Bengali Hindu intelligentsia learned a valuable political lesson from this "white mutiny": the effectiveness of well-orchestrated agitation through demonstrations in the streets and publicity in the media when seeking redress for real and imagined grievances.

THE INDEPENDENCE MOVEMENT

Origins of the Congress and the Muslim League

The decades following the Sepoy Rebellion were a period of growing political awareness, manifestation of Indian public opinion, and emergence of Indian leadership at national and provincial levels. Ominous economic uncertainties created by British colonial rule and the limited opportunities that awaited the ever-expanding number of Western-educated graduates began to dominate the rhetoric of leaders who had begun to think of themselves as a "nation," despite fissures along the lines of region, religion, language, and caste. Inspired by the suggestion made by A.O. Hume, a retired British civil servant, seventy-three Indian delegates met in Bombay in 1885 and founded the Indian National Congress (Congress). They were mostly members of the upwardly mobile and successful Western-educated provincial elites, engaged in professions such as law, teaching, and journalism. They had acquired political experience from regional competition in the professions and from their aspirations in securing nomination to various positions in legislative councils, universities, and special commissions. At its inception, the Congress had no well-defined ideology and commanded few of the resources essential to a political organization. It functioned more as a debating society that met annually to express its loyalty to the Raj and passed numerous resolutions on less controversial issues such as civil rights or opportunities in government, especially the civil service. These resolutions were submitted to the viceroy's government and, occasionally, to the British Parliament, but the Congress's early gains were meager. Despite its claim to represent all India, the Congress voiced the interests of urban elites; the number of participants from other economic backgrounds remained negligible.

By 1900, although the Congress had emerged as an all-India political organization, its achievement was undermined by its singular failure to attract Muslims, who had by then begun to realize their inadequate education and underrepresentation in government service. Muslim leaders saw that their community had fallen behind the Hindus. Attacks by Hindu reformers against religious conversion, cow killing, and the preservation of Urdu in Arabic script deepened their fears of minority status and denial of their rights if the Congress alone were to represent the people of India. For many Muslims, loyalty to the British crown seemed preferable to cooperation with Congress leaders. Sir Sayyid Ahmad Khan (1817-98) launched a movement for Muslim regeneration that culminated in the founding in 1875 of the Muhammadan Anglo-Oriental College at Aligarh, Uttar Pradesh (renamed Aligarh Muslim University in 1921). Its objective was to educate wealthy students by emphasizing the compatibility of Islam with modern Western knowledge. The diversity among India's Muslims, however, made it impossible to bring about uniform cultural and intellectual regeneration.

Sir George Curzon, the governor-general (1899-1905), ordered the partition of Bengal in 1905. He wanted to improve administrative efficiency in that huge and populous region, where the Bengali Hindu intelligentsia exerted considerable influence on local and national politics. The partition created two provinces: Eastern Bengal and Assam, with its capital at Dhaka (then spelled Dacca), and West Bengal, with its capital at Calcutta (which also served as the capital of British India). An ill-conceived and hastily implemented action, the partition outraged Bengalis. Not only had the government failed to consult Indian public opinion but the action appeared to reflect the British resolve to "divide and rule." Widespread agitation ensued in the streets and in the press, and the Congress advocated boycotting British products under the banner of *swadeshi* (home-made).

The Congress-led boycott of British goods was so successful that it unleashed anti-British forces to an extent unknown since the Sepoy Rebellion. A cycle of violence, terrorism, and repression ensued in some parts of the country. The British tried to mitigate the situation by announcing a series of constitutional reforms in 1909 and by appointing a few moderates to the imperial and provincial councils. In 1906 a Muslim deputation met with the viceroy, Gilbert John Elliot (1905-10), seeking concessions from the impending constitutional reforms, including special considerations in government service and electorates. The All-India Muslim League (Muslim League) was founded the same year to promote loyalty to the British and to advance Muslim political rights, which the British recognized by increasing the number of elective offices reserved for Muslims in the India Councils Act of 1909. The Muslim League insisted on its separateness from the Hindu-dominated Congress, as the voice of a "nation within a nation."

In what the British saw as an additional goodwill gesture, in 1911 King-Emperor George V (r. 1910-36) visited India for a durbar (a traditional court held for subjects to express fealty to their ruler), during which he announced the reversal of the partition of Bengal and the transfer of the capital from Calcutta to a newly planned city to be built immediately south of Delhi, which became New Delhi.

POLITICAL IMPASSE AND INDEPENDENCE

The Congress neither acknowledged the Muslim League's performance, albeit poor, in the elections nor deigned to form a coalition government with the League, a situation that led to the collapse of negotiations and mutual trust between the leaders. Mohammad Ali Jinnah, a Western-educated Muslim lawyer, took over the presidency of the moribund Muslim League and galvanized it into a national force under the battle cry of "Islam in danger." Jinnah doubted the motives of Gandhi and Nehru and accused them of practicing Hindu chauvinism. He relentlessly attacked the Congress-led ministries, accusing them of casteism, corruption, and nepotism. Skillfully, he succeeded in unifying various regional Islamic organizations and factions in Punjab and Bengal under the umbrella of the Muslim League.

Electoral gains by the Congress in 1937 were rendered ephemeral as its leaders ordered provincial ministries to resign in November 1939, when the viceroy (Victor Alexander John Hope, Marquis of Linlithgow—1936-43) declared India's entrance into World War II without consulting Indian leaders. Jinnah and the Muslim League welcomed the Congress withdrawal from government as a timely opportunity and observed a day of thanksgiving on December 22, 1939. Jinnah persuaded the participants at the annual Muslim League session in Lahore in 1940 to adopt what later came to be known as the Pakistan Resolution, demanding the division of India into two separate sovereign states, one Muslim, the other Hindu. Although the idea of Pakistan had been introduced as early as 1930 at Allahabad, very few had responded to it. However, the volatile political climate, the personal hostilities between the leaders, and the opportunism of Jinnah transformed the idea of Pakistan into a popular demand.

Between 1940 and 1942, the Congress launched two abortive agitations against the British, and 60,000 Congress members were arrested, including Gandhi and Nehru. Unlike the uncooperative and belligerent Congress, the Muslim League supported the British during World War II. Belated but perhaps sincere British attempts to accommodate the demands of the two rival parties, while preserving the unitary state in India, seemed unacceptable to both as they alternately rejected whatever proposal was put forward during the war years. As a result, a three-way impasse settled in: the Congress and the Muslim League doubted British motives in handing over power to Indians, while the British struggled to retain some hold on India while offering to give greater autonomy.

The Congress wasted precious time denouncing the British rather than allaying Muslim fears during the highly charged election campaign of 1946. Even the more mature Congress leaders, especially Gandhi and Nehru, failed to see how genuinely afraid the Muslims were and how exhausted and weak the British had become in the aftermath of the war. When it appeared that the Congress had no desire to share power with the Muslim League at the center, Jinnah declared August 16, 1946, Direct Action Day, which brought communal rioting and massacre in many places in the north. Partition seemed preferable to civil war. On June 3, 1947, Viscount Louis Mountbatten, the viceroy (1947) and governor-general (1947-48), announced plans for partition of the British Indian Empire into the nations of India and Pakistan, which itself was divided into east and west wings on either side of India. At midnight, on August 15, 1947, India strode to freedom amidst ecstatic shouting of *"Jai Hind"* (roughly, Long Live India), when Nehru delivered a memorable and moving speech on India's "tryst with destiny."

INDEPENDENT INDIA

National Integration

The euphoria of independence was short-lived as partition brought disastrous consequences for India in the wake of communal conflict. Partition unleashed untold misery and loss of lives and property as millions of Hindu and Muslim refugees fled either Pakistan or India. Both nations were also caught up in a number of conflicts involving the allocation of assets, demarcation of boundaries, equitable sharing of water resources, and control over Kashmir. At the same time, Indian leaders were faced with the stupendous task of national integration and economic development.

When the British relinquished their claims to paramountcy, the 562 independent princely states were given the option to join either of the two nations. A few princely states readily joined Pakistan, but the rest—except Hyderabad (the largest of the princely states with 132,000 square kilometers and a population of more than 14 million), Jammu and Kashmir (with 3 million inhabitants), and Junagadh (with a population of 545,000)—merged with India. India successfully annexed Hyderabad and Junagadh after "police actions" and promises of privileges to the rulers.

The Hindu maharajah of predominantly Muslim Jammu and Kashmir remained uncommitted until armed tribesmen and regular troops from Pakistan infiltrated his domain, inducing him to sign the Instrument of Accession to India on October 27, 1947. Pakistan refused to accept the legality of the accession, and, as a result, war broke out. Kashmir remains a source of friction between the neighbors. The assassination of Mahatma Gandhi on January 30, 1948, in New Delhi, by a Hindu extremist opposed to Gandhi's openness to Muslims ended the tenuous celebration of independence and deepened the hatred and mutual suspicion in Hindu-Muslim relations.

Economic backwardness was one of the serious challenges that India faced at independence. Under three successive five-year plans, inaugurated between 1951 and 1964 under Nehru's leadership, India produced increasing amounts of food. Although food production did not allow self-sufficiency until fiscal year (FY) 1984, India has emerged as the nation with the seventh largest gross national product (GNP) in the world.

Linguistic regionalism eventually reached a crisis stage and undermined the Congress' attempts at nation building. Whereas in the early 1920s, the Congress had deemed that the use of regional vernaculars in education and administration would facilitate the governance of the country, partition made the leaders, especially Nehru, realize how quickly such provincial or subnational interests would dismantle India's fragile unity. However, in the face of widespread agitation for linguistic separation of states, beginning with the Telangana Movement in 1953, in 1956 Nehru reluctantly accepted the recommendations of the States Reorganisation Commission, and the number of states grew by reorganization along linguistic lines. The states became the loci for democratization of political processes at district levels, for expression of regional culture and popular demands against a national culture and unity, for economic development at strategic localities in the rural areas, and for proliferation of opposition parties that ended the possibility of a pan-Indian two-party system.

2

SOCIETY AND RELIGION

It is impossible to know India without understanding its religious beliefs and practices, which have a large impact on the personal lives of most Indians and influence public life on a daily basis. Indian religions have deep historical roots that are recollected by contemporary Indians. The ancient culture of South Asia, going back at least 4,500 years, has come down to India primarily in the form of religious texts. The artistic heritage, as well as intellectual and philosophical contributions, has always owed much to religious thought and symbolism. Contacts between India and other cultures have led to the spread of Indian religions throughout the world, resulting in the extensive influence of Indian thought and practice on Southeast and East Asia in ancient times and, more recently, in the diffusion of Indian religions to Europe and North America. Within India, on a day-to-day basis, the vast majority of people engage in ritual actions that are motivated by religious systems that owe much to the past but are continuously evolving. Religion, then, is one of the most important facets of Indian history and contemporary life.

A number of world religions originated in India, and others that started elsewhere found fertile ground for growth there. Devotees of Hinduism, a varied grouping of philosophical and devotional traditions, officially numbered 687.6 million people, or 82 percent of the population in the 1991 census. Buddhism and Jainism, ancient monastic traditions, have had a major influence on Indian art, philosophy, and society and remain important minority religions in the late twentieth century. Buddhists represented 0.8 percent of the total population while Jains represented 0.4 percent in 1991.

Islam spread from the West throughout South Asia, from the early eighth century, to become the largest minority religion in India. In fact, with 101.5 million Muslims (12.1 percent of the population), India has at least the fourth largest Muslim population in the world (after Indonesia with 174.3 million, Pakistan with 124 million, and Bangladesh with 103 million; some analysts put the number of Indian Muslims even higher—128 million in 1994, which would give India the second largest Muslim population in the world).

Sikhism, which started in Punjab in the sixteenth century, has spread throughout India and the world since the mid-nineteenth century. With nearly 16.3 million adherents, Sikhs represent 1.9 percent of India's population.

Christianity, represented by almost all denominations, traces its history in India back to the time of the apostles and counted 19.6 million members in India in 1991. Judaism and Zoroastrianism, arriving originally with traders and exiles from the West, are represented by small populations, mostly concentrated on India's west coast. A variety of independent tribal religious groups also are lively carriers of unique ethnic traditions.

The listing of the major belief systems only scratches the surface of the remarkable diversity in Indian religious life. The complex doctrines and institutions of the great traditions, preserved through written documents, are divided into numerous schools of thought, sects, and paths of devotion. In many cases, these divisions stem from the teachings of great masters, who arise continually to lead bands of followers with a new revelation or path to salvation. In contemporary India, the migration of large numbers of people to urban centers and the impact of modernization have led to the emergence of new religions, revivals, and reforms within the great traditions that create original bodies of teaching and kinds of practice. In other cases, diversity appears through the integration or acculturation of entire social groups—each with its own vision of the divine—within the world of village farming communities that base their culture on literary and ritual traditions preserved in Sanskrit or in regional languages. The local interaction between great traditions and local forms of worship and belief, based on village, caste, tribal, and linguistic differences, creates a range of ritual forms and mythology that varies widely throughout the country. Within this range of differences, Indian religions have demonstrated for many centuries a considerable degree of tolerance for alternate visions of the divine and of salvation.

Religious tolerance in India finds expression in the definition of the nation as a secular state, within which the government since independence has officially remained separate from any one religion, allowing all forms of belief equal status before the law. In practice it has proven difficult to divide religious affiliation from public life. In states where the majority of the population embrace one religion, the boundary between government and religion becomes permeable; in Tamil Nadu, for example, the state government manages Hindu temples, while in Punjab an avowedly Sikh political party usually controls the state assembly. One of the most notable features of Indian politics, particularly since the 1960s, has been the steady growth of militant ideologies that see in only one religious tradition the way toward salvation and demand that public institutions conform to their interpretations of scripture. The vitality of religious fundamentalism and its impact on public life in the form of riots and religion-based political parties have been among the greatest challenges to Indian political institutions in the 1990s.

THE VEDAS AND POLYTHEISM

Hinduism in India traces its source to the Vedas, ancient hymns composed and recited in Punjab as early as 1500 B.C. Three main collections of the Vedas—the Rig, Sama, and Yajur—consist of chants that were originally recited by priests while offering plant and animal sacrifices in sacred fires. A fourth collection, the Atharva Veda, contains a number of formulas for requirements as varied as medical cures and love magic. The majority of modern Hindus revere these hymns as sacred sounds passed down to humanity from the greatest antiquity and as the source of Hindu tradition.

The vast majority of Vedic hymns are addressed to a pantheon of deities who are attracted, generated, and nourished by the offerings into the sacred flames and the precisely chanted mantras (mystical formulas of invocation) based on the hymns. Each of these deities may appear to be the supreme god in his or her own hymns, but some gods stand out as most significant. Indra, god of the firmament and lord of the weather, is the supreme deity of the Vedas. Indra also is a god of war who, accompanied by a host of storm gods, uses thunderbolts as weapons to slay the serpent demon Vritra (the name means storm cloud), thus releasing the rains for the earth. Agni, the god of fire, accepts the sacrificial offerings and transmits them to all the gods. Varuna passes judgment, lays down the law, and protects the cosmic order. Yama, the god of death, sends earthly dwellers signs of old age, sickness, and approaching mortality as exhortations to lead a moral life. Surya is the sun god, Chandra the moon god, Vayu the wind god, and Usha the dawn goddess.

Some of the later hymns of the Rig Veda contain speculations that form the basis for much of Indian religious and philosophical thought. From one perspective, the universe originates through the evolution of an impersonal force manifested as male and female principles. Other hymns describe a personal creator, Prajapati, the Lord of creatures, from whom came the heavens and the earth and all the other gods. One hymn describes the universe as emerging from the sacrifice of a cosmic man (*purusha*) who was the source of all things but who was in turn offered into the fire by gods. Within the Vedic accounts of the origin of things, there is a tension between visions of the highest reality as an impersonal force, or as a creator god, or as a group of gods with different jobs to do in the universe. Much of Hinduism tends to accept all these visions simultaneously, claiming that they are all valid as different facets of a single truth, or ranks them as explanations with different levels of sophistication. It is possible, however, to follow only one of these explanations, such as believing in a single personal god while rejecting all others, and still claim to be following the Vedas. In sum, Hinduism does not exist as a single belief system with one textual explanation of the origin of the universe or the nature of God, and a wide range of philosophies and practices can trace their beginnings somewhere in the hymns of the Vedas.

By the sixth century B.C., the Vedic gods were in decline among the people, and few people care much for Indra, Agni, or Varuna in contemporary India. These gods might appear as background characters in myths and stories about more important deities, such as Shiva or Vishnu; in some Hindu temples, there also are small statues of Vedic deities. Sacrificial fire, which once accompanied major political activities, such as the crowning of kings or the conquest of territory, still forms the heart of household rituals for many Hindus, and some Brahman families pass down the skill of memorizing the hymns and make a living as professional reciters of the Vedas. One of the main legacies of Brahmanical sacrifice, seen even among traditions that later denied its usefulness, was a concentration on precise ritual actions and a belief in sacred sound as a powerful tool for manifesting the sacred in daily life.

JAINISM

The oldest continuous monastic tradition in India is Jainism, the path of the Jinas, or victors. This tradition is traced to Vardhamana Mahavira (The Great Hero; ca. 599-527 B.C.), the twenty-fourth and last of the Tirthankaras (Sanskrit for fordmakers). According to legend, Mahavira was born to a ruling family in the town of Vaishali, located in the modern state of Bihar. At the age of thirty, he renounced his wealthy life and devoted himself to fasting and self-mortification in order to purify his consciousness and discover the meaning of existence. He never again dwelt in a house, owned property, or wore clothing of any sort. Following the example of the teacher Parshvanatha (ninth century B.C.), he attained enlightenment and spent the rest of his life meditating and teaching a dedicated group of disciples who formed a monastic order following rules he laid down. His life's work complete, he entered a final fast and deliberately died of starvation.

The ancient belief system of the Jains rests on a concrete understanding of the working of karma, its effects on the living soul (*jiva*), and the conditions for extinguishing action and the soul's release. According to the Jain view, the soul is a living substance that combines with various kinds of nonliving matter and through action accumulates particles of matter that adhere to it and determine its fate. Most of the matter perceptible to human senses, including all animals and plants, is attached in various degrees to living souls and is in this sense alive. Any action has consequences that necessarily follow the embodied soul, but the worst accumulations of matter come from violence against other living beings. The ultimate Jain discipline, therefore, rests on complete inactivity and absolute nonviolence (ahimsa) against any living beings. Some Jain monks and nuns wear face masks to avoid accidently inhaling small organisms, and all practicing believers try to remain vegetarians. Extreme renunciation, including the refusal of all food, lies at the heart of a discipline that purges the mind and body of all desires and actions and, in the process, burns off the consequences of actions performed in the past. In this sense, Jain renunciants may recognize or revere deities, but they do not view the Vedas as sacred texts and instead concentrate on the atheistic, individual quest for purification and removal of karma. The final goal is the extinguishing of self, a "blowing out" (nirvana) of the individual self.

By the first century A.D., the Jain community evolved into two main divisions based on monastic discipline: the Digambara or "sky-clad" monks who wear no clothes, own nothing, and collect donated food in their hands; and the Svetambara or "white-clad" monks and nuns who wear white robes and carry bowls for donated food. The Digambara do not accept the possibility of women achieving liberation, while the Svetambara do. Western and southern India have been Jain strongholds for many centuries; laypersons have typically formed minority communities concentrated primarily in urban areas and in mercantile occupations. In the mid-1990s, there were about 7 million Jains, the majority of whom live in the states of Maharashtra (mostly the city of Bombay, or Mumbai in Marathi), Rajasthan, and Gujarat. Karnataka, traditionally a stronghold of Digambaras, has a sizable Jain community.

The Jain laity engage in a number of ritual activities that resemble those of the Hindus around them. Special shrines in residences or in public temples include images of the Tirthankaras, who are not worshiped but remembered and revered; other shrines house the gods who are more properly invoked to intercede with worldly problems. Daily rituals may include meditation and bathing; bathing the images; offering food, flowers, and lighted lamps for the images; and reciting mantras in Ardhamagadhi, an ancient language of northeast India related to Sanskrit. Many Jain laity engage in sacramental ceremonies during life-cycle rituals, such as the first taking of solid food, marriage, and death, resembling those enacted by Hindus. Jains may also worship local gods and participate in local Hindu or Muslim celebrations without compromising their fundamental devotion to the path of the Jinas. The most important festivals of Jainism celebrate the five major events in the life of Mahavira: conception, birth, renunciation, enlightenment, and final release at death.

At a number of pilgrimage sites associated with great teachers of Jainism, the gifts of wealthy donors made possible the building of architectural wonders. Shatrunjaya Hills (Siddhagiri) in Gujarat is a major Svetambara site, an entire city of about 3,500 temples. Mount Abu in Rajasthan, with one Digambara and five Svetambara temples, is the site of some of India's greatest architecture, dating from the eleventh through thirteenth centuries A.D. In Karnataka, on the hill of Sravana Belgola, stands the monolithic seventeen-meter-high statue of the naked Bhagwan Bahubali (Gomateshvara), the first person in the world believed by the faithful to have attained enlightenment, so deep in meditation that vines are growing around his legs. At this site every twelve years, a major concourse of Jain ascetics and laity participate in a purification ceremony in which the statue is anointed from head to toe. Carved in 981, the statue is considered the holiest Jain shrine. In addition to its lavish patronage of shrines, the Jain community, with its long scriptural tradition and wealth gained from trade, has always been known for its philanthropy and especially for its support of education and learning. Prestigious Jain schools are located in most major cities. The largest concentrations of Jains are in Maharashtra (more than 965,000) and Rajasthan (nearly 563,000), with sizable numbers also in Gujarat and Madhya Pradesh.

BUDDHISM

Buddhism began with the life of Siddhartha Gautama (ca. 563-483 B.C.), a prince from the small Shakya Kingdom located in the foothills of the Himalayas in Nepal. Brought up in luxury, the prince abandoned his home and wandered forth as a religious beggar, searching for the meaning of existence. The stories of his search presuppose the Jain tradition, as Gautama was for a time a practitioner of intense austerity, at one point almost starving himself to death. He decided, however, that self-torture weakened his mind while failing to advance him to enlightenment and therefore turned to a milder style of renunciation and concentrated on advanced meditation techniques. Eventually, under a tree in the forests of Gaya (in modern Bihar), he resolved to stir no farther until he had solved the mystery of existence. Breaking through the final barriers, he achieved the knowledge that he later expressed as the Four Noble Truths: all of life is suffering; the cause of suffering is desire; the end of desire leads to the end of suffering; and the means to end desire is a path of discipline and meditation. Gautama was now the Buddha, or the awakened one, and he spent the remainder of his life traveling about northeast India converting large numbers of disciples. At the age of eighty, the Buddha achieved his final passing away (*parinirvana*) and died, leaving a thriving monastic order and a dedicated lay community to continue his work.

By the third century B.C., the still-young religion based on the Buddha's teachings was being spread throughout South Asia through the agency of the Mauryan Empire (ca. 326-184 B.C.; see The

Mauryan Empire, ch. 1). By the seventh century A.D., having spread throughout East Asia and Southeast Asia, Buddhism probably had the largest religious following in the world.

For centuries Indian royalty and merchants patronized Buddhist monasteries and raised beautiful, hemispherical stone structures called stupas over the relics of the Buddha in reverence to his memory. Since the 1840s, archaeology has revealed the huge impact of Buddhist art, iconography, and architecture in India. The monastery complex at Nalanda in Bihar, in ruins in 1993, was a world center for Buddhist philosophy and religion until the thirteenth century. But by the thirteenth century, when Turkic invaders destroyed the remaining monasteries on the plains, Buddhism as an organized religion had practically disappeared from India. It survived only in Bhutan and Sikkim, both of which were then independent Himalayan kingdoms; among tribal groups in the mountains of northeast India; and in Sri Lanka. The reasons for this disappearance are unclear, and they are many: shifts in royal patronage from Buddhist to Hindu religious institutions; a constant intellectual struggle with dynamic Hindu intellectual schools, which eventually triumphed; and slow adoption of popular religious forms by Buddhists while Hindu monastic communities grew up with the same style of discipline as the Buddhists, leading to the slow but steady amalgamation of ideas and trends in the two religions.

Buddhism began a steady and dramatic comeback in India during the early twentieth century, spurred on originally by a combination of European antiquarian and philosophical interest and the dedicated activities of a few Indian devotees. The foundation of the Mahabodhi Society (Society of Great Enlightenment) in 1891, originally as a force to wrest control of the Buddhist shrine at Gaya from the hands of Hindu managers, gave a large stimulus to the popularization of Buddhist philosophy and the importance of the religion in India's past.

A major breakthrough occurred in 1956 after some thirty years of Untouchable, or Dalit , agitation when Bhimrao Ramji (B.R.) Ambedkar, leader of the Untouchable wing within the Congress , announced that he was converting to Buddhism as a way to escape from the impediments of the Hindu caste system. He brought with him masses of Untouchables—also known as Harijans or Dalits—and members of Scheduled Castes , who mostly came from Maharashtra and border areas of neighboring states and from the Agra area in Uttar Pradesh. By the early 1990s, there were more than 5 million Buddhists in Maharashtra, or 79 percent of the entire Buddhist community in India, almost all recent converts from low castes. When added to longtime Buddhist populations in hill areas of northeast India (West Bengal, Assam, Sikkim, Mizoram, and Tripura) and high Himalayan valleys (Ladakh District in Jammu and Kashmir, Himachal Pradesh, and northern Uttar Pradesh), and to the influx of Tibetan Buddhist refugees who fled from Tibet with the Dalai Lama in 1959 and thereafter, the recent converts raised the number of Buddhists in India to 6.4 million by 1991. This was a 35.9 percent increase since 1981 and made Buddhism the fifth largest religious group in the country.

The forms of Buddhism practiced by Himalayan communities and Tibetan refugees are part of the Vajrayana, or "Way of the Lightning Bolt," that developed after the seventh century A.D. as part of Mahayana (Great Path) Buddhism. Although retaining the fundamental importance of individual spiritual advancement, the Vajrayana stresses the intercession of bodhisattvas, or enlightened beings, who remain in this world to aid others on the path. Until the twentieth century, the Himalayan kingdoms supported a hierarchy in which Buddhist monks, some identified from birth as bodhisattvas, occupied the highest positions in society.

Most other Buddhists in India follow Theravada Buddhism, the "Doctrine of the Elders," which traces its origin through Sri Lankan and Burmese traditions to scriptures in the Pali language, a Sanskritic dialect in eastern India. Although replete with miraculous events and legends, these scriptures stress a more human Buddha and a democratic path toward enlightenment for everyone. Ambedkar's plan for the expanding Buddhist congregation in India visualized Buddhist monks and nuns developing themselves through service to others. Convert communities, by embracing Buddhism, have embarked on social transformations, including a decline in alcoholism, a simplification of marriage ceremonies and abolition of ruinous marriage expenses, a greater emphasis on education, and a heightened sense of identity and self-worth.

The Tradition of the Enlightened Master

A number of avowedly Hindu monastic communities have grown up over time and adopted some of the characteristics associated with early Buddhism and Jainism, while remaining dedicated to the Hindu philosophical traditions. One of the oldest and most respected of the Hindu orders traces its origin to the teacher Shankara (788-820), believed by many devotees to have lived hundreds of years earlier. Shankara's philosophy is a primary source of Vedanta, or the "End of the Veda," the final commentary on revealed truth, which is one of the most influential trends in modern Hinduism. His interpretation of the Upanishads portrays *brahman* as absolutely one and without qualities. The phenomenal world is illusion (*maya*), which the embodied soul must transcend in order to achieve oneness with *brahman*. As a wandering monk, Shankara traveled throughout India, combating Buddhist atheism and founding five seats of learning at Badrinath (Uttar Pradesh), Dwaraka (Gujarat), Puri (Orissa), Sringeri (Karnataka), and Kanchipuram (Tamil Nadu). In the 1990s, those seats are still held by successors to Shankara's philosophy (Shankara Acharyas), who head an order of orange-clad monks that is highly respected by the Hindu community throughout India. Activities of the *acharyas* , including their periodic trips away from their home monasteries to visit and preach to devotees, receive exposure in regional and national media. Their conservative viewpoints and pronouncements on a variety of topics, although not binding on most believers, attract considerable public attention.

The initiation of a renunciant usually depends on the judgment of an *acharya* who determines whether a candidate is dedicated and prepared or not; he then gives to the disciple training and instructions including the initiate's own secret formula or mantra. After initiation, the disciple may remain with his teacher or in a monastery for an indefinite period or may wander forth in a variety of careers. The Ramanandi order in North India, for example, includes holy men (sadhus) who practice ascetic disciplines, militant members of fortified temples, and priests in charge of temple administration and ritual.

There are other orders of renunciants who lead still more austere existences, including naked ascetics who wander begging for their food and assemble for spectacular parades at major festivals. A few dedicated seekers still withdraw to the fastness of the Himalayas or other remote spots and work on their meditation and yoga in total obscurity. Others beg in populated areas, sometimes engaging in fierce austerities such as piercing their bodies with pins and knives. They are a reminder to all people that the path of renunciation waits for anyone who has the dedication and the courage to leave the world behind.

Another kind of renunciation appears in the cult of Sai Baba, who achieved national and international fame in the twentieth century. The first person known by this name was a holy man—Sai Baba (died 1918)—who appeared in 1872 in Maharashtra and lived a humble life that blended meditation and devotional techniques from a variety of sources. This saint has a small but dedicated following throughout India. A later incarnation was Satya Sai Baba (*satya* means true), born in 1926 in Andhra Pradesh. At age thirteen, he experienced the first of several seizures that resulted in a changed personality and intense devotional activity, leading to his statement that he is the second incarnation of Sai Baba. By 1950 he had set up a retreat at Puttaparti in what later became Andhra Pradesh and was accepting disciples. His fame spread along with numerous apocryphal stories of his ability to perform miracles, including the manifestation of sacred ash and, according to some accounts, watches or other objects, from thin air or from his own body. The cult has expanded to include publishing, social service, and education institutions and includes an international association of thousands of believers. Devotion to Satya Sai Baba does not preclude attachment to other religious observances but concentrates instead on worship and veneration of the holy man himself, often in the form of a photograph. Thousands of pilgrims have traveled to his retreat annually to participate in group activities, obtain mementos, and perhaps a view of the teacher himself.

THE WORSHIP OF PERSONAL GODS

For the vast majority of Hindus, the most important religious path is *bhakti* (devotion) to personal gods. There are a wide variety of gods to choose from, and although sectarian adherence to particular deities is often strong, there is a widespread acceptance of choice in the desired god (*ishta devata*) as the most appropriate focus for any particular person. Most devotees are therefore polytheists, worshiping all or part of the vast pantheon of deities, some of whom have come down from Vedic times. In practice, a worshiper tends to concentrate prayers on one deity or on a small group of deities with whom there is a close personal relationship.

Puja (worship) of the gods consists of a range of ritual offerings and prayers typically performed either daily or on special days before an image of the deity, which may be in the form of a person or a symbol of the sacred presence. In its more developed forms, *puja* consists of a series of ritual stages beginning with personal purification and invocation of the god, followed by offerings of flowers, food, or other objects such as clothing, accompanied by fervent prayers. Some dedicated worshipers perform these ceremonies daily at their home shrines; others travel to one or more temples to perform *puja* , alone or with the aid of temple priests who receive offerings and present these offerings to the gods. The gifts given to the gods become sacred through contact with their images or with their shrines, and may be received and used by worshipers as the grace (*prasada*) of the divine. Sacred ash or saffron powder, for example, is often distributed after *puja* and smeared on the foreheads of devotees. In the absence of any of these ritual objects, however, *puja* may take the form of a simple prayer sent toward the image of the divine, and it is common to see people stop for a moment before roadside shrines to fold their hands and offer short invocations to the gods. Since at least the seventh century A.D., the devotional path has spread from the south throughout India through the literary and musical activities of saints who have been some of the most important representatives of regional languages and traditions. The hymns of these saints and their successors, mostly in vernacular forms, are memorized and performed at all levels of society. Every state in India has its own *bhakti* tradition and poets who are studied and revered. In Tamil Nadu, groups called Nayanmars (devotees of Shiva) and Alvars (devotees of Vishnu) were composing beautiful poetry in the Tamil language as early as the sixth century. In Bengal one of the greatest poets was Chaitanya (1485-1536), who spent much of his life in a state of mystical ecstasy. One of the greatest North Indian saints was Kabir (ca. 1440-1518), a common leatherworker who stressed faith in God without devotion to images, rituals, or scriptures. Among female poets, Princess Mirabai (ca. 1498-1546) from Rajasthan stands out as one whose love for Krishna was so intense that she suffered persecution for her public singing and dancing for the lord.

A recurring motif that emerges from the poetry and the hagiographies of these saints is the equality of all men and women before God and the ability of people from all castes and occupations to find their way to union with God if they have enough faith and devotion. In this sense, the *bhakti* tradition serves as one of the equalizing forces in Indian society and culture.

VISHNU

As one of the most important gods in the Hindu pantheon, Vishnu is surrounded by a number of extremely popular and well-known stories and is the focus of a number of sects devoted entirely to his worship. Vishnu contains a number of personalities, often represented as ten major descents (avatars) in which the god has taken on physical forms in order to save earthly creatures from destruction. In one story, the earth was drowning in a huge flood, so to save it Vishnu took on the body of a giant turtle and lifted the earth on his back out of the waters. A tale found in the Vedas describes a demon who could not be conquered. Responding to the pleas of the gods, Vishnu appeared before the demon as a dwarf. The demon, in a classic instance of pride, underestimated this dwarf and granted him as much of the world as he could tread in three steps. Vishnu then assumed his universal form and in three strides spanned the entire universe and beyond, crushing the demon in the process.

The incarnation of Vishnu known to almost everyone in India is his life as Ram (Rama in Sanskrit), a prince from the ancient north Indian kingdom of Ayodhya, in the cycle of stories known as the *Ramayana* (The Travels of Ram). On one level, this is a classic adventure story, as Ram is exiled from the kingdom and has to wander in the forests of southern India with his beautiful wife Sita and his loyal younger brother Lakshman. After many adventures, during which Ram befriends the king of the monkey kingdom and joins forces with the great monkey hero Hanuman, the demon king Ravana kidnaps Sita and takes her to his fortress on the island of Lanka (modern Sri Lanka). A huge war then ensues, as Ram with his animal allies attacks the demons, destroys them all, and returns in triumph to North India to occupy his lawful throne. Village storytellers, street theater players, the movies, and the national television network all have their versions of this story. In many parts of the country, but especially in North India, the annual festival of Dussehra celebrates Ram's adventures and his final triumph and includes the public burning of huge effigies of Ravana at the end of several days of parties. Everyone knows that Ram is really Vishnu, who came down to rid the earth of the demons and set up an ideal kingdom of righteousness—Ram Raj—which stands as an ideal in contemporary India. Sita is in reality his consort, the goddess Lakshmi, the ideal of feminine beauty and devotion to her husband. Lakshmi, also known as Shri, eventually became the goddess of fortune, surplus, and happiness. Hanuman, as the faithful sidekick with great physical and magical powers, is one of the most beloved images in the Hindu pantheon with temples of his own throughout the country.

Another widely known incarnation is Krishna. In the *Mahabharata* (Great Battle of the Descendants of Bharata), the gigantic, multivolume epic of ancient North Indian kingdoms, Krishna appears as the ruler of one of the many states allied either with the heroic Pandava brothers or with their treacherous cousins, the Kauravas. Bharata was an ancient king whose achievements are celebrated in the *Mahabharata* and from whose name derives one of the names for modern India, that is Bharat. During the final battle, Krishna serves as charioteer for the hero Arjuna, and before the fighting starts he bolsters Arjuna's faltering will to fight against his kin. Krishna reveals himself as Vishnu, the supreme godhead, who has set up the entire conflict to cleanse the earth of evildoers according to his inscrutable will. This section of the epic, the *Bhagavad Gita* , or Song of the Lord, is one of the great jewels of world religious literature and of central importance in modern Hinduism. One of its main themes is *karma-yoga* , or selfless discipline in offering all of one's allotted tasks in life as a devotion to God and without attachment to consequences. The true reality is the soul that neither slays nor is slain and that can rejoin God through selfless dedication and through Krishna's saving grace.

A completely different cycle of stories portrays Krishna as a young cowherd, growing up in the country after he was saved from an evil uncle who coveted his kingdom. In this incarnation, Krishna often appears as a happy, roly-poly infant, well known for his pranks and thefts of butter. Although his enemies send evil agents to destroy him, the baby miraculously survives their attacks and kills his demonic assailants. Later, as he grows into an adolescent, he continues to perform miracles such as saving the cowherds and their flocks from a dangerous storm by holding up a mountain over their heads until the weather clears. His most striking exploits, however, are his affairs as a young adult with the *gopis* (cowherding maidens), all of whom are in love with him because of his good looks and talent with the flute.

These explicitly sexual activities, including stealing the clothes of the maidens while they are bathing, are the basis for a wide range of poetry and songs to Krishna as a lover; the devotee of the god takes on a female role and directs toward the beloved lord the heartfelt longing for union with the divine. Krishna's relationship with Radha, his favorite among the *gopis* , has served as a model for male and female love in a variety of art forms, and since the sixteenth century appears prominently as a motif in North Indian paintings. Unlike many other deities, who are depicted as very fair in color, Krishna appears in all these adventures as a dark lord, either black or blue in color. In this sense, he is a figure who constantly overturns accepted conventions of order, hierarchy, and propriety, and introduces a playful and mischievous aspect of a god who hides from his worshipers but saves them in the end. The festival of Holi at the spring equinox, in which people of all backgrounds play in the streets and squirt each other with colored water, is associated with Krishna.

In iconography Vishnu may appear as any of his ten incarnations but often stands in sculpture as a princely male with four arms that bear a club, discus, conch, and lotus flower. He may also appear lying on his back on the thousand-headed king of the serpents, Shesha-Naga, in the milk ocean at the center of time, with his feet massaged by Lakshmi, and with a lotus growing from his navel giving birth to the god Brahma, a four-headed representation of the creative principle. Vishnu in this representation is the ultimate source of the universe that he causes to expand and contract at regular cosmic intervals measuring millions of years. On a more concrete level, Vishnu may become incarnate at any moment on earth in order to continue to bring sentient creatures back to himself, and a number of great religious teachers (including, for example, Chaitanya in Bengal) are identified by their followers as incarnations of Vishnu.

SHIVA

The god Shiva is the other great figure in the modern pantheon. In contrast to the regal attributes of Vishnu, Shiva is a figure of renunciation. A favorite image portrays him as an ascetic, performing meditation alone in the fastness of the Himalayas. There he sits on a tiger skin, clad only in a loincloth, covered with sacred ash that gives his skin a gray color. His trident is stuck into the ground next to him. Around his neck is a snake. From his matted hair, tied in a topknot, the river Ganga (Ganges) descends to the earth. His neck is blue, a reminder of the time he drank the poison that emerged while gods and demons competed to churn the milk ocean. Shiva often appears in this image as an antisocial being, who once burned up Kama, the god of love, with a glance. But behind this image is the cosmic lord who, through the very power of his meditating consciousness, expands the entire universe and all beings in it. Although he appears to be hard to attain, in reality Shiva is a loving deity who saves those devotees who are wholeheartedly dedicated to him.

The *bhakti* literature of South India, where Shiva has long been important, describes the numerous instances of pure-hearted devotion to the beautiful lord and the final revelation of himself as Shiva after testing his devotees. Shiva often appears on earth in disguise, perhaps as a wandering Brahman priest, to challenge the charity or belief of a suffering servant, only to appear eventually in his true nature. Many of these divine plays are connected directly with specific people and specific sites, and almost every ancient Shiva temple can claim a famous poem or a famous miracle in its history. The hundreds of medieval temples in Tamil Nadu, almost all dedicated to Shiva, contain sculptured panels depicting the god in a variety of guises: Bhikshatana, the begging lord; Bhairava, a horrible, destructive image; or Nataraja, the lord of the dance, beating a drum that keeps time while he manifests the universe.

Because he withholds his sexual urges and controls them, Shiva is able to transmute sexual energy into creative power, by generating intense heat. It is, in fact, the heat generated from discipline and austerity (*tapas*) that is seen as the source for the generative power of all renunciants, and in this sense Shiva is often connected with wandering orders of monks in modern India. For the average worshiper, the sexual power of Shiva is seen in the most common image that represents him, the lingam. This is typically a cylindrical stone several feet tall, with a rounded top, standing in a circular base. On one level, this is the most basic image of divinity, providing a focus for worship with a minimum of artistic embellishment, attempting to represent the infinite. The addition of carved anatomical details on many lingams, however, leaves no doubt for the worshiper that this is an erect male sexual organ, showing the procreative power of God at the origin of all things. The concept of reality as the complex interplay of opposite principles, male and female, thus finds its highest form in the mythology of Shiva and his consort Parvati (also known as Shakti, Kali, or Durga), the daughter of the mountains. This most controlled deity, the meditating Shiva, then has still another form, as the erotic lover of Parvati, embracing her passionately.

Shiva and Parvati have two sons, who have entire cycles of myths and legends and *bhakti* cults in their own right. One son is called variously Karttikeya (identified with the planet Mars) or Skanda (the god of war or Subrahmanya). He is extremely handsome, carries a spear, and rides a peacock. According to some traditions, he emerged motherless from Shiva when the gods needed a great warrior to conquer an indestructible demon. In southern India, where he is called Murugan, he is a lord of mountain places and a great friend of those who dedicate themselves to him. Some devotees vow to carry on their shoulders specially carved objects of wood for a determined number of weeks, never putting them down during that time. Others may go further, and insert knives or long pins into their bodies for extended periods.

Another son of Shiva and Parvati is Ganesh, or Ganapati, the Lord of the Ganas (the hosts of Shiva), who has a male human's body with four arms and the head of an elephant. One myth claims that he originated directly from Parvati's body and entered into a quarrel with Shiva, who cut off his human head and replaced it later with the head of the first animal he found, which happened to be an elephant. For most worshipers, Ganesh is the first deity invoked during any ceremony because he is the god of wisdom and remover of obstacles. People worship Ganesh when beginning anything, for example, at the start of a trip or the first day of the new school year. He is often pictured next to his mount, the rat, symbol of the ability to get in anywhere. Ganesh is therefore a clever figure, a trickster in many stories, who presents a benevolent and friendly image to those worshipers who placate him. His image is perhaps the most widespread and public in India, visible in streets and transportation terminals everywhere. The antics of Ganesh and Karttikeya and the interactions of Shiva and Parvati have generated a series of entertaining myths of Shiva as a henpecked husband, who would prefer to keep meditating but instead is drawn into family problems, providing a series of morality tales in households throughout India.

BRAHMA AND THE HINDU TRINITY

It is often said that the Hindu pantheon has three gods at its head: Brahma, the creator of the universe; Vishnu, the preserver of life; and Shiva, the destroyer of ignorance. Brahma is a representation of the impersonal *brahman* in a human form, usually with four faces facing the cardinal directions and four arms. In reality, Brahma receives little devotion from worshipers, who may mention him in passing while giving their attention to the other main gods. There are few temples in India dedicated to him; instead, his image may stand in niches on the walls of temples built for other deities. Religious stories usually place Brahma as an intermediate authority who cannot handle a problem and passes it on to either Vishnu or Shiva. The concept of the trinity (*trimurti*), expressed in beautiful art works or invoked even by believers, is in practice a philosophical construct that unites all deistic traditions within Hinduism into one overarching symbol.

THE GODDESS

Philosophical musings as far back as the Rig Veda contemplated the universe as the result of an interplay between the male principle (*purusha*), the prime source of generative power but quiescent, and a female principle that came to be known as *prakriti* , an active principle that manifests reality, or power (*shakti*), at work in the world. On a philosophical level, this female principle ultimately rests in the oneness of the male, but on a practical level it is the female that is most significant in the world. The vast array of iconography and mythology that surround the gods such as Vishnu and Shiva is a backdrop for the worship of their female consorts, and the male deities fade into the background. Thus it is that the divine is often female in India.

Vishnu's consort, Lakshmi, has a number of well-known incarnations that are the center of cults in their own right. In the *Ramayana* , for example, female characters are responsible for most of the important events, and the dutiful Sita, who resists the advances of lustful Ravana, is a much beloved figure of devotion. Lakshmi receives direct worship along with Ram during the big national festival of Dipavali (Diwali), celebrated with massive fireworks demonstrations, when people pray for success and wealth during the coming year. The *Mahabharata* is equally packed with tales of male and female relationships in which women hold their own, and the beautiful Draupadi, wife of the five Pandava heroes, has her own cult in scattered locations throughout India.

Parvati, in a variety of forms, is the most common focus of devotion in India. She presents two main facets to her worshipers: a benign and accepting personality that provides assistance and a powerful and dangerous personality that must be placated. The benign vision exists in many temples to Shiva throughout the country, where the goddess has her own shrine that is in practice the most frequented site of heartfelt devotion. During annual festivals in which the god and goddess emerge from their shrines and travel in processions, it is often the goddess who is most eagerly anticipated. In North India, for example, life-like statues of the loving goddess Kali, who is ultimately a manifestation of Parvati, are carried through huge crowds that line village and city streets. In South India, where gigantic temples are the physical and social centers of town life, the shrines and their annual festivals are often known by the names of their goddesses. One of the more famous is the sixteenth- and seventeenth-century Minakshi Temple in Madurai, Tamil Nadu. The temple is named after the "fish-eyed goddess" Minakshi, described in myths as a dark queen born with three breasts, who set out to conquer the universe. After overrunning the world and vanquishing the gods, Minakshi finally met Shiva and, when her third breast disappeared, accepted him as her lord. This motif of physical power and energy appears in many stories where the goddess is a warrior or conqueror of demons who in the end joins with Shiva.

Alternative visions, however, portray a goddess on the loose, with the potential for causing havoc in the world unless appeased. The goddess Durga is a great warrior who carries swords and a shield, rides a tiger, and destroys demons when the gods prove incapable; in this incarnation, she never submits, but remains capable of terrible deeds of war. The goddess Kali often appears as an even more horrific vision of the divine, with garlands of human skulls around her neck and a severed head in her hand; her bloody tongue hangs from her mouth, and the weapons in her arms drip gore. This image attempts to capture the destructive capacity of the divine, the suffering in the world, and the ultimate return of all things to the goddess at death.

In many small shrines throughout India, in marked contrast to the large and ornate temples dominated by Brahmanical principles and the philosophy of nonviolence, the female divinity receives regular gifts of blood sacrifices, usually chickens and goats. In addition, the goddess may manifest herself as the bearer of a number of diseases.

The goddess of smallpox, known as Shitala in North India and Mariamman in South India, remains a feared and worshiped figure even after the official elimination of the disease, for she is still capable of afflicting people with a number of fevers and poxes. Many more localized forms of goddesses, known by different names in different regions, are the focus for prayers and vows that lead worshipers to undertake acts of austerity and pilgrimages in return for favors.

LOCAL DEITIES

Along many paths in the countryside, and in some urban neighborhoods, there are sacred spots at the base of trees, or small stones set in niches, or simply made statues with flowers or a small flame burning in front of them. These are shrines for deities who are locally honored for protecting the people from harm caused by natural disasters or evil influences. Worshipers often portray these protectors as warriors, and, in some cases, they may be traced back to great human fighters who died for their village and later became immortalized. In South India, there are thousands of hero stones, simple representations of warriors on slabs of stone, found in and around agricultural settlements, in memory of nameless local fighters who may have died while protecting their communities hundreds of years ago. At one time, these stones may have received regular signs of devotion, but they are mostly ignored in contemporary India. In the fields on the outskirts of many villages, there are large, multicolored, terra-cotta figures of warriors with raised swords or figures of war horses; these are open-air shrines of the god Aiyanar, who serves as the village protector and who has very few connections with the great tradition of Hinduism.

Local deities may begin to attract the attention of worshipers from a wide geographical area, which may include many villages or neighborhoods, or from a large percentage of the members of particular castes, who come to the deity seeking protection or boons. These deities have their own shrines, which may be simple, independent enclosures with pillared halls or may stand as separate establishments attached to temples of Shiva, Vishnu, or any other great god.

Deities at this level attract expressive and ecstatic forms of worship and tend to possess special devotees on a regular basis or enter into their believers during festivals. People who are possessed by the god may speak to their families and friends concerning important personal or social problems, predicting the future or clarifying mysteries. These local gods often expect offerings of animals, usually goats or chickens, which are killed in the vicinity of the shrines and then consumed in communal meals by families and friends.

In the twentieth century, there has been an increase in the number of new, regional gods attracting worshipers from many different groups, spurred by vast improvements in transport and communication. For example, in the hills bordering the states of Tamil Nadu and Kerala is a shrine for the god Ayyappan, whose origin is uncertain but who is sometimes called the offspring of Shiva and Vishnu in his female form. Ayyappan's annual festival is a time of pilgrimage for ever-growing numbers of men from throughout South India.

These devotees fast and engage in austerities under the leadership of a teacher for weeks beforehand and then travel in groups to the shrine for a glimpse of the god. Bus tickets are hard to obtain for several weeks as masses of elated men, clad in distinctive ritual dhotis of various colors, throng public transportation during their trip to the shrine. In northwestern India, the popularity of the goddess Vaishno Devi has risen meteorically since independence. Vaishno Devi, who combines elements of Lakshmi and Durga, is an extremely benevolent manifestation of the eternal virgin who gives material well-being to her worshipers. One million pilgrims travel annually to her cave shrine in the foothills of the Himalayas, about fifty kilometers north of the city of Jammu.

Since the 1950s, the most spectacular example of a deity's increasing influence throughout northern and central India is the cult of Santoshi Ma (Mother of Contentment). Her myths recount the sufferings of a young woman left alone by her working husband and abused by her in-laws, who nevertheless remains loving and faithful to her man and, by performing simple vows to the goddess (fasting one day every week), eventually sees the return of her now-rich husband and moves with him into her own house. Santoshi Ma, thought to be the daughter of Ganesh, is worshiped mostly by lower middle-class women who also pray for material goods. In the 1980s and early 1990s, her shrines were spreading everywhere and even taking over older temples, aided by the release in the 1970s of an extremely popular film version of her story, *Jay Santoshi Ma.*

THE CEREMONIES OF HINDUISM

The ritual world of Hinduism, manifestations of which differ greatly among regions, villages, and individuals, offers a number of common features that link all Hindus into a greater Indian religious system and influence other religions as well. The most notable feature in religious ritual is the division between purity and pollution. Religious acts presuppose some degree of impurity or defilement for the practitioner, which must be overcome or neutralized before or during ritual procedures. Purification, usually with water, is thus a typical feature of most religious action. Avoidance of the impure—taking animal life, eating flesh, associating with dead things, or body fluids—is another feature of Hindu ritual and is important for repressing pollution. In a social context, those individuals or groups who manage to avoid the impure are accorded increased respect. Still another feature is a belief in the efficacy of sacrifice, including survivals of Vedic sacrifice. Thus, sacrifices may include the performance of offerings in a regulated manner, with the preparation of sacred space, recitation of texts, and manipulation of objects. A third feature is the concept of merit, gained through the performance of charity or good works, that will accumulate over time and reduce sufferings in the next world.

DOMESTIC WORSHIP

The home is the place where most Hindus conduct their worship and religious rituals. The most important times of day for performance of household rituals are dawn and dusk, although especially devout families may engage in devotion more often. For many households, the day begins when the women in the house draw auspicious geometric designs in chalk or rice flour on the floor or the doorstep. For orthodox Hindus, dawn and dusk are greeted with recitation from the Rig Veda of the Gayatri Mantra for the sun—for many people, the only Sanskrit prayer they know. After a bath, there is personal worship of the gods at a family shrine, which typically includes lighting a lamp and offering foodstuffs before the images, while prayers in Sanskrit or a regional language are recited. In the evenings, especially in rural areas, mostly female devotees may gather together for long sessions of singing hymns in praise of one or more of the gods.

Minor acts of charity punctuate the day. During daily baths, there are offerings of a little water in memory of the ancestors. At each meal, families may set aside a handful of grain to be donated to beggars or needy persons, and daily gifts of small amounts of grain to birds or other animals serve to accumulate merit for the family through their self-sacrifice.

LIFE-CYCLE RITUALS

A detailed series of life-cycle rituals (*samskara* , or refinements) mark major transitions in the life of the individual. Especially orthodox Hindu families may invite Brahman priests to their homes to officiate at these rituals, complete with sacred fire and recitations of mantras. Most of these rituals, however, do not occur in the presence of such priests, and among many groups who do not revere the Vedas or respect Brahmans, there may be other officiants or variations in the rites.

Ceremonies may be performed during pregnancy to ensure the health of the mother and growing child. The father may part the hair of the mother three times upward from the front to the back, to assure the ripening of the embryo. Charms may serve to ward off the evil eye and witches or demons. At birth, before the umbilical cord is severed, the father may touch the baby's lips with a gold spoon or ring dipped in honey, curds, and ghee.

The word *vak* (speech) is whispered three times into the right ear, and mantras are chanted to ensure a long life. A number of rituals for the infant include the first visit outside to a temple, the first feeding with solid food (usually cooked rice), an ear-piercing ceremony, and the first haircut (shaving the head) that often occurs at a temple or during a festival when the hair is offered to a deity.

A crucial event in the life of the orthodox, upper-caste Hindu male is an initiation (*upanayana*) ceremony, which takes place for some young males between the ages of six and twelve to mark the transition to awareness and adult religious responsibilities. At the ceremony itself, the family priest invests the boy with a sacred thread to be worn always over the left shoulder, and the parents instruct him in pronouncing the Gayatri Mantra. The initiation ceremony is seen as a new birth; those groups entitled to wear the sacred thread are called the twice-born. In the ancient categorization of society associated with the Vedas, only the three highest groups—Brahman, warrior (Kshatriya), and commoner or merchant (Vaishya)—were allowed to wear the thread, to make them distinct from the fourth group of servants (Shudra). Many individuals and groups who are only hazily associated with the old "twice-born" elites perform the *upanayana* ceremony and claim the higher status it bestows. For young Hindu women in South India, a different ritual and celebration occurs at the first menses.

The next important transition in life is marriage. For most people in India, the betrothal of the young couple and the exact date and time of the wedding are matters decided by the parents in consultation with astrologers. At Hindu weddings, the bride and bridegroom represent the god and the goddess, although there is a parallel tradition that sees the groom as a prince coming to wed his princess. The groom, decked in all his finery, often travels to the wedding site on a caparisoned white horse or in an open limousine, accompanied by a procession of relatives, musicians, and bearers of ornate electrified lamps. The actual ceremonies in many cases become extremely elaborate, but orthodox Hindu marriages typically have at their center the recitation of mantras by priests. In a crucial rite, the new couple take seven steps northward from a sacred household fire, turn, and make offerings into the flames. Independent traditions in regional languages and among different caste groups support wide variations in ritual.

After the death of a family member, the relatives become involved in ceremonies for preparation of the body and a procession to the burning or burial ground. For most Hindus, cremation is the ideal method for dealing with the dead, although many groups practice burial instead; infants are buried rather than cremated. At the funeral site, in the presence of the male mourners, the closest relative of the deceased (usually the eldest son) takes charge of the final rite and, if it is cremation, lights the funeral pyre. After a cremation, ashes and fragments of bone are collected and eventually immersed in a holy river. After a funeral, everyone undergoes a purifying bath. The immediate family remains in a state of intense pollution for a set number of days (sometimes ten, eleven, or thirteen). At the end of that period, close family members meet for a ceremonial meal and often give gifts to the poor or to charities. A particular feature of the Hindu ritual is the preparation of rice balls (*pinda*) offered to the spirit of the dead person during memorial services. In part these ceremonies are seen as contributing to the merit of the deceased, but they also pacify the soul so that it will not linger in this world as a ghost but will pass through the realm of Yama, the god of death.

PILGRIMAGE

India is covered with holy sites associated with the exploits of the gods, the waters of a sacred river, or the presence of holy men. Texts called the Puranas (ancient lore in Sanskrit) contain lengthy sections that describe numerous sacred places and the merit gained by traveling to them in a devout manner. Bathing at such sites is a specially meritorious act. With the expansion of public transportation in the twentieth century, there has been a vast increase in the numbers of people who visit these spots to partake of the divine and visit new places. In fact, for many Indians pilgrimage is the preferred form of tourism, involving family and community groups in enjoyable and uplifting vacations.

Certain important sites are well-known throughout India and attract hundreds of thousands of pilgrims annually. Probably the most significant is Varanasi (also known as Banaras, Benares, or Kashi) in southeastern Uttar Pradesh on the north bank of the Ganga. It is sacred to Hindus, Buddhists, and Jains, who flock to the ghats, or steps, leading from temples down to the banks of the sacred Ganga in their search for an auspicious site for death, cremation, or immersion of ashes. Hardwar, in northwestern Uttar Pradesh, far up the Ganga in the foothills of the Himalayas, is theVaranasi of northwest India for Hindus living there and is a favorite spot for ritual bathing. There are numerous destinations in the Himalayas, including Badrinath and Kedarnath, isolated sites in northern Uttar Pradesh that once required a long journey on foot. In southern India, the rivers Kaveri, Krishna, and Godavari attract pilgrims to a large number of bathing sites, and the coastline features major temples such as the Ramalingesvara Temple in Ramesvaram, Tamil Nadu, where Ram and his army crossed over to Lanka to rescue Sita. Pandharpur, in Maharashtra, is the destination for many thousands of devotees of Vitthala, an incarnation of Vishnu, whose tradition goes back at least to the thirteenth century and was written about by the great Marathi *bhakti* poets Namdev, Tukaram, and Eknath. There are smaller sites near almost every river or scenic hilltop.

For many pilgrims, the process of getting to their destination involves preliminary vows and fasting, intensive cooperative efforts among different families and groups, extensive traveling on foot, and the constant singing of devotional songs. On arrival, groups of pilgrims often make contact with priests who specialize in the pilgrim trade and for a fee plan the group's schedule and ritual activity. At some of the major sites, the families of the priests have served as hereditary guides for groups of pilgrims over many generations. Where a shrine is the focus, the devotee may circumambulate the buildings and wait in line for long hours just for a glimpse of the deity's image as security personnel move the crowds along. At auspicious bathing sites, pilgrims may have to wade through the crush of other devotees to dip into the sacred waters of a river or a tank. Worshipers engaged in special vows or in praying for the cure of a loved one may purchase shrine amulets to give to the god (which are circulated back to the shrine's shop) or purchase foodstuffs, sanctified by the god's presence, to take to friends and family. Nearby, souvenir hawkers and shopkeepers and sometimes even amusement parks contribute to a lively atmosphere that is certainly part of the attraction of many pilgrimage sites.

FESTIVALS

A vast number of local Hindu festivals revolve around the worship of gods at the neighborhood, village, or caste level. All over India, at least once a year the images of the gods are taken from their shrines to travel in processions around their domains. The images are carried on palanquins that require human bearers or on human-drawn, large-wheeled carts. The images may be intricately made up in order for the stone or wooden statues to appear lifelike. They may wear costly vestments, and flower garlands may surround their necks or entire shrines. The gods move down village or city streets in parades that may include multiple palanquins and, at sites of major temples, even elephants decked out in traditional vestments. As the parade passes, throngs of worshipers pray and make vows to the gods while the community as a whole looks on and participates in the spectacle. In many locations, these public parades go on for a number of days and include special events where the gods engage in "play" (*lila*) that may include mock battles and the defeat of demons. The ceremonial bathing of the images and displays of the gods in all their finery in public halls also occur. In the south, where temples stand at the geographic and psychological heart of village and town, some "chariots" of the gods stand many stories tall and require the concerted effort of dozens of men to pull them through the streets.

There are a number of Hindu religious festivals that are officially recognized by the government as "closed holidays," on which work stops throughout the country. The biggest of these occur within two blocks of time after the end of the southwest monsoon. The first comes at the end of the ten-day festival of Dussehra, late in the month of Asvina (September-October) according to the Shaka calendar, India's official calendar. This festival commemorates Ram's victory over Ravana and the rescue of his wife Sita. On the ninth day of Dusshera, people bless with sandalwood paste the "weapons" of their business life, including everything from plows to computers. On the final day of Dussehra, in North India celebrating crowds set fire to huge paper effigies of Ravana. Several weeks later comes Dipavali (Diwali), or the Festival of Lights, in the month of Kartika (October-November). This is officially a one-day holiday, but in reality it becomes a week-long event when many people take vacations. One tradition links this festival to the victory of Krishna over the demon Naraka, but for most devotees the holiday is a recreation of Ram's triumphant return with Sita, his wife, from his adventures. People light rows of lamps and place them on sills around their houses, set off gigantic amounts of fireworks, pray for wealth and good fortune, distribute sweets, and send greeting cards to friends and business associates.

The other closed holidays associated with Hindu festivals include Mahashivaratri, or the great night of Shiva, during the month of Magha (January-February). This festival celebrates Shiva's emanation of the universe through his cosmic dance, and is a day of fasting, visiting temples, and in many places staying up all night to sing devotional songs. On the fourth day in the month of Bhadra (August-September) comes the festival of Ganesh Chaturthi. Families and businesses prepare for this festival by purchasing brightly painted images of Ganesh and worshiping them for a number of days. On the festival itself, with great celebration, participants bathe the images (and in most cases permanently dump them) in nearby rivers, lakes, or seas. Janmashtami, the birthday of Krishna, also occurs in the month of Bhadra.

There are a large number of "restricted holidays" celebrated by the vast majority of the population and resulting in closures of business establishments. Major Hindu events include Ramanavami, the birthday of Ram in the month of Chaitra (March-April), and Holi, celebrated at the end of the month of Phalguna (February-

March), when people engage in cross-dressing, play tricks on each other, and squirt colored water or powder on each other. These primarily northern festivals receive varying amounts of attention in other parts of the country. A separate series of restricted holidays allow regional cultures to celebrate their own feasts, such as the harvest festival of Pongal in Tamil Nadu in mid-January, which celebrates the harvest and the sun's entrance into Capricorn.

ISLAM

Islam is India's largest minority religion, with Muslims officially comprising 12.1 percent of the country's population, or 101.6 million people as of the 1991 census. The largest concentrations—about 52 percent of all Muslims in India—live in the states of Bihar (12 million), West Bengal (16 million), and Uttar Pradesh (24 million), according to the 1991 census. Muslims represent a majority of the local populations only in Jammu and Kashmir (not tabulated in 1991 but 65 percent in 1981) and Lakshadweep (94 percent). As a faith with its roots outside South Asia, Islam also offers some striking contrasts to those religions that originated in India.

Origins and Tenets

Islam began with the ministry of the Prophet Muhammad (570-632), who belonged to a merchant family in the trading town of Mecca in Arabia. In his middle age, Muhammad received visions in which the Archangel Gabriel revealed the word of God to him. After 620 he publicly preached the message of these visions, stressing the oneness of God (Allah), denouncing the polytheism of his fellow Arabs, and calling for moral uplift of the population. He attracted a dedicated band of followers, but there was intense opposition from the leaders of the city, who profited from pilgrimage trade to the shrine called the Kaaba. In 622 Muhammad and his closest supporters migrated to the town of Yathrib (now renamed Medina) to the north and set up a new center of preaching and opposition to the leadership of Mecca. This move, the hijrah or hegira, marks the beginning of the Islamic calendar and the origin of the new religion of Islam. After a series of military engagements, Muhammad and his followers were able to defeat the authorities in Mecca and return to take control of the city. Before his death in 632, Muhammad was able to bring most of the tribes of Arabia into the fold of Islam. Soon after his death, the united Arabs conquered present-day Syria, Iraq, Egypt, and Iran, making Islam into a world religion by the end of the seventh century.

Islam means submission to God, and a Muslim is one who has submitted to the will of God. At the center of the religion is an intense concentration on the unity of God and the separation between God and his creatures. No physical representation of God is allowed. There are no other gods. The duty of humanity is to profess the simple testimony: "There is no god but God (Allah), and Muhammad is his Prophet." Obedience to God's will rests on following the example of the Prophet in one's own life and faithfulness to the revelations collected into the most sacred text, the Quran. The Five Pillars of Islam are reciting the profession of faith; praying five times a day; almsgiving to the poor; fasting (abstaining from dawn to dusk from food, drink, sexual relations, and smoking) during the month of Ramazan (the ninth month of the Islamic calendar, known as Ramadan in Arab countries), the holy month when God's revelations were received by Muhammad; and making the pilgrimage (hajj) to Mecca at least once during one's life if possible. People who obey God's commandments and live a good life will go to heaven after death; those who disobey will go to hell. All souls will be resurrected for a last judgment at the end of the world. Muslims view themselves as followers of the same tradition preserved in the Judaic and Christian scriptures, accept the prophetic roles of Ibrahim (Abraham), Musa (Moses), and Isa (Jesus), and view Islam as the final statement of revealed truth for the entire world.

Regulation of the Muslim community rests primarily on rules in the Quran, then on authenticated tales of the conduct (*sunna*) of the Prophet Muhammad, then on reasoning, and finally on the consensus of opinion. By the end of the eighth century, four main schools of Muslim jurisprudence had emerged in Sunni Islam to interpret the sharia (Islamic law). Prominent among these groups was the Hanafi school, which dominated most of India, and the Shafii school, which was more prevalent in South India. Because Islam has no ordained priesthood, direction of the Muslim community rests on the learning of religious scholars (ulama) who are expert in understanding the Quran and its appended body of commentaries.

Early leadership controversies within the Muslim community led to divisions that still have an impact on the body of believers. When Muhammad died, leadership fell to his father-in-law, Abu Bakr, who became the first caliph (*khalifa* , or successor), a position that combined spiritual and secular power. A separate group advocated the leadership of Ali, the cousin and son-in-law of the Prophet, who had married his daughter Fatima. Leadership could have fallen to Ali's son Husayn, but, in the power struggle that followed, in 680 Husayn and seventy-two followers were murdered at Karbala (now in modern Iraq).

This leadership dispute formed the most crucial dividing point in Islamic history: the victorious party went on to found the Umayyad Dynasty (661-750), which had its headquarters at Damascus, leading the majority of Muslims in the Sunni path. The disaffected Shiat Ali (or Party of Ali) viewed only his line as legitimate and continued to follow descendants of Husayn as their leader (imam). Among the followers of this Shia path, there is a party of "Seveners" who trace the lineage of imams down to Ismail (d. 762), the Seventh Imam and eldest son of the Sixth Imam. The Ismailis are the largest Shia group in India, and are concentrated in Maharashtra and Gujarat. A second group, the "Twelvers" (the most numerous Shia group worldwide), traces the lineage of imams through twelve generations, believing that the last or Twelfth Imam became "hidden" and will reappear in the world as a savior, or Mahdi, at some time in the future.

The division between Sunni and Shia dates back to purely political struggles in the seventh century, but over time between the two major communities many divisive differences in ritual and legal interpretations have evolved. The vast majority of Muslims are Sunni, and in contemporary India 90 percent of Muslims follow this path. Sunnis have recognized no legitimate caliph after the position was abolished in Turkey in 1924, placing the direction of the community clearly with the ulama.

Public worship for the average Muslim consists of going to a mosque (*masjid*)—normally on Fridays, although mosques are well attended throughout the week—for congregational prayers led by a local imam, following the public call to prayer, which may be intoned from the top of a minaret (*minar*) at the mosque. After leaving their footwear at the door, men and women separate; men usually sit in front, women in back, either inside the mosque or in an open courtyard. The prayer leader gives a sermon in the local regional language, perhaps interspersed with Arabic or Farsi (sometimes called Persian or Parsi) quotations, depending on his learning and the sophistication of the audience. Announcements of events of interest that may include political commentary are often included. Then follow common prayers that involve responses from the worshipers who stand, bow, and kneel in unison during devotions.

SIKHISM

Sikhism has about 20 million believers worldwide but has an importance far beyond those numbers because Sikhs have played a disproportionately large role in the armed forces and public affairs in India for the last 400 years. Although most Indian Sikhs (79 percent) remain concentrated in the state of Punjab, nearly 3.5 million Sikhs live outside the state, while about 4 million live abroad. This Sikh diaspora, driven by ambition and economic success, has made Sikhism a world religion as well as a significant minority force within the country.

Early History and Tenets

Sikhism began with Guru Nanak (1469-1539), a member of a trading caste in Punjab who seems to have been employed for some time as a government servant, was married and had two sons, and at age forty-five became a religious teacher. At the heart of his message was a philosophy of universal love, devotion to God, and the equality of all men and women before God. He set up congregations of believers who ate together in free communal kitchens in an overt attempt to break down caste boundaries based on food prohibitions. As a poet, musician, and enlightened master, Nanak's reputation spread, and by the time he died he had founded a new religion of "disciples" (*shiksha* or sikh) that followed his example.

Nanak's son, Baba Sri Chand, founded the Udasi sect of celibate ascetics, which continued in the 1990s. However, Nanak chose as his successor not his son but Angad (1504-52), his chief disciple, to carry on the work as the second guru. Thus began a lineage of teachers that lasted until 1708 and amounted to ten gurus in the Sikh tradition, each of whom is viewed as an enlightened master who propounded directly the word of God. The third guru, Amar Das (1479-1574), established missionary centers to spread the message and was so well respected that the Mughal emperor Akbar visited him. Amar Das appointed his son-in-law Ram Das (1534-81) to succeed him, establishing a hereditary succession for the position of guru. He also built a tank for water at Amritsar in Punjab, which, after his death, became the holiest center of Sikhism.

By the late sixteenth century, the influence of the Sikh religion on Punjabi society was coming to the notice of political authorities. The fifth guru, Arjun Das (1563-1606), was executed in Lahore by the Mughal emperor Jahangir (r. 1605-27) for alleged complicity in a rebellion. In response, the next guru, Hargobind (d. 1644), militarized and politicized his position and fought three battles with Mughal forces. Hargobind established a militant tradition of resistance to persecution by the central government in Delhi that remains an important motif in Sikh consciousness. Hargobind also established at Amritsar, in front of the Golden Temple, the central shrine devoted to Sikhism, the Throne of the Eternal God (Akal Takht) from which the guru dispensed justice and administered the secular affairs of the community, clearly establishing the tradition of a religious state that remains a major issue. The ninth guru, Tegh Bahadur (1621-75), because he refused Mughal emperor Aurangzeb's order to convert to Islam, was brought to Delhi and beheaded on a site that later became an important *gurdwara* (abode of the guru, a Sikh temple) on Chandni Chauk, one of the old city's main thoroughfares.

These events led the tenth guru, Gobind Singh (1666-1708), to transform the Sikhs into a militant brotherhood dedicated to defense of their faith at all times. He instituted a baptism ceremony involving the immersion of a sword in sugared water that initiates Sikhs into the Khalsa (*khalsa* , from the Persian term for "the king's own," often taken to mean army of the pure) of dedicated devotion. The outward signs of this new order were the "Five Ks" to be observed at all times: uncut hair (*kesh*), a long knife (*kirpan*), a comb (*kangha*), a steel bangle (*kara*), and a special kind of breeches not reaching below the knee (*kachha*). Male Sikhs took on the surname Singh (meaning lion), and women took the surname Kaur (princess). All made vows to purify their personal behavior by avoiding intoxicants, including alcohol and tobacco. In modern India, male Sikhs who have dedicated themselves to the Khalsa do not cut their beards and keep their long hair tied up under turbans, preserving a distinctive personal appearance recognized throughout the world.

Much of Guru Gobind Singh's later life was spent on the move, in guerrilla campaigns against the Mughal Empire, which was entering the last days of its effective authority under Aurangzeb (1658-1707). After Gobind Singh's death, the line of gurus ended, and their message continued through the *Adi Granth* (Original Book), which dates from 1604 and later became known as the *Guru Granth Sahib* (Holy Book of the Gurus). The *Guru Granth Sahib* is revered as a continuation of the line of gurus and as the living word of God by all Sikhs and stands at the heart of all ceremonies.

Most of the Sikh gurus were excellent musicians, who composed songs that conveyed their message to the masses in the saints' own language, which combined variants of Punjabi with Hindi and Braj and also contained Arabic and Persian vocabulary. Written in

Gurmukhi script, these songs are one of the main sources of early Punjabi language and literature. There are 5,894 hymns in all, arranged according to the musical measure in which they are sung. An interesting feature of this literature is that 937 songs and poems are by well-known *bhakti* saints who were not members of the lineage of Sikh gurus, including the North Indian saint Kabir and five Muslim devotees. In the *Guru Granth Sahib* , God is called by all the Hindu names and by Allah as well. From its beginnings, then, Sikhism was an inclusive faith that attempted to encompass and enrich other Indian religious traditions.

The belief system propounded by the gurus has its origins in the philosophy and devotions of Hinduism and Islam, but the formulation of Sikhism is unique. God is the creator of the universe and is without qualities or differentiation in himself. The universe (*samsar*) is not sinful in its origin but is covered with impurities; it is not suffering, but a transitory opportunity for the soul to recognize its true nature and break the cycle of rebirth. The unregenerate person is dominated by self-interest and remains immersed in illusion (*maya*), leading to bad karma. Meanwhile, God desires that his creatures escape and achieve enlightenment (nirvana) by recognizing his order in the universe. He does this by manifesting his grace as a holy word, attainable through recognition and recitation of God's holy name (*nam*). The role of the guru, who is the manifestation of God in the world, is to teach the means for prayer through the *Guru Granth Sahib* and the community of believers. The guru in this system, and by extension the *Guru Granth Sahib* , are coexistent with the divine and play a decisive role in saving the world.

Where the *Guru Granth Sahib* is present, that place becomes a *gurdwara.* Many Sikh homes contain separate rooms or designated areas where a copy of the book stands as the center of devotional ceremonies. Throughout Punjab, or anywhere there is a substantial body of believers, there are special shrines where the *Guru Granth Sahib* is displayed permanently or is installed daily in a ceremonial manner. These public *gurdwaras* are the centers of Sikh community life and the scene of periodic assemblies for worship. The typical assembly involves group singing from the *Guru Granth Sahib* , led by distinguished believers or professional singers attached to the shrine, distribution of holy food, and perhaps a sermon delivered by the custodian of the shrine.

As for domestic and life-cycle rituals, well into the twentieth century many Sikhs followed Hindu customs for birth, marriage, and death ceremonies, including readings from Hindu scriptures and the employment of Brahmans as officiants. Reform movements within the Sikh community have purged many of these customs, substituting instead readings from the *Guru Granth Sahib* as the focus for rituals and the employment of Sikh ritual specialists. At major public events—weddings, funerals, or opening a new business—patrons may fund a reading of the entire *Guru Granth Sahib* by special reciters.

TRIBAL RELIGIONS

Among the 68 million citizens of India who are members of tribal groups, the religious concepts, terminologies, and practices are as varied as the hundreds of tribes, but members of these groups have one thing in common: they are under constant pressure from the major organized religions. Some of this pressure is intentional, as outside missionaries work among tribal groups to gain converts. Most of the pressure, however, comes from the process of integration within a national political and economic system that brings tribes into increasing contact with other groups and different, prestigious belief systems. In general, those tribes that remain geographically isolated in desert, hill, and forest regions or on islands are able to retain their traditional cultures and religions longer. Those tribes that make the transition away from hunting and gathering and toward sedentary agriculture, usually as low-status laborers, find their ancient religious forms in decay and their place filled by practices of Hinduism, Islam, Christianity, or Buddhism.

One of the most studied tribal religions is that of the Santal of Orissa, Bihar, and West Bengal, one of the largest tribes in India, having a population estimated at 4.2 million. According to the 1991 census, however, only 23,645 people listed Santal as their religious belief. According to the Santal religion, the supreme deity, who ultimately controls the entire universe, is Thakurji. The weight of belief, however, falls on a court of spirits (*bonga*), who handle different aspects of the world and who must be placated with prayers and offerings in order to ward off evil influences. These spirits operate at the village, household, ancestor, and subclan level, along with evil spirits that cause disease, and can inhabit village boundaries, mountains, water, tigers, and the forest. A characteristic feature of the Santal village is a sacred grove on the edge of the settlement where many spirits live and where a series of annual festivals take place.

The most important spirit is Maran Buru (Great Mountain), who is invoked whenever offerings are made and who instructed the first Santals in sex and brewing of rice beer. Maran Buru's consort is the benevolent Jaher Era (Lady of the Grove).

A yearly round of rituals connected with the agricultural cycle, along with life-cycle rituals for birth, marriage and burial at death, involves petitions to the spirits and offerings that include the sacrifice of animals, usually birds. Religious leaders are male specialists in medical cures who practice divination and witchcraft. Similar beliefs are common among other tribes of northeast and central India such as the Kharia, Munda, and Oraon.

Smaller and more isolated tribes often demonstrate less articulated classification systems of the spiritual hierarchy, described as animism or a generalized worship of spiritual energies connected with locations, activities, and social groups. Religious concepts are intricately entwined with ideas about nature and interaction with local ecological systems. As in Santal religion, religious specialists are drawn from the village or family and serve a wide range of spiritual functions that focus on placating potentially dangerous spirits and coordinating rituals.

Unlike the Santal, who have a large population long accustomed to agriculture and a distinguished history of resistance to outsiders, many smaller tribal groups are quite sensitive to ecological degradation caused by modernization, and their unique religious beliefs are under constant threat. Even among the Santal, there are 300,000 Christians who are alienated from traditional festivals, although even among converts the belief in the spirits remains strong. Among the Munda and Oraon in Bihar, about 25 percent of the population are Christians. Among the Kharia of Bihar (population about 130,000), about 60 percent are Christians, but all are heavily influenced by Hindu concepts of major deities and the annual Hindu cycle of festivals. Tribal groups in the Himalayas were similarly affected by both Hinduism and Buddhism in the late twentieth century. Even the small hunting-and-gathering groups in the union territory of Andaman and Nicobar Islands have been under severe pressure because of immigration to this area and the resulting reduction of their hunting area.

CHRISTIANITY

The first Christians in India, according to tradition and legend, were converted by Saint Thomas the Apostle, who arrived on the Malabar Coast of India in A.D. 52. After evangelizing and performing miracles in Kerala and Tamil Nadu, he is believed to have been martyred in Madras and buried on the site of San Thomé Cathedral. Members of the Syro-Malabar Church, an eastern rite of the Roman Catholic Church, adopted the Syriac liturgy dating from fourth century Antioch. They practiced what is also known as the Malabar rite until the arrival of the Portuguese in the late fifteenth century. Soon thereafter, the Portuguese attempted to latinize the Malabar rite, an action which, by the mid-sixteenth century, led to charges of heresy against the Syro-Malabar Church and a lengthy round of political machinations. By the middle of the next century, a schism occurred when the adherents of the Malankar rite (or Syro-Malankara Church) broke away from the Syro-Malabar Church. Fragmentation continued within the Syro-Malabar Church up through the early twentieth century when a large contingent left to join the Nestorian Church, which had had its own roots in India since the sixth or seventh century. By 1887, however, the leaders of the Syro-Malabar Church had reconciled with Rome, which formally recognized the legitimacy of the Malabar rite. The Syro-Malankara Church was reconciled with Rome in 1930 and, while retaining the Syriac liturgy, adopted the Malayalam language instead of the ancient Syriac language.

Throughout this period, foreign missionaries made numerous converts to Christianity. Early Roman Catholic missionaries, particularly the Portuguese, led by the Jesuit Saint Francis Xavier (1506-52), expanded from their bases on the west coast making many converts, especially among lower castes and outcastes. The miraculously undecayed body of Saint Francis Xavier is still on public view in a glass coffin at the Basilica of Bom Jesus in Goa. Beginning in the eighteenth century, Protestant missionaries began to work throughout India, leading to the growth of Christian communities of many varieties.

The total number of Christians in India according to the 1991 census was 19.6 million, or 2.3 percent of the population. About 13.8 million of these Christians were Roman Catholics, including 300,000 members of the Syro-Malankara Church. The remainder of Roman Catholics were under the Catholic Bishops' Conference of India. In January 1993, after centuries of self-government, the 3.5-million-strong Latin-rite Syro-Malabar Church was raised to archepiscopate status as part of the Roman Catholic Church. In total, there were nineteen archbishops, 103 bishops, and about 15,000 priests in India in 1995.

Most Protestant denominations are represented in India, the result of missionary activities throughout the country, starting with the onset of British rule. Most denominations, however, are almost exclusively staffed by Indians, and the role of foreign missionaries is limited. The largest Protestant denomination in the country is the Church of South India, since 1947 a union of Presbyterian, Reformed, Congregational, Methodist, and Anglican congregations with approximately 2.2 million members. A similar Church of North India has 1 million members. There are 473,000 Methodists, 425,000 Baptists, and about 1.3 million Lutherans. Orthodox churches of the Malankara and Malabar rites total 2 million and 700,000 members, respectively.

All Christian churches have found the most fertile ground for expansion among Dalits, Scheduled Castes, and Scheduled Tribe groups. During the twentieth century, the fastest growing Christian communities have been located in the northeast, among the Khasis, Mizos, Nagas, and other hill tribes. Christianity offers a non-Hindu mode of acculturation during a period when the state and modern economy have been radically transforming the life-styles of the hill peoples. Missionaries have led the way in the development of written languages and literature for many tribal groups. Christian churches have provided a focus for unity among different ethnic groups and have brought with them a variety of charitable services.

ZOROASTRIANISM

According to the 1991 census, there were 79,382 members of the Zoroastrian faith. Some 79 percent lived in Maharashtra (primarily in Bombay) and most of the rest in Gujarat. Zoroastrians are primarily descendants of tenth-century immigrants from Persia who preserved the religion of Zoroaster, a prophet of Iran who taught probably in the sixth century B.C. Although the number of Parsis steadily declined during the twentieth century as a result of emigration and low birth rates, their religion is significant because of the financial influence wielded by this mostly trading community and because they represent the world's largest surviving group of believers in this ancient faith.

Originally, the Parsis were shipbuilders and traders located in the ports and towns of Gujarat. Their freedom from food or occupational restrictions based on caste affiliation enabled them to take advantage of the numerous commercial opportunities that accompanied the colonial expansion of trade and control. Substantial numbers moved to Bombay, which served as a base for expanding their business activities throughout India and abroad. A combination of Western commercial contacts and English-language education during the colonial period made the Parsis arguably the most cosmopolitan community in India. Socially, they were equally at home with Indians and Westerners; Parsi women enjoyed freedom of movement earlier than most high-caste Hindu or upper-class Muslim women. In contemporary India, Parsis are the most urban, elite, and wealthy of any of the nation's religious groups. Their role in the development of trade, industry, finance, and philanthropy has earned them an important place in the country's social and economic life, and several have achieved high rank in government.

The source of Parsi religion is a body of texts called the *Avesta* , which includes a number of sections in archaic language attributed to Zoroaster himself, and which preserve the cult of the fire sacrifice as the focus of ritual life. The supreme spirit is Ahura Mazda (or Ohrmazd), whose will is manifest in the world through the actions of bountiful immortals or good spiritual attributes that support life and love. Opposing the supreme spirit is the force of evil, Angra Mainyu (or Ahriman), which is the cause of all destruction and corruption in the world. Equipped with free will, humans can choose sides in this struggle and after death will appear at the bridge of judgment. People who choose to do good deeds go to heaven, those who commit evil go to hell. The opposed cosmic forces battle through the history of the universe, until at the end of time there will be a final judgment and a resurrection of the dead to a perfect world.

The extensive ritual life of devout Parsis revolves around sacred fires, of which there are three grades dependent on extensive ceremonial preparation. The highest two grades can only be maintained in fire temples by hereditary priests, who undergo extensive purificatory rites and wear special face masks to prevent polluting the flames with breath or saliva, while the third grade of fire can exist in the household. The most important rite for most lay people is the Navjote, which occurs between the seventh and fifteenth year of life, and initiates the young person into the adult community. The ceremony involves purifying bathing, reciting *Avesta* -based scriptures, and being invested with a sacred shirt (*sudrah*) and waist thread (*kusti*) that should always be worn thereafter. Marriage is also an important rite, complete with scriptural recitations. At death, great care is taken to avoid pollution from the body, and funeral services usually take place within twenty-four hours. The dead are then disposed of by exposure to vultures on large, circular "towers of silence" (*dakhma*). Most rituals take place in the home or in special pavilions; congregational worship at fire temples is limited to spring and autumn festivals.

The towns of Sanjan, Nausari, and Udvada in Gujarat are of prime importance to Parsis, having long served as community centers before mass migration to Bombay in the nineteenth century. Bombay is home to 70 percent of India's Parsis, where the management of Parsi affairs rests in the hands of a *panchayat* , the assembly that serves as a charitable and educational organization providing a comprehensive social welfare system at the local level.

JUDAISM

Trade contacts between the Mediterranean region and the west coast of India probably led to the presence of small Jewish settlements in India as long ago as the early first millennium B.C. In Kerala a community of Jews tracing its origin to the fall of Jerusalem in A.D. 70 has remained associated with the cities of Cranganore and Kochi (formerly known as Cochin) for at least 1,000 years. The Pardesi Synagogue in Kochi, rebuilt in 1568, is in the architectural style of Kerala but preserves the archaic ritual style of the Sephardic rite, with Babylonian and Yemenite influence as well. The Jews of Kochi, concentrated mostly in the old "Jew Town," were completely integrated into local culture, speaking Malayalam and taking local names while preserving their knowledge of Hebrew and contacts with Southwest Asia. A separate community of Jews, called the Bene Israel, had lived along the Konkan Coast in and around Bombay, Pune, and Ahmadabad for almost 2,000 years. Unlike the Kochi Jews, they became a village-based society and maintained little contact with other Jewish communities. They always remained within the orthodox Jewish fold, practicing the Sephardic rite without rabbis, with the synagogue as the center of religious and cultural life. A third group of Jews immigrated to India, beginning at the end of the eighteenth century, following the trade contacts established by the British Empire. These Baghdad Jews came mostly from the area of modern Iraq and settled in Bombay and Calcutta, where many of them became wealthy and participated in the economic leadership of these growing cities.

The population of the Kochi Jews, always small, had decreased from 5,000 in 1951 to about fifty in the early 1990s. During the same period, the Bene Israel decreased from about 20,000 to 5,000, while the Baghdad Jews declined from 5,000 to 250. Emigration to Australia, Israel, Britain, and North America accounts for most of this decline. According to the 1981 Indian census, there were 5,618 Jews in India, down from 5,825 in 1971. The 1991 census showed a further decline to 5,271, most of whom lived in Maharashtra and Mizoram.

3

CULTURE AND THE SOCIETY

India is justly famous for its complex social systems. Indian society is multifaceted to an extent perhaps unknown in any other of the world's great civilizations. Virtually no generalization made about Indian society is valid for all of the nation's multifarious groups. Comprehending the complexities of Indian social structure has challenged scholars and other observers over many decades.

The ethnic and linguistic diversity of Indian civilization is more like the diversity of an area as variable as Europe than like that of any other single nation-state. Living within the embrace of the Indian nation are vast numbers of different regional, social, and economic groups, each with different cultural practices. Particularly noteworthy are differences between social structures in the north and the south, especially in the realm of kinship systems. Throughout the country, religious differences can be significant, especially between the Hindu majority and the large Muslim minority; and other Indian groups—Buddhists, Christians, Jains, Jews, Parsis, Sikhs, and practitioners of tribal religions—all pride themselves on being unlike members of other faiths.

Access to wealth and power varies considerably, and vast differences in socioeconomic status are evident everywhere. The poor and the wealthy live side by side in urban and rural areas. It is common in city life to see a prosperous, well-fed man or woman chauffeured in a fine car pass gaunt street dwellers huddled beneath burlap shelters along the roadway. In many villages, solid cement houses of landowners rise not far from the flimsy thatched shacks of landless laborers. Even when not so obvious, distinctions of class are found in almost every settlement in India.

Urban-rural differences can be immense. Nearly 74 percent of India's population dwells in villages, with agriculture providing support for most of these rural residents. In villages, mud-plastered walls ornamented with traditional designs, dusty lanes, herds of grazing cattle, and the songs of birds at sunset provide typical settings for the social lives of most Indians. In India's great cities, however, millions of people live amidst cacophony—roaring vehicles, surging crowds, jammed apartment buildings, busy commercial establishments, loudspeakers blaring movie tunes—while breathing the poisons of industrial and automotive pollution.

Gender distinctions are pronounced. The behavior expected of men and women can be quite different, especially in villages, but also in urban centers. Prescribed ideal gender roles help shape the actions of both sexes as they move between family and the world outside the home.

Crosscutting and pervading all of these differences of region, language, wealth, status, religion, urbanity, and gender is the special feature of Indian society that has received most attention from observers: caste. The people of India belong to thousands of castes and castelike groups—hierarchically ordered, named groups into which members are born. Caste members are expected to marry within the group and follow caste rules pertaining to diet, avoidance of ritual pollution, and many other aspects of life.

Given the vast diversity of Indian society, any observation must be tempered with the understanding that it cannot apply to all Indians. Still, certain themes or underlying principles of life are widely accepted in India.

THEMES IN INDIAN SOCIETY

India is a hierarchical society. Within Indian culture, whether in the north or the south, Hindu or Muslim, urban or village, virtually all things, people, and groups of people are ranked according to various essential qualities. If one is attuned to the theme of hierarchy in India, one can discern it everywhere. Although India is a political democracy, in daily life there is little advocacy of or adherence to notions of equality.

Castes and castelike groups—those quintessential groups with which almost all Indians are associated—are ranked. Within most villages or towns, everyone knows the relative rankings of each locally represented caste, and people's behavior toward one another is constantly shaped by this knowledge. Between the extremes of the very high and very low castes, however, there is sometimes disagreement on the exact relative ranking of castes clustered in the middle.

Castes are primarily associated with Hinduism but also exist among other Indian religious groups. Muslims sometimes expressly deny that they have castes—they state that all Muslims are brothers under God—but observation of Muslim life in various parts of India reveals the existence of castelike groups and clear concern with social hierarchy. Among Indian Christians, too, differences in caste are acknowledged and maintained.

Throughout India, individuals are also ranked according to their wealth and power. For example, there are "big men" (*bare admi* , in Hindi) and "little men" (*chhote admi*) everywhere. "Big men" sit confidently on chairs, while "little men" come before them to make requests, either standing or crouching down on their haunches, certainly not presuming to sit beside a man of high status as an equal. Even men of nearly equal status who might share a string cot to sit on take their places carefully—the higher-ranking man at the head of the cot, the lower-ranking man at the foot.

Within families and kinship groupings, there are many distinctions of hierarchy. Men outrank women of the same or similar age, and senior relatives outrank junior relatives. Several other kinship relations involve formal respect. For example, in northern India, a daughter-in-law of a household shows deference to a daughter of a household. Even among young siblings in a household, there is constant acknowledgment of age differences: younger siblings never address an older sibling by name, but rather by respectful terms for elder brother or elder sister. However, an older sibling may address the younger by name.

Even in a business or academic setting, where colleagues may not openly espouse traditional observance of caste or class ranking behavior, they may set up fictive kinship relations, addressing one another by kinship terms reflecting family or village-style hierarchy. For example, a younger colleague might respectfully address an older colleague as *chachaji* (respected father's younger brother), gracefully acknowledging the superior position of the older colleague.

Purity and Pollution

Many status differences in Indian society are expressed in terms of ritual purity and pollution. Notions of purity and pollution are extremely complex and vary greatly among different castes, religious groups, and regions. However, broadly speaking, high status is associated with purity and low status with pollution. Some kinds of purity are inherent, or inborn; for example, gold is purer than copper by its very nature, and, similarly, a member of a high-ranking Brahman , or priestly, caste is born with more inherent purity than a member of a low-ranking Sweeper (Mehtar, in Hindi) caste. Unless the Brahman defiles himself in some extraordinary way, throughout his life he will always be purer than a Sweeper. Other kinds of purity are more transitory—a Brahman who has just taken a bath is more ritually pure than a Brahman who has not bathed for a day. This situation could easily reverse itself temporarily, depending on bath schedules, participation in polluting activities, or contact with temporarily polluting substances.

Purity is associated with ritual cleanliness—daily bathing in flowing water, dressing in properly laundered clothes of approved materials, eating only the foods appropriate for one's caste, refraining from physical contact with people of lower rank, and avoiding involvement with ritually impure substances. The latter include body wastes and excretions, most especially those of another adult person. Contact with the products of death or violence are typically polluting and threatening to ritual purity.

During her menstrual period, a woman is considered polluted and refrains from cooking, worshiping, or touching anyone older than an infant. In much of the south, a woman spends this time "sitting outside," resting in an isolated room or shed. During her period, a Muslim woman does not touch the Quran. At the end of the period, purity is restored with a complete bath. Pollution also attaches to birth, both for the mother and the infant's close kin, and to death, for close relatives of the deceased.

Members of the highest priestly castes, the Brahmans, are generally vegetarians (although some Bengali and Maharashtrian Brahmans eat fish) and avoid eating meat, the product of violence and death. High-ranking Warrior castes (Kshatriyas), however, typically consume nonvegetarian diets, considered appropriate for their traditions of valor and physical strength.

A Brahman born of proper Brahman parents retains his inherent purity if he bathes and dresses himself properly, adheres to a vegetarian diet, eats meals prepared only by persons of appropriate rank, and keeps his person away from the bodily exuviae of others (except for necessary contact with the secretions of family infants and small children).

If a Brahman happens to come into bodily contact with a polluting substance, he can remove this pollution by bathing and changing his clothing. However, if he were to eat meat or commit other transgressions of the rigid dietary codes of his particular caste, he would be considered more deeply polluted and would have to undergo various purifying rites and payment of fines imposed by his caste council in order to restore his inherent purity.

In sharp contrast to the purity of a Brahman, a Sweeper born of Sweeper parents is considered to be born inherently polluted. The touch of his body is polluting to those higher on the caste hierarchy than he, and they will shrink from his touch, whether or not he has bathed recently. Sweepers are associated with the traditional occupation of cleaning human feces from latrines and sweeping public lanes of all kinds of dirt. Traditionally, Sweepers remove these polluting materials in baskets carried atop the head and dumped out in a garbage pile at the edge of the village or neighborhood. The involvement of Sweepers with such filth accords with their low-status position at the bottom of the Hindu caste hierarchy, even as their services allow high-status people, such as Brahmans, to maintain their ritual purity.

Members of the Leatherworker (Chamar) caste are ascribed a very low status consonant with their association with the caste occupation of skinning dead animals and tanning the leather. Butchers (Khatiks, in Hindi), who kill and cut up the bodies of animals, also rank low on the caste hierarchy because of their association with violence and death.

However, castes associated with ruling and warfare—and the killing and deaths of human beings—are typically accorded high rank on the caste hierarchy. In these instances, political power and wealth outrank association with violence as the key determinant of caste rank.

Maintenance of purity is associated with the intake of food and drink, not only in terms of the nature of the food itself, but also in terms of who has prepared it or touched it. This requirement is especially true for Hindus, but other religious groups hold to these principles to varying degrees. Generally, a person risks pollution—and lowering his own status—if he accepts beverages or cooked foods from the hands of people of lower caste status than his own. His status will remain intact if he accepts food or beverages from people of higher caste rank. Usually, for an observant Hindu of any but the very lowest castes to accept cooked food from a Muslim or Christian is regarded as highly polluting.

In a clear example of pollution associated with dining, a Brahman who consumed a drink of water and a meal of wheat bread with boiled vegetables from the hands of a Sweeper would immediately become polluted and could expect social rejection by his caste fellows. From that moment, fellow Brahmans following traditional pollution rules would refuse food touched by him and would abstain from the usual social interaction with him. He would not be welcome inside Brahman homes—most especially in the ritually pure kitchens—nor would he or his close relatives be considered eligible marriage partners for other Brahmans.

Generally, the acceptance of water and ordinary foods cooked in water from members of lower-ranking castes incurs the greatest pollution. In North India, such foods are known as *kaccha khana* , as contrasted with fine foods cooked in butter or oils, which are known as *pakka khana.* Fine foods can be accepted from members of a few castes slightly lower than one's own. Local hierarchies differ on the specific details of these rules.

Completely raw foods, such as uncooked grains, fresh unpeeled bananas, mangoes, and uncooked vegetables can be accepted by anyone from anyone else, regardless of relative status. Toasted or parched foods, such as roasted peanuts, can also be accepted from anyone without ritual or social repercussions. (Thus, a Brahman may accept gifts of grain from lower-caste patrons for eventual preparation by members of his own caste, or he may purchase and consume roasted peanuts or tangerines from street vendors of unknown caste without worry.)

Water served from an earthen pot may be accepted only from the hands of someone of higher or equal caste ranking, but water served from a brass pot may be accepted even from someone slightly lower on the caste scale. Exceptions to this rule are members of the Waterbearer (Bhoi, in Hindi) caste, who are employed to carry water from wells to the homes of the prosperous and from whose hands members of all castes may drink water without becoming polluted, even though Waterbearers are not ranked high on the caste scale.

These and a great many other traditional rules pertaining to purity and pollution constantly impinge upon interaction between people of different castes and ranks in India. Although to the non-Indian these rules may seem irrational and bizarre, to most of the people of India they are a ubiquitous and accepted part of life. Thinking about and following purity and pollution rules make it necessary for people to be constantly aware of differences in status. With every drink of water, with every meal, and with every contact with another person, people must ratify the social hierarchy of which they are a part and within which their every act is carried out. The fact that expressions of social status are intricately bound up with events that happen to everyone every day—eating, drinking, bathing, touching, talking—and that transgressions of these rules, whether deliberate or accidental, are seen as having immediately polluting effects on the person of the transgressor, means that every ordinary act of human life serves as a constant reminder of the importance of hierarchy in Indian society.

There are many Indians, particularly among the educated urban elite, who do not follow traditional purity and pollution practices. Dining in each others' homes and in restaurants is common among well-educated people of diverse backgrounds, particularly when they belong to the same economic class. For these people, guarding the family's earthen water pot from inadvertent touch by a low-ranking servant is not the concern it is for a more traditional villager. However, even among those people whose words and actions denigrate traditional purity rules, there is often a reluctance to completely abolish consciousness of purity and pollution from their thinking.

It is surely rare for a Sweeper, however well-educated, to invite a Brahman to dinner in his home and have his invitation unself-consciously accepted. It is less rare, however, for educated urban colleagues of vastly different caste and religious heritage to enjoy a cup of tea together. Some high-caste liberals pride themselves on being free of "casteism" and seek to accept food from the hands of very low-caste people, or even deliberately set out to marry someone from a significantly lower caste or a different religion. Thus, even as they deny it, these progressives affirm the continuing significance of traditional rules of purity, pollution, and hierarchy in Indian society.

Social Interdependence

One of the great themes pervading Indian life is social interdependence. People are born into groups—families, clans, subcastes, castes, and religious communities—and live with a constant sense of being part of and inseparable from these groups. A corollary is the notion that everything a person does properly involves interaction with other people. A person's greatest dread, perhaps, is the possibility of being left alone, without social support, to face the necessary challenges of life. This sense of interdependence is extended into the theological realm: the very shape of a person's life is seen as being greatly influenced by divine beings with whom an ongoing relationship must be maintained.

Social interaction is regarded as being of the highest priority, and social bonds are expected to be long lasting. Even economic activities that might in Western culture involve impersonal interactions are in India deeply imbedded in a social nexus. All social interaction involves constant attention to hierarchy, respect, honor, the feelings of others, rights and obligations, hospitality, and gifts of food, clothing, and other desirable items. Finely tuned rules of etiquette help facilitate each individual's many social relationships.

Western visitors to India are sometimes startled to find that important government and business officials have left their posts—often for many days at a time—to attend a cousin's wedding or participate in religious activities in a distant part of the country. "He is out of station and will be back in a week or two," the absent official's officemates blandly explain to the frustrated visitor. What is going on is not laziness or hedonistic recreation, but is the official's proper recognition of his need to continually maintain his social ties with relatives, caste fellows, other associates, and God. Without being enmeshed in such ties throughout life, a person cannot hope to maintain long-term efficacy in either economic or social endeavors. Social bonds with relatives must be reinforced at family events or at rites crucial to the religious community. If this is not done, people who could offer vital support in many phases of life would be alienated.

In every activity, there is an assumption that social ties can help a person and that their absence can bring failure. Seldom do people carry out even the simplest task on their own. From birth onward, a child learns that his "fate" has been "written" by divine forces and that his life will be shaped by a plan decided by more powerful beings. When a small child eats, his mother puts the mouthfuls of food into his mouth with her own hand. When a boy climbs a tree to pluck mangoes, another stands below with a basket to receive them. When a girl fetches water from the well in pots on her head, someone at her home helps her unload the pots. When a farmer stacks sheaves of grain onto his bullock cart, he stands atop the cart, catching the sheaves tossed up to him by his son.

A student applying to a college hopes that he has an influential relative or family friend who can put in a good word for him with the director of admissions. At the age of marriage, a young person expects that parents will take care of finding the appropriate bride or groom and arranging all the formalities. At the birth of a child, the new mother is assured that the child's kin will help her attend to the infant's needs. A businessman seeking to arrange a contract relies not only on his own abilities but also on the assistance of well-connected friends and relatives to help finalize the deal. And finally, when facing death, a person is confident that offspring and other relatives will carry out the appropriate funeral rites, including a commemorative feast when, through gifts of clothing and food, continuing social ties are reaffirmed by all in attendance.

FAMILY

Family Ideals

In India, people learn the essential themes of cultural life within the bosom of a family. In most of the country, the basic units of society are the patrilineal family unit and wider kinship groupings.

The most widely desired residential unit is the joint family, ideally consisting of three or four patrilineally related generations, all living under one roof, working, eating, worshiping, and cooperating together in mutually beneficial social and economic activities. Patrilineal joint families include men related through the male line, along with their wives and children. Most young women expect to live with their husband's relatives after marriage, but they retain important bonds with their natal families.

Despite the continuous and growing impact of urbanization, secularization, and Westernization, the traditional joint household, both in ideal and in practice, remains the primary social force in the lives of most Indians. Loyalty to family is a deeply held ideal for almost everyone.

Large families tend to be flexible and well-suited to modern Indian life, especially for the 67 percent of Indians who are farmers or agricultural workers or work in related activities. As in most primarily agricultural societies, few individuals can hope to achieve economic security without being part of a cooperating group of kinsmen. The joint family is also common in cities, where kinship ties can be crucial to obtaining scarce jobs or financial assistance. Numerous prominent Indian families, such as the Tatas, Birlas, and Sarabhais, retain joint family arrangements even as they work together to control some of the country's largest financial empires.

The joint family is an ancient Indian institution, but it has undergone some change in the late twentieth century. Although several generations living together is the ideal, actual living arrangements vary widely depending on region, social status, and economic circumstance. Many Indians live in joint families that deviate in various ways from the ideal, and many live in nuclear families—a couple with their unmarried children—as is the most common pattern in the West. However, even where the ideal joint family is seldom found (as, for example, in certain regions and among impoverished agricultural laborers and urban squatters), there are often strong networks of kinship ties through which economic assistance and other benefits are obtained. Not infrequently, clusters of relatives live very near each other, easily available to respond to the give and take of kinship obligations. Even when relatives cannot actually live in close proximity, they typically maintain strong bonds of kinship and attempt to provide each other with economic help, emotional support, and other benefits.

As joint families grow ever larger, they inevitably divide into smaller units, passing through a predictable cycle over time. The breakup of a joint family into smaller units does not necessarily represent the rejection of the joint family ideal. Rather, it is usually a response to a variety of conditions, including the need for some members to move from village to city, or from one city to another to take advantage of employment opportunities. Splitting of the family is often blamed on quarrelling women—typically, the wives of coresident brothers. Although women's disputes may, in fact, lead to family division, men's disagreements do so as well. Despite cultural ideals of brotherly harmony, adult brothers frequently quarrel over land and other matters, leading them to decide to live under separate roofs and divide their property. Frequently, a large joint family divides after the demise of elderly parents, when there is no longer a single authority figure to hold the family factions together. After division, each new residential unit, in its turn, usually becomes joint when sons of the family marry and bring their wives to live in the family home.

Variations in Family Structure

Some family types bear special mention because of their unique qualities. In the sub-Himalayan region of Uttar Pradesh, polygyny is commonly practiced. There, among Hindus, a simple polygynous family is composed of a man, his two wives, and their unmarried children. Various other family types occur there, including the supplemented subpolygynous household—a woman whose husband lives elsewhere (perhaps with his other wife), her children, plus other adult relatives. Polygyny is also practiced in other parts of India by a tiny minority of the population, especially in families in which the first wife has not been able to bear children. Among the Buddhist people of the mountainous Ladakh District of Jammu and Kashmir, who have cultural ties to Tibet, fraternal polyandry is practiced, and a household may include a set of brothers with their common wife or wives. This family type, in which brothers also share land, is almost certainly linked to the extreme scarcity of cultivable land in the Himalayan region, because it discourages fragmentation of holdings.

The peoples of the northeastern hill areas are known for their matriliny, tracing descent and inheritance in the female line rather than the male line. One of the largest of these groups, the Khasis—an ethnic or tribal people in the state of Meghalaya—are divided into matrilineal clans; the youngest daughter receives almost all of the inheritance including the house. A Khasi husband goes to live in his wife's house. Khasis, many of whom have become Christian, have the highest literacy rate in India, and Khasi women maintain notable authority in the family and community.

Perhaps the best known of India's unusual family types is the traditional Nayar *taravad* , or great house. The Nayars are a cluster of castes in Kerala. High-ranking and prosperous, the Nayars maintained matrilineal households in which sisters and brothers and their children were the permanent residents.

After an official prepuberty marriage, each woman received a series of visiting husbands in her room in the *taravad* at night. Her children were all legitimate members of the *taravad*. Property, matrilineally inherited, was managed by the eldest brother of the senior woman. This system, the focus of much anthropological interest, has been disintegrating in the twentieth century, and in the 1990s probably fewer than 5 percent of the Nayars live in matrilineal *taravads*. Like the Khasis, Nayar women are known for being well-educated and powerful within the family.

Malabar rite Christians, an ancient community in Kerala, adopted many practices of their powerful Nayar neighbors, including naming their sons for matrilineal forebears. Their kinship system, however, is patrilineal. Kerala Christians have a very high literacy rate, as do most Indian Christian groups.

Large Kinship Groups

In most of Hindu India, people belong not only to coresident family groups but to larger aggregates of kin as well. Subsuming the family is the patrilineage (known in northern and central India as the *khandan* , *kutumb* , or *kul*), a locally based set of males who trace their ancestry to a common progenitor a few generations back, plus their wives and unmarried daughters. Larger than the patrilineage is the clan, commonly known as the *gotra* or *got* , a much larger group of patrilineally related males and their wives and daughters, who often trace common ancestry to a mythological figure. In some regions, particularly among the high-ranking Rajputs of western India, clans are hierarchically ordered. Some people also claim membership in larger, more amorphous groupings known as *vansh* and *sakha*.

Hindu lineages and clans are strictly exogamous—that is, a person may not marry or have a sexual alliance with a member of his own lineage or clan; such an arrangement would be considered incestuous. In North India, rules further prohibit marriage between a person and his mother's lineage members as well. Among some high-ranking castes of the north, exogamy is also extended to the mother's, father's mother's, and mother's mother's clans. In contrast, in South India, marriage to a member of the mother's kin group is often encouraged.

Muslims also recognize kinship groupings larger than the family. These include the *khandan* , or patrilineage, and the *azizdar* , or kindred. The *azizdar* group differs slightly for each individual and includes all relatives linked to a person by blood or marriage. Muslims throughout India encourage marriage within the lineage and kindred, and marriages between the children of siblings are common.

Within a village or urban neighborhood, members of a lineage recognize their kinship in a variety of ways. Mutual assistance in daily work, in emergencies, and in factional struggles is expected. For

Hindus, cooperation in specific annual rituals helps define the kin group. For example, in many areas, at the worship of the goddess deemed responsible for the welfare of the lineage, patrilineally related males and their wives join in the rites and consume specially consecrated fried breads or other foods. Unmarried daughters of the lineage are only spectators at the rites and do not share in the special foods. Upon marriage, a woman becomes a member of her husband's lineage and then participates regularly in the worship of her husband's lineage goddess. Lineage bonds are also evident at life-cycle observances, when kin join together in celebrating births, marriages, and religious initiations. Upon the death of a lineage member, other lineage members observe ritual death pollution rules for a prescribed number of days and carry out appropriate funeral rites and feasts.

For some castes, especially in the north, careful records of lineage ties are kept by a professional genealogist, a member of a caste whose traditional task is maintaining genealogical tomes. These itinerant bards make their rounds from village to village over the course of a year or more, recording births, deaths, and glorious accomplishments of the patrilineal descent group. These genealogical services have been especially crucial among Rajputs, Jats, and similar groups whose lineages own land and where power can depend on fine calculations of pedigree and inheritance rights.

Some important kinship linkages are not traced through men but through women. These linkages involve those related to an individual by blood and marriage through a mother, married sisters, or married daughters, and for a man, through his wife. Anthropologist David Mandelbaum has termed these "feminal kin." Key relationships are those between a brother and sister, parents and daughters, and a person and his or her mother's brother. Through bonds with these close kin, a person has links with several households and lineages in many settlements. Throughout most of India, there are continuous visits—some of which may last for months and include the exchange of gifts at visits, life-cycle rites, and holidays, and many other key interactions between such relatives. These relationships are often characterized by deep affection and willingly offered support. These ties cut across the countryside, linking each person with kin in villages and towns near and far. Almost everywhere a villager goes—especially in the north, where marriage networks cover wide distances—he can find some kind of relative. Moral support, a place to stay, economic assistance, and political backing are all available through these kinship networks.

The multitude of kinship ties is further extended through the device of fictive kinship. Residents of a single village usually use kinship terms for one another, and especially strong ties of fictive kinship can be ceremonially created with fellow religious initiates or fellow pilgrims of one's village or neighborhood.

In the villages and cities of the north, on the festival of Raksha Bandhan (the Tying of the Protective Thread, during which sisters tie sacred threads on their brothers' wrists to symbolize the continuing bond between them), a female may tie a thread on the wrist of an otherwise unrelated male and "make him her brother." Fictive kinship bonds cut across caste and class lines and involve obligations of hospitality, gift-giving, and variable levels of cooperation and assistance.

Neighbors and friends may also create fictive kinship ties by informal agreement. Actually, any strong friendship between otherwise unrelated people is typically imbued with kinship-like qualities. In such friendships, kinship terms are adopted for address, and the give and take of kinship may develop. Such bonds commonly evolve between neighbors in urban apartment buildings, between special friends at school, and between close associates at work. The use of kinship terms enhances affection in the relationship. In Gujarat, personal names usually include the word for "sister" and "brother," so that the use of someone's personal name automatically sounds affectionate and caring.

Family Authority and Harmony

In the Indian household, lines of hierarchy and authority are clearly drawn, shaping structurally and psychologically complex family relationships. Ideals of conduct are aimed at creating and maintaining family harmony.

All family members are socialized to accept the authority of those ranked above them in the hierarchy. In general, elders rank above juniors, and among people of similar age, males outrank females. Daughters of a family command the formal respect of their brothers' wives, and the mother of a household is in charge of her daughters-in-law. Among adults in a joint family, a newly arrived daughter-in-law has the least authority. Males learn to command others within the household but expect to accept the direction of senior males. Ideally, even a mature adult man living in his father's household acknowledges his father's authority on both minor and major matters. Women are especially strongly socialized to accept a position subservient to males, to control their sexual impulses, and to subordinate their personal preferences to the needs of the family and kin group. Reciprocally, those in authority accept responsibility for meeting the needs of others in the family group.

There is tremendous emphasis on the unity of the family grouping, especially as differentiated from persons outside the kinship circle. Internally, efforts are made to deemphasize ties between spouses and between parents and their own children in order to enhance a wider sense of harmony within the entire household. Husbands and wives are discouraged from openly displaying affection for one another, and in strictly traditional households, they may not even properly speak to one another in the presence of anyone else, even their own children. Young parents are inhibited by "shame" from ostentatiously dandling their own young children but are encouraged to play with the children of siblings.

Psychologically, family members feel an intense emotional interdependence with each other and the family as an almost organic unit. Ego boundaries are permeable to others in the family, and any notion of a separate self is often dominated by a sense of what psychoanalyst Alan Roland has termed a more inclusive "familial self." Interpersonal empathy, closeness, loyalty, and interdependency are all crucial to life within the family.

Family resources, particularly land or businesses, have traditionally been controlled by family males, especially in high-status groups. Customarily, according to traditional schools of Hindu law, women did not inherit land or buildings and were thus beholden to their male kin who controlled these vital resources. Under Muslim customary law, women are entitled to inherit real estate and often do so, but their shares have typically been smaller than those of similarly situated males. Under modern law, all Indian women can inherit land.

VEILING AND THE SECLUSION OF WOMEN

A particularly interesting aspect of Indian family life is purdah (from the Hindi *parda* , literally, curtain), or the veiling and seclusion of women. In much of northern and central India, particularly in rural areas, Hindu and Muslim women follow complex rules of veiling the body and avoidance of public appearance, especially in the presence of relatives linked by marriage and before strange men. Purdah practices are inextricably linked to patterns of authority and harmony within the family. Rules of Hindu and Muslim purdah differ in certain key ways, but female modesty and decorum as well as concepts of family honor are essential to the various forms of purdah. In most areas, purdah restrictions are stronger for women of high-status families.

The importance of purdah is not limited to family life; rather, these practices all involve restrictions on female activity and access to power and the control of vital resources in a male-dominated society. Restriction and restraint for women in virtually every aspect of life are the basic essentials of purdah. In India, both males and females are circumscribed in their actions by economic disabilities, hierarchical rules of deference in kinship groups, castes, and the larger society. But for women who observe purdah, there are additional constraints.

For almost all women, modest dress and behavior are important. Clothing covering most of the body is common; only in tribal groups and among a few castes do women publicly bare their legs or upper bodies. In most of the northern half of India, traditionally dressed women cover the tops of their heads with the end of the sari or scarf (*dupatta*). Generally, females are expected to associate only with kin or companions approved by their families and to remain sexually chaste. Women are not encouraged to roam about on pleasure junkets, but rather travel only for explicit family-sanctioned purposes. In North India, women do relatively little shopping; most shopping is done by men. In contrast to females, males have much more freedom of movement and observe much less body modesty.

For both males and females, free association with the opposite sex is limited, and dating in the Western sense is essentially limited to members of the educated urban elite. In all areas, illicit liaisons do occur. Although the male may escape social repudiation if such liaisons become known, the female may suffer lasting damage to her own reputation and bring dishonor to her family. Further, if a woman is sexually linked with a man of lower caste status, the woman is regarded as being irremediably polluted, "like an earthen pot." A male so sullied can be cleansed of his temporary pollution, "like a brass pot," with a ritual bath.

Such rules of feminine modesty are not considered purdah but merely proper female behavior. For traditional Hindus of northern and central India, purdah observances begin at marriage, when a woman acquires a husband and in-laws. Although she almost never observes purdah in her natal home or before her natal relatives, a woman does observe purdah in her husband's home and before his relatives. As a young woman, she remains inside her husband's house much of the time (rather than going out into lanes or fields), absents herself or covers her face with her sari in the presence of senior males and females related by marriage, and, when she does leave the house in her marital village, covers her face with her sari.

Through use of the end of the sari as a face veil and deference of manner, a married woman shows respect to her affinal kin who are older than or equal to her husband in age, as well as certain other relatives. She may speak to the women before whom she veils, but she usually does not converse with the men. Exceptions to this are her husband's younger brothers, before whom she may veil her face, but with whom she has a warm joking relationship involving verbal banter. Initially almost faceless and voiceless in her marital home, a married woman matures and gradually relaxes some of these practices, especially as elder in-laws become senescent or die and she herself assumes senior status. In fact, after some years, a wife may neglect to veil her face in front of her husband when others are present and may even speak to her husband in public.

Such practices help shield women from unwanted male advances and control women's sexuality but also express relations within and between groups of kin. Familial prestige, household harmony, social distance, affinal respect, property ownership, and local political power are all linked to purdah.

Restricting women to household endeavors rather than involving them in tasks in fields and markets is associated with prestige and high rank in northern India. There the wealthiest families employ servants to carry water from the well and to work in the fields alongside family males. Mature women of these families may make rare appearances in the fields to bring lunch to the family males working there and sometimes to supervise laborers. Thus elitism is expressed in women's exclusive domesticity, with men providing economic necessities for the family.

Only women of poor and low-ranking groups engage in heavy manual labor outside the home, especially for pay. Such women work long hours in the fields, on construction gangs, and at many other tasks, often veiling their faces as they work.

For Muslim women, purdah practices involve less emphasis on veiling from in-laws and more emphasis on protecting women from contact with strangers outside the sphere of kinship. Because Muslims often marry cousins, a woman's in-laws may also be her natal relatives, so veiling her face within the marital home is often inappropriate. Unlike Hindus, Muslim women do not veil from other women as do Hindus. Traditional Muslim women and even unmarried girls, however, often refrain from appearing in public, or if they do go out, they wear an all-covering garment known as a *burka* , with a full face covering. A *burka* protects a woman—and her family—from undue familiarity with unknown outsiders, thus emphasizing the unity of the family vis-à-vis the outside world. Because Muslim women are entitled to a share in the family real estate, controlling their relationships with males outside the family can be crucial to the maintenance of family property and prestige.

In rural communities and in older sections of cities, purdah observances remain vital, although they are gradually diminishing in intensity. Among the educated urban and rural elite, purdah practices are rapidly vanishing and for many have all but disappeared. Chastity and female modesty are still highly valued, but, for the elite, face-veiling and the *burka* are considered unsophisticated. As girls and women become more widely and more highly educated, female employment outside the home is commonplace, even for women of elite families.

LIFE PASSAGES

In India, the ideal stages of life have been most clearly articulated by Hindus. The ancient Hindu ideal rests on childhood, followed by four stages: undergoing religious initiation and becoming a celibate student of religious texts, getting married and becoming a householder, leaving home to become a forest hermit after becoming a grandparent, and becoming a homeless wanderer free of desire for all material things. Although few actually follow this scheme, it serves as a guide for those attempting to live according to valued standards. For Hindus, dharma (a divinely ordained code of proper conduct), karma (the sum of one's deeds in this life and in past lives), and *kismat* (fate) are considered relevant to the course of life. Crucial transitions from one phase of life to another are marked by sometimes elaborate rites of passage.

Children and Childhood

Throughout much of India, a baby's birth is celebrated with rites of welcome and blessing—songs, drums, happy distribution of sweets, auspicious unguents, gifts for infant and mother, preparation of horoscopes, and inscriptions in the genealogist's record books. In general, children are deeply desired and welcomed, their presence regarded as a blessing on the household. Babies are often treated like small deities, pampered and coddled, adorned with makeup and trinkets, and carried about and fed with the finest foods available to the family. Young girls are worshiped as personifications of Hindu goddesses, and little boys are adulated as scions of the clan.

In their children, parents see the future of the lineage and wider kin group, helpers in daily tasks, and providers of security in the parents' old age. These delightful ideals are articulated and enacted over and over again; yet, a coexisting harsher reality emerges from a close examination of events and statistics. Many children lead lives of striking hardship, and many die premature deaths. In general, conditions are significantly worse for girls than for boys.

Birth celebrations for baby daughters are more muted than for sons and are sometimes absent altogether. Although India was once led by a woman prime minister, Indira Gandhi, and Indian women currently hold a wide range of powerful positions in every walk of life, there is a strong cultural bias toward males. Girls are frequently victims of underfeeding, medical neglect, sex-selective abortion, and outright infanticide. According to the 1991 census final population totals, there were 927 females per 1,000 males in India—a figure that has gradually declined from 972 females per 1,000 males in 1901 and from 934 just since 1981. Much of this imbalance is attained through neglecting the nutritional and health needs of female children, and much is also the result of inadequate health care for women of childbearing years. The sex ratio is even more imbalanced in urban areas (894 per 1,000 in 1991) than in rural areas (938 per 1,000 in 1991), partially because a large number of village men go to work in cities, leaving their wives and children behind in their rural homes.

That girls are victims of fatal neglect and murder has been thoroughly discussed in the Indian press and in scholarly investigations. It has been noted that infant girls are killed with potions of opium in Rajasthan and pastes of poisonous oleander in Tamil Nadu—most especially girls preceded by the birth of several sisters. Clinics offering ultrasound and amniocentesis in order to detect and abort female fetuses have become popular in various parts of the country, and many thousands of female fetuses have been so destroyed. In Maharashtra, Rajasthan, and Punjab such selective abortions have been outlawed because of pressure from feminist groups. More usually, girls are simply fed and cared for less well than their brothers.

The sex ratio is particularly unfavorable to females in the central northern section of the country. For example, in Uttar Pradesh there are only eighty-eight females per 100 males; in Haryana, eighty-seven per 100; and in Rajasthan ninety-one per 100. By contrast, in Kerala, on the southwest coast, a region traditionally noted for matriliny, the sex ratio is reversed, with females outnumbering males 104 to 100. In Andhra Pradesh and Tamil Nadu, two large southern states, there are ninety-seven females per 100 males.

Parents favor boys for various reasons. In the north, a boy's value in agricultural endeavors is higher than a girl's, and after marriage a boy continues to live with his parents, ideally supporting them in their old age. Political scientist Philip Oldenburg notes that in some violence-prone regions of the north, having sons may enhance families' capacity to defend themselves and to exercise power. A girl, however, moves away to live with her husband's relatives, and with her goes a dowry. In the late twentieth century, the values of dowries have been increasing, and, furthermore, groups that never gave dowries in the past are being pressured to do so. Thus, a girl child can represent a significant economic liability to her parents. In rice-growing areas, especially in the south, girls receive better treatment, and there is some evidence that the better treatment is related to the value of women as field workers in wet-rice cultivation. Throughout most of India, for Hindus it is important to have a son conduct funeral rites for his parents; a daughter, as a member of her husband's lineage, has not traditionally been able to do so.

For both boys and girls, infant mortality rates tend to be high, and in the absence of confidence that their infants will live, parents tend to produce numerous offspring in the hope that at least two sons will survive to adulthood. Family planning measures are used to a modest degree in India; perhaps 37.5 percent of couples use contraceptives at least occasionally. Abortion is legal, condoms are advertised on colorful billboards, and government health services offer small bounties for patients undergoing vasectomies and tubal ligations. In some regions, most notably Kerala, better health care and higher infant survival rates are associated with lowered fertility rates.

Most children survive infancy and do not fall victim to the cultural and economic pressures alluded to above. The majority of children grow up as valued members of a family, treasured by their parents and encouraged to participate in appropriate activities. Although relative ages of children are always known and reflected in linguistic and deference behavior, there is little age-grading in daily life. Children of all ages associate with each other and with adults, unlike the situation in the West, where age-grading is common.

Studies of Indian psychology by Sudhir Kakar, Alan Roland, and others stress that the young Indian child grows up in intimate emotional contact with the mother and other mothering persons. Because conjugal marital relationships are deemphasized in the joint household, a woman looks to her children to satisfy some of her intimacy needs. Her bond to her children, especially her sons but also her daughters, becomes enormously strong and lasting. A child is suckled on demand, sometimes for years, sleeps with a parent or grandparent, is bathed by doting relatives, and is rarely left alone. Massaged with oil, carried about, gently toilet-trained, and gratified with treats, the young child develops an inner core of well-being and a profound sense of expectation of protection from others. Such indulgent and close relationships produce a symbiotic mode of relating to others and effect the development of a person with a deeply held sense of involvement with relatives, so vital to the Indian family situation.

The young child learns early about hierarchy within the family, as he watches affectionate and respectful relationships between seniors and juniors, males and females. A young child is often carried about by an older sibling, and strong and close sibling bonds usually develop. Bickering among siblings is not as common as it is in the West; rather, most siblings learn to think of themselves as part of a family unit that must work together as it meets the challenges of the outside world.

Young children are encouraged to participate in the numerous rituals that emphasize family ties. The power of sibling relationships is recognized, for example, when a brother touches his sister's feet, honoring in her the principle of feminine divinity, which, if treated appropriately, can bring him prosperity. In calendrical and life-cycle rituals in both the north and the south, sisters bless their brothers and also symbolically request their protection throughout life.

After about four or five years of indulgence, children typically experience greater demands from family members. In villages, children learn the rudiments of agricultural labor, and young children often help with weeding, harvesting, threshing, and the like. Girls learn domestic chores, and boys are encouraged to take cattle for grazing, learn plowing, and begin to drive bullock carts and ride bicycles. City children also learn household duties, and children of poor families often work as servants in the homes of the prosperous. Some even pick through garbage piles to find shreds of food and fuel.

In some areas, children work as exploited laborers in factories, where they weave carpets for the export market and make matches, glass bangles, and other products. At Sivakasi, in Tamil Nadu, some 45,000 children work in the match, fireworks, and printing industries, comprising perhaps the largest single concentration of child labor in the world. Children reportedly as young as four years old work long hours each day.

Education in a school setting is available for most of India's children, and many young people attend school. Officials state that education is "compulsory," but the reality is that a significant percentage of children—especially girls—fail to become literate and instead carry out many other tasks in order to contribute to family income. More than half of India's children between the ages of six and fourteen—82.2 million—are not in school. Instead they participate in the labor force, even as more privileged children study at government and private schools and prepare for more prestigious jobs. Thus children learn early the realities of socioeconomic and urban-rural differentiation and grow up to perpetuate India's hierarchical society.

For many children, especially boys, an important event of young adolescence is religious initiation. Initiation rituals vary among different regions, religious communities, and castes. In the north, girls reach puberty without public notice and in an atmosphere of shyness, whereas in much of the south, puberty celebrations joyously announce to the family and community that a young girl has grown to maturity.

MARRIAGE

In India there is no greater event in a family than a wedding, dramatically evoking every possible social obligation, kinship bond, traditional value, impassioned sentiment, and economic resource. In the arranging and conducting of weddings, the complex permutations of Indian social systems best display themselves.

Marriage is deemed essential for virtually everyone in India. For the individual, marriage is the great watershed in life, marking the transition to adulthood. Generally, this transition, like everything else in India, depends little upon individual volition but instead occurs as a result of the efforts of many people. Even as one is born into a particular family without the exercise of any personal choice, so is one given a spouse without any personal preference involved. Arranging a marriage is a critical responsibility for parents and other relatives of both bride and groom. Marriage alliances entail some redistribution of wealth as well as building and restructuring social realignments, and, of course, result in the biological reproduction of families.

Some parents begin marriage arrangements on the birth of a child, but most wait until later. In the past, the age of marriage was quite young, and in a few small groups, especially in Rajasthan, children under the age of five are still united in marriage. In rural communities, prepuberty marriage for girls traditionally was the rule. In the late twentieth century, the age of marriage is rising in villages, almost to the levels that obtain in cities. Legislation mandating minimum marriage ages has been passed in various forms over the past decades, but such laws have little effect on actual marriage practices. Essentially, India is divided into two large regions with regard to Hindu kinship and marriage practices, the north and the south. Additionally, various ethnic and tribal groups of the central, mountainous north, and eastern regions follow a variety of other practices. These variations have been extensively described and analyzed by anthropologists, especially Irawati Karve, David G. Mandelbaum, and Clarence Maloney.

Broadly, in the Indo-Aryan-speaking north, a family seeks marriage alliances with people to whom it is not already linked by ties of blood. Marriage arrangements often involve looking far afield. In the Dravidian-speaking south, a family seeks to strengthen existing kin ties through marriage, preferably with blood relatives. Kinship terminology reflects this basic pattern. In the north, every kinship term clearly indicates whether the person referred to is a blood relation or an affinal relation; all blood relatives are forbidden as marriage mates to a person or a person's children. In the south, there is no clear-cut distinction between the family of birth and the family of marriage. Because marriage in the south commonly involves a continuing exchange of daughters among a few families, for the married couple all relatives are ultimately blood kin. Dravidian terminology stresses the principle of relative age: all relatives are arranged according to whether they are older or younger than each other without reference to generation.

On the Indo-Gangetic Plain, marriages are contracted outside the village, sometimes even outside of large groups of villages, with members of the same caste beyond any traceable consanguineal ties.

In much of the area, daughters should not be given into villages where daughters of the family or even of the natal village have previously been given. In most of the region, brother-sister exchange marriages (marriages linking a brother and sister of one household with the sister and brother of another) are shunned. The entire emphasis is on casting the marriage net ever-wider, creating new alliances. The residents of a single village may have in-laws in hundreds of other villages.

In most of North India, the Hindu bride goes to live with strangers in a home she has never visited. There she is sequestered and veiled, an outsider who must learn to conform to new ways. Her natal family is often geographically distant, and her ties with her consanguineal kin undergo attenuation to varying degrees.

In central India, the basic North Indian pattern prevails, with some modifications. For example, in Madhya Pradesh, village exogamy is preferred, but marriages within a village are not uncommon. Marriages between caste-fellows in neighboring villages are frequent. Brother-sister exchange marriages are sometimes arranged, and daughters are often given in marriage to lineages where other daughters of their lineage or village have previously been wed.

In South India, in sharp contrast, marriages are preferred between cousins (especially cross-cousins, that is, the children of a brother and sister) and even between uncles and nieces (especially a man and his elder sister's daughter). The principle involved is that of return—the family that gives a daughter expects one in return, if not now, then in the next generation. The effect of such marriages is to bind people together in relatively small, tight-knit kin groups. A bride moves to her in-laws' home—the home of her grandmother or aunt—and is often comfortable among these familiar faces. Her husband may well be the cousin she has known all her life that she would marry.

Many South Indian marriages are contracted outside of such close kin groups when no suitable mates exist among close relatives, or when other options appear more advantageous. Some sophisticated

South Indians, for example, consider cousin marriage and uncle-niece marriage outmoded.

Rules for the remarriage of widows differ from one group to another. Generally, lower-ranking groups allow widow remarriage, particularly if the woman is relatively young, but the highest-ranking castes discourage or forbid such remarriage. The most strict adherents to the nonremarriage of widows are Brahmans. Almost all groups allow widowers to remarry. Many groups encourage a widower to marry his deceased wife's younger sister (but never her older sister).

Among Muslims of both the north and the south, marriage between cousins is encouraged, both cross-cousins (the children of a brother and sister) and parallel cousins (the children of two same-sex siblings). In the north, such cousins grow up calling each other "brother" and "sister", yet they may marry. Even when cousin marriage does not occur, spouses can often trace between them other kinship linkages.

Some tribal people of central India practice an interesting permutation of the southern pattern. Among the Murias of Bastar in southeastern Madhya Pradesh, as described by anthropologist Verrier Elwin, teenagers live together in a dormitory (*ghotul*), sharing life and love with one another for several blissful years. Ultimately, their parents arrange their marriages, usually with cross-cousins, and the delights of teenage romance are replaced with the serious responsibilities of adulthood. In his survey of some 2,000 marriages, Elwin found only seventy-seven cases of *ghotul* partners eloping together and very few cases of divorce. Among the Muria and Gond tribal groups, cross-cousin marriage is called "bringing back the milk," alluding to the gift of a girl in one generation being returned by the gift of a girl in the next.

Finding the perfect partner for one's child can be a challenging task. People use their social networks to locate potential brides and grooms of appropriate social and economic status. Increasingly, urban dwellers use classified matrimonial advertisements in newspapers. The advertisements usually announce religion, caste, and educational qualifications, stress female beauty and male (and in the contemporary era, sometimes female) earning capacity, and may hint at dowry size.

In rural areas, matches between strangers are usually arranged without the couple meeting each other. Rather, parents and other relatives come to an agreement on behalf of the couple. In cities, however, especially among the educated classes, photographs are exchanged, and sometimes the couple are allowed to meet under heavily chaperoned circumstances, such as going out for tea with a group of people or meeting in the parlor of the girl's home, with her relatives standing by. Young professional men and their families may receive inquiries and photographs from representatives of several girls' families. They may send their relatives to meet the most promising candidates and then go on tour themselves to meet the young women and make a final choice. In the early 1990s, increasing numbers of marriages arranged in this way link brides and grooms from India with spouses of Indian parentage resident in Europe, North America, and the Middle East.

Almost all Indian children are raised with the expectation that their parents will arrange their marriages, but an increasing number of young people, especially among the college-educated, are finding their own spouses. So-called love marriages are deemed a slightly scandalous alternative to properly arranged marriages. Some young people convince their parents to "arrange" their marriages to people with whom they have fallen in love. This process has long been possible for Indians from the south and for Muslims who want to marry a particular cousin of the appropriate marriageable category. In the upper classes, these semi-arranged love marriages increasingly occur between young people who are from castes of slightly different rank but who are educationally or professionally equal. If there are vast differences to overcome, such as is the case with love marriages between Hindus and Muslims or between Hindus of very different caste status, parents are usually much less agreeable, and serious family disruptions can result.

In much of India, especially in the north, a marriage establishes a structural opposition between the kin groups of the bride and groom—bride-givers and bride-takers. Within this relationship, bride-givers are considered inferior to bride-takers and are forever expected to give gifts to the bride-takers. The one-way flow of gifts begins at engagement and continues for a generation or two. The most dramatic aspect of this asymmetrical relationship is the giving of dowry.

In many communities throughout India, a dowry has traditionally been given by a bride's kin at the time of her marriage. In ancient times, the dowry was considered a woman's wealth—property due a beloved daughter who had no claim on her natal family's real estate—and typically included portable valuables such as jewelry and household goods that a bride could control throughout her life. However, over time, the larger proportion of the dowry has come to consist of goods and cash payments that go straight into the hands of the groom's family. In the late twentieth century, throughout much of India, dowry payments have escalated, and a groom's parents sometimes insist on compensation for their son's higher education and even for his future earnings, to which the bride will presumably have access. Some of the dowries demanded are quite oppressive, amounting to several years' salary in cash as well as items such as motorcycles, air conditioners, and fancy cars. Among some lower-status groups, large dowries are currently replacing traditional bride-price payments. Even among Muslims, previously not given to demanding large dowries, reports of exorbitant dowries are increasing.

The dowry is becoming an increasingly onerous burden for the bride's family. Antidowry laws exist but are largely ignored, and a bride's treatment in her marital home is often affected by the value of her dowry. Increasingly frequent are horrible incidents, particularly in urban areas, where a groom's family makes excessive demands on the bride's family—even after marriage—and when the demands are not met, murder the bride, typically by setting her clothes on fire in a cooking "accident." The groom is then free to remarry and collect another sumptuous dowry. The male and female in-laws implicated in these murders have seldom been punished.

Such dowry deaths have been the subject of numerous media reports in India and other countries and have mobilized feminist groups to action. In some of the worst areas, such as the National Capital Territory of Delhi, where hundreds of such deaths are reported annually and the numbers are increasing yearly, the law now requires that all suspicious deaths of new brides be investigated.

Official government figures report 1,786 registered dowry deaths nationwide in 1987; there is also an estimate of some 5,000 dowry deaths in 1991. Women's groups sometimes picket the homes of the in-laws of burned brides. Some analysts have related the growth of this phenomenon to the growth of consumerism in Indian society.

Fears of impoverishing their parents have led some urban middle-class young women, married and unmarried, to commit suicide. However, through the giving of large dowries, the newly wealthy are often able to marry their treasured daughters up the status hierarchy so reified in Indian society.

After marriage arrangements are completed, a rich panoply of wedding rituals begins. Each religious group, region, and caste has a slightly different set of rites. Generally, all weddings involve as many kin and associates of the bride and groom as possible. The bride's family usually hosts most of the ceremonies and pays for all the arrangements for large numbers of guests for several days, including accommodation, feasting, decorations, and gifts for the groom's party.

These arrangements are often extremely elaborate and expensive and are intended to enhance the status of the bride's family. The groom's party usually hires a band and brings fine gifts for the bride, such as jewelry and clothing, but these are typically far outweighed in value by the presents received from the bride's side.

After the bride and groom are united in sacred rites attended by colorful ceremony, the new bride may be carried away to her in-laws' home, or, if she is very young, she may remain with her parents until they deem her old enough to depart. A prepubescent bride usually stays in her natal home until puberty, after which a separate consummation ceremony is held to mark her departure for her conjugal home and married life. The poignancy of the bride's weeping departure for her new home is prominent in personal memory, folklore, literature, song, and drama throughout India.

ADULTHOOD

In their new status, a young married couple begin to accept adult responsibilities. These include work inside and outside of the home, childbearing and childrearing, developing and maintaining social relationships, fulfilling religious obligations, and enhancing family prosperity and prestige as much as possible.

The young husband usually remains resident with his natal family, surrounded by well-known relatives and neighbors. The young bride, however, is typically thrust into a strange household, where she is expected to follow ideal patterns of chaste and cheerfully obedient behavior.

Ideally, the Hindu wife should honor her husband as if he were her personal god. Through her marriage, a woman becomes an auspicious wife (*suhagan*), adorned with bangles and amulets designed to protect her husband's life and imbued with ritual powers to influence prosperity and procreation.

At her wedding, the Hindu bride is likened to Lakshmi, the Goddess of Wealth, in symbolic recognition of the fact that the groom's patrilineage can increase and prosper only through her fertility and labors. Despite this simile, elegantly stated in the nuptial ritual, the young wife is pressed into service as the most subordinate member of her husband's family.

If any misfortunes happen to befall her affinal family after her arrival, she may be blamed as the bearer of bad luck. Not surprisingly, some young women find adjusting to these new circumstances extremely upsetting. A small percentage experience psychological distress so severe that they seem to be possessed by outspoken ghosts and spirits.

In these difficult early days of a marriage, and later on throughout her life, a woman looks to her natal kin for moral and often economic support. Although she has become part of another household and lineage, she depends on her natal relatives—especially her brothers—to back her up in a variety of circumstances. A wide range of long visits home, ritual obligations, gifts, folklore, and songs reflect the significance of a woman's lifelong ties to her blood relatives.

By producing children, especially highly valued sons, and, ultimately, becoming a mother-in-law herself, a woman gradually improves her position within the conjugal household. In motherhood the married woman finds social approval, economic security, and emotional satisfaction.

A man and his wife owe respect and obedience to his parents and other senior relatives. Ideally, all cooperate in the joint family enterprise. Gradually, as the years pass, members of the younger generation take the place of the older generation and become figures of authority and respect. As this transition occurs, it is generally assumed that younger family members will physically care for and support elders until their demise.

In their adult years, men and women engage in a wide variety of tasks and occupations strongly linked to socioeconomic status, including caste membership, wealth, place of residence, and many other factors.

In general, the higher the status of a family, the less likely its members are to engage in manual labor and the more likely its members are to be served by employees of lower status. Although educated women are increasingly working outside the home, even in urbane circles some negative stigma is still attached to women's employment. In addition, students from high-status families do not work at temporary menial jobs as they do in many Western countries.

People of low status work at the many menial tasks that high-status people disdain. Poor women cannot afford to abstain from paid labor, and they work alongside their menfolk in the fields and at construction projects. In low-status families, women are less likely than high-status women to unquestioningly accept the authority of men and even of elders because they are directly responsible for providing income for the family.

Among Sweepers, very low-status latrine cleaners, women carry out more of the traditional tasks than do men and hold a relatively less subordinate position in their families than do women of traditional high-status families. Such women are, nonetheless, less powerful in the society at large than are women of economically prosperous high-status families, who control and influence the control of more assets than do poor women.

Along with economically supporting themselves, their elders, and their children, adults must maintain and add to the elaborate social networks upon which life depends. Offering gracious hospitality to guests is a key ingredient of proper adult behavior. Adults must also attend to religious matters, carrying out rites intended to protect their families and communities. In these efforts, men and women constantly work for the benefit of their kin groups, castes, and other social units.

DEATH AND BEYOND

The death of an infant or young child—a common event in India—causes sorrow but usually not major social disruption. The death of a married adult has wider repercussions. Among Hindus, the demise of a lineage member immediately ritually pollutes the entire lineage for a period of several days. As part of the mourning process, closely related male mourners have their heads and facial hair shaved, thus publicly declaring their close links to the deceased. Various funeral rites, feasts, and mourning practices affirm kinship ties with the deceased and among survivors. Crucial social bonds become visible to all concerned.

Although a man may grieve for his deceased wife, a widow may face not only a personal loss but a major restructuring of her life.

Becoming a widow in India is not a benign or neutral event. A man's death, particularly if it occurs when he is young, may be attributed to ill fortune brought upon him by his wife, possibly because of her sins in a past life.

With the death of her husband, a woman's auspicious wifehood ends, and she is plunged into dreaded widowhood. The very word *widow* is used as an epithet. As a widow, a woman is devoid of reason to adorn herself. If she follows tradition, she may shave her head, shed her jewelry, and wear only plain white or dark clothing.

Widows of low-ranking groups have always been allowed to remarry, but widows of high rank have been expected to remain unmarried and chaste until death. In earlier times, for child brides married to older men and widowed young, these strictures caused great hardship and inspired reform movements in some parts of the country.

In past centuries, the ultimate rejection of widowhood occurred in the burning of the Hindu widow on her husband's funeral pyre, a practice known as sati (meaning, literally, true or virtuous one). Women who so perished in the funeral flames were posthumously adulated, and even in the late twentieth century are worshiped at memorial tablets and temples erected in their honor.

In western India, Rajput lineages proudly point to satis in their history. Sati was never widespread, and it has been illegal since 1829, but a few cases of sati still occur in India every year. In choosing to die with her husband, a woman evinces great merit and power and is considered able to bring boons to her husband's patrilineage and to others who honor her. Thus, through her meritorious death, a widow avoids disdain and achieves glory, not only for herself, but for all of her kin as well.

By restricting widow remarriage, high-status groups limit restructuring of the lineage on the death of a male member. An unmarried widow remains a member of her husband's lineage, with no competing ties to other groups of in-laws. Her rights to her husband's property, traditionally limited though they are to management rather than outright inheritance, remain uncomplicated by remarriage to a man from another lineage. It is among lower-ranking groups with lesser amounts of property and prestige that widow remarriage is most frequent.

Most Indians see their present lifetimes as but a prelude to an afterlife, the quality of which depends on their behavior in this life. Muslims envision heaven and hell, but Hindus conceptualize a series of rebirths ideally culminating in union with the divine. Some Hindus believe they are destined to marry the same person in each of their lifetimes. Thus people feel connected with different permutations of themselves and others over cosmic cycles of time.

4

CASTE AND CLASS IN INDIAN SOCIETY

Varna, Caste, and Other Divisions

Although many other nations are characterized by social inequality, perhaps nowhere else in the world has inequality been so elaborately constructed as in the Indian institution of caste. Caste has long existed in India, but in the modern period it has been severely criticized by both Indian and foreign observers. Although some educated Indians tell non-Indians that caste has been abolished or that "no one pays attention to caste anymore," such statements do not reflect reality.

Caste has undergone significant change since independence, but it still involves hundreds of millions of people. In its preamble, India's constitution forbids negative public discrimination on the basis of caste. However, caste ranking and caste-based interaction have occurred for centuries and will continue to do so well into the foreseeable future, more in the countryside than in urban settings and more in the realms of kinship and marriage than in less personal interactions.

Castes are ranked, named, endogamous (in-marrying) groups, membership in which is achieved by birth. There are thousands of castes and subcastes in India, and these large kinship-based groups are fundamental to South Asian social structure. Each caste is part of a locally based system of interde-pendence with other groups, involving occupational specialization, and is linked in complex ways with networks that stretch across regions and throughout the nation. The word *caste* derives from the Portuguese *casta* , meaning breed, race, or kind. Among the Indian terms that are sometimes translated as caste are *varna* , *jati* , *jat* , *biradri* , and *samaj*. All of these terms refer to ranked groups of various sizes and breadth. *Varna* , or color, actually refers to large divisions that include various castes; the other terms include castes and subdivisions of castes sometimes called subcastes.

Many castes are traditionally associated with an occupation, such as high-ranking Brahmans; middle-ranking farmer and artisan groups, such as potters, barbers, and carpenters; and very low-ranking "Untouchable" leatherworkers, butchers, launderers, and latrine cleaners. There is some correlation between ritual rank on the caste hierarchy and economic prosperity. Members of higher-ranking castes tend, on the whole, to be more prosperous than members of lower-ranking castes. Many lower-caste people live in conditions of great poverty and social disadvantage.

According to the Rig Veda, sacred texts that date back to oral traditions of more than 3,000 years ago, progenitors of the four ranked *varna* groups sprang from various parts of the body of the primordial man, which Brahma created from clay. Each group had a function in sustaining the life of society—the social body. Brahmans, or priests, were created from the mouth. They were to provide for the intellectual and spiritual needs of the community. Kshatriyas, warriors and rulers, were derived from the arms. Their role was to rule and to protect others. Vaishyas—landowners and merchants—sprang from the thighs, and were entrusted with the care of commerce and agriculture. Shudras—artisans and servants—came from the feet. Their task was to perform all manual labor.

Later conceptualized was a fifth category, "Untouchable" menials, relegated to carrying out very menial and polluting work related to bodily decay and dirt. Since 1935 "Untouchables" have been known as Scheduled Castes, referring to their listing on government rosters, or schedules. They are also often called by

Mohandas Karamchand (Mahatma) Gandhi's term Harijans, or "Children of God." Although the term *Untouchable* appears in literature produced by these low-ranking castes, in the 1990s, many politically conscious members of these groups prefer to refer to themselves as Dalit , a Hindi word meaning oppressed or downtrodden. According to the 1991 census, there were 138 million Scheduled Caste members in India, approximately 16 percent of the total population.

The first four *varnas* apparently existed in the ancient Aryan society of northern India. Some historians say that these categories were originally somewhat fluid functional groups, not castes. A greater degree of fixity gradually developed, resulting in the complex ranking systems of medieval India that essentially continue in the late twentieth century.

Although a *varna* is not a caste, when directly asked for their caste affiliation, particularly when the questioner is a Westerner, many Indians will reply with a *varna* name. Pressed further, they may respond with a much more specific name of a caste, or *jati* , which falls within that *varna.* For example, a Brahman may specify that he is a member of a named caste group, such as a Jijotiya Brahman, or a Smartha Brahman, and so on. Within such castes, people may further belong to smaller subcaste categories and to specific clans and lineages. These finer designations are particularly relevant when marriages are being arranged and often appear in newspaper matrimonial advertisements.

Members of a caste are typically spread out over a region, with representatives living in hundreds of settlements. In any small village, there may be representatives of a few or even a score or more castes.

Numerous groups usually called tribes (often referred to as Scheduled Tribes) are also integrated into the caste system to varying degrees. Some tribes live separately from others—particularly in the far northeast and in the forested center of the country, where tribes are more like ethnic groups than castes. Some tribes are themselves divided into groups similar to subcastes. In regions where members of tribes live in peasant villages with nontribal peoples, they are usually considered members of separate castes ranking low on the hierarchical scale.

Inequalities among castes are considered by the Hindu faithful to be part of the divinely ordained natural order and are expressed in terms of purity and pollution. Within a village, relative rank is most graphically expressed at a wedding or death feast, when all residents of the village are invited. At the home of a high-ranking caste member, food is prepared by a member of a caste from whom all can accept cooked food (usually by a Brahman). Diners are seated in lines; members of a single caste sit next to each other in a row, and members of other castes sit in perpendicular or parallel rows at some distance. Members of Dalit castes, such as Leatherworkers and Sweepers, may be seated far from the other diners—even out in an alley. Farther away, at the edge of the feeding area, a Sweeper may wait with a large basket to receive discarded leavings tossed in by other diners. Eating food contaminated by contact with the saliva of others not of the same family is considered far too polluting to be practiced by members of any other castes. Generally, feasts and ceremonies given by Dalits are not attended by higher-ranking castes.

Among Muslims, although status differences prevail, brotherhood may be stressed. A Muslim feast usually includes a cloth laid either on clean ground or on a table, with all Muslims, rich and poor, dining from plates placed on the same cloth. Muslims who wish to provide hospitality to observant Hindus, however, must make separate arrangements for a high-caste Hindu cook and ritually pure foods and dining area.

Castes that fall within the top four ranked *varnas* are sometimes referred to as the "clean castes," with Dalits considered "unclean." Castes of the top three ranked *varnas* are often designated "twice-born," in reference to the ritual initiation undergone by male members, in which investiture with the Hindu sacred thread constitutes a kind of ritual rebirth. Non-Hindu castelike groups generally fall outside these designations.

Each caste is believed by devout Hindus to have its own dharma, or divinely ordained code of proper conduct. Accordingly, there is often a high degree of tolerance for divergent lifestyles among different castes. Brahmans are usually expected to be nonviolent and spiritual, according with their traditional roles as vegetarian teetotaler priests. Kshatriyas are supposed to be strong, as fighters and rulers should be, with a taste for aggression, eating meat, and drinking alcohol. Vaishyas are stereotyped as adept businessmen, in accord with their traditional activities in commerce. Shudras are often described by others as tolerably pleasant but expectably somewhat base in behavior, whereas Dalits—especially Sweepers—are often regarded by others as followers of vulgar life-styles. Conversely, lower-caste people often view people of high rank as haughty and unfeeling.

The chastity of women is strongly related to caste status. Generally, the higher ranking the caste, the more sexual control its women are expected to exhibit. Brahman brides should be virginal, faithful to one husband, and celibate in widowhood. By contrast, a Sweeper bride may or may not be a virgin, extramarital affairs may be tolerated, and, if widowed or divorced, the woman is encouraged to remarry. For the higher castes, such control of female sexuality helps ensure purity of lineage—of crucial importance to maintenance of high status. Among Muslims, too, high status is strongly correlated with female chastity.

Within castes explicit standards are maintained. Transgressions may be dealt with by a caste council (*panchayat*— .), meeting periodically to adjudicate issues relevant to the caste. Such councils are usually formed of groups of elders, almost always males. Punishments such as fines and outcasting, either temporary or permanent, can be enforced. In rare cases, a person is excommunicated from the caste for gross infractions of caste rules. An example of such an infraction might be marrying or openly cohabiting with a mate of a caste lower than one's own; such behavior would usually result in the higher-caste person dropping to the status of the lower-caste person.

Activities such as farming or trading can be carried out by anyone, but usually only members of the appropriate castes act as priests, barbers, potters, weavers, and other skilled artisans, whose occupational skills are handed down in families from one generation to another. As with other key features of Indian social structure, occupational specialization is believed to be in accord with the divinely ordained order of the universe.

The existence of rigid ranking is supernaturally validated through the idea of rebirth according to a person's karma, the sum of an individual's deeds in this life and in past lives. After death, a person's life is judged by divine forces, and rebirth is assigned in a high or a low place, depending upon what is deserved. This supernatural sanction can never be neglected, because it brings a person to his or her position in the caste hierarchy, relevant to every transaction involving food or drink, speaking, or touching.

In past decades, Dalits in certain areas (especially in parts of the south) had to display extreme deference to high-status people, physically keeping their distance—lest their touch or even their shadow pollute others—wearing neither shoes nor any upper body covering (even for women) in the presence of the upper castes. The lowest-ranking had to jingle a little bell in warning of their polluting approach. In much of India, Dalits were prohibited from entering temples, using wells from which the "clean" castes drew their water, or even attending schools. In past centuries, dire punishments were prescribed for Dalits who read or even heard sacred texts.

Such degrading discrimination was made illegal under legislation passed during British rule and was protested against by preindependence reform movements led by Mahatma Gandhi and Bhimrao Ramji (B.R.) Ambedkar, a Dalit leader. Dalits agitated for the right to enter Hindu temples and to use village wells and effectively pressed for the enactment of stronger laws opposing disabilities imposed on them. After independence, Ambedkar almost singlehandedly wrote India's constitution, including key provisions barring caste-based discrimination. Nonetheless, discriminatory treatment of Dalits remains a factor in daily life, especially in villages, as the end of the twentieth century approaches.

In modern times, as in the past, it is virtually impossible for an individual to raise his own status by falsely claiming to be a member of a higher-ranked caste. Such a ruse might work for a time in a place where the person is unknown, but no one would dine with or intermarry with such a person or his offspring until the claim was validated through kinship networks. Rising on the ritual hierarchy can only be achieved by a caste as a group, over a long period of time, principally by adopting behavior patterns of higher-ranked groups. This process, known as Sanskritization, has been described by M.N. Srinivas and others. An example of such behavior is that of some Leatherworker castes adopting a policy of not eating beef, in the hope that abstaining from the defiling practice of consuming the flesh of sacred bovines would enhance their castes' status. Increased economic prosperity for much of a caste greatly aids in the process of improving rank.

Intercaste Relations

In a village, members of different castes are often linked in what has been called the *jajmani* system, after the word *jajman* , which in some regions means patron. Members of various service castes perform tasks for their patrons, usually members of the dominant, that is, most powerful landowning caste of the village (commonly castes of the Kshatriya *varna*).

Households of service castes are linked through hereditary bonds to a household of patrons, with the lower-caste members providing services according to traditional occupational specializations. Thus, client families of launderers, barbers, shoemakers, carpenters, potters, tailors, and priests provide customary services to their patrons, in return for which they receive customary seasonal payments of grain, clothing, and money. Ideally, from generation to generation, clients owe their patrons political allegiance in addition to their labors, while patrons owe their clients protection and security.

The harmonious qualities of the *jajmani* system have been overidealized and variations of the system overlooked by many observers. Further, the economic interdependence of the system has weakened since the 1960s. Nevertheless, it is clear that members of different castes customarily perform a number of functions for one another in rural India that emphasize cooperation rather than competition. This cooperation is revealed in economic arrangements, in visits to farmers' threshing floors by service caste members to claim traditional payments, and in rituals emphasizing interdependence at life crises and calendrical festivals all over South Asia. For example, in rural Karnataka, in an event described by anthropologist Suzanne Hanchett, the annual procession of the village temple cart bearing images of the deities responsible for the welfare of the village cannot go forward without the combined efforts of representatives of all castes. It is believed that the sacred cart will literally not move unless all work together to move it, some pushing and some pulling.

Some observers feel that the caste system must be viewed as a system of exploitation of poor low-ranking groups by more prosperous high-ranking groups. In many parts of India, land is largely held by dominant castes—high-ranking owners of property—that economically exploit low-ranking landless laborers and poor artisans, all the while degrading them with ritual emphases on their so-called god-given inferior status. In the early 1990s, blatant subjugation of low-caste laborers in the northern state of Bihar and in eastern Uttar Pradesh was the subject of many news reports. In this region, scores of Dalits who have attempted to unite to protest low wages have been the victims of lynchings and mass killings by high-caste landowners and their hired assassins.

In 1991 the news magazine *India Today* reported that in an ostensibly prosperous village about 160 kilometers southeast of Delhi, when it became known that a rural Dalit laborer dared to have a love affair with the daughter of a high-caste landlord, the lovers and their Dalit go-between were tortured, publicly hanged, and burnt by agents of the girl's family in the presence of some 500 villagers. A similar incident occurred in 1994, when a Dalit musician who had secretly married a woman of the Kurmi cultivating caste was beaten to death by outraged Kurmis, possibly instigated by the young woman's family. The terrified bride was stripped and branded as punishment for her transgression. Dalit women also have been the victims of gang rapes by the police. Many other atrocities, as well as urban riots resulting in the deaths of Dalits, have occurred in recent years. Such extreme injustices are infrequent enough to be reported in outraged articles in the Indian press, while much more common daily discrimination and exploitation are considered virtually routine.

Changes in the Caste System

Despite many problems, the caste system has operated successfully for centuries, providing goods and services to India's many millions of citizens. The system continues to operate, but changes are occurring. India's constitution guarantees basic rights to all its citizens, including the right to equality and equal protection before the law. The practice of untouchability, as well as discrimination on the basis of caste, race, sex, or religion, has been legally abolished. All citizens have the right to vote, and political competition is lively. Voters from every stratum of society have formed interest groups, overlapping and crosscutting castes, creating an evolving new style of integrating Indian society.

Castes themselves, however, far from being abolished, have certain rights under Indian law. As described by anthropologist Owen M. Lynch and other scholars, in the expanding political arena caste groups are becoming more politicized and forced to compete with other interest groups for social and economic benefits. In the growing cities, traditional intercaste interdependencies are negligible.

Independent India has built on earlier British efforts to remedy problems suffered by Dalits by granting them some benefits of protective discrimination. Scheduled Castes are entitled to reserved electoral offices, reserved jobs in central and state governments, and special educational benefits. The constitution mandates that one-seventh of state and national legislative seats be reserved for members of Scheduled Castes in order to guarantee their voice in government. Reserving seats has proven useful because few, if any, Scheduled Caste candidates have ever been elected in nonreserved constituencies.

Educationally, Dalit students have benefited from scholarships, and Scheduled Caste literacy increased (from 10.3 percent in 1961 to 21.4 percent in 1981, the last year for which such figures are available), although not as rapidly as among the general population. Improved access to education has resulted in the emergence of a substantial group of educated Dalits able to take up white-collar occupations and fight for their rights.

There has been tremendous resistance among non-Dalits to this protective discrimination for the Scheduled Castes, who constitute some 16 percent of the total population, and efforts have been made to provide similar advantages to the so-called Backward Classes , who constitute an estimated 52 percent of the population. In August 1990, Prime Minister Vishwanath Pratap (V.P.) Singh announced his intention to enforce the recommendations of the Backward Classes Commission (Mandal Commission), issued in December 1980 and largely ignored for a decade. The report, which urged special advantages for obtaining civil service positions and admission to higher education for the Backward Classes, resulted in riots and self-immolations and contributed to the fall of the prime minister. The upper castes have been particularly adamant against these policies because unemployment is a major problem in India, and many feel that they are being unjustly excluded from posts for which they are better qualified than lower-caste applicants.

As an act of protest, many Dalits have rejected Hinduism with its rigid ranking system. Following the example of their revered leader, Dr. Ambedkar, who converted to Buddhism four years before his death in 1956, millions of Dalits have embraced the faith of the Buddha. Over the past few centuries, many Dalits have also converted to Christianity and have often by this means raised their socioeconomic status. However, Christians of Dalit origin still often suffer from discrimination by Christians—and others—of higher caste backgrounds.

Despite improvements in some aspects of Dalit status, 90 percent of them live in rural areas in the mid-1990s, where an increasing proportion—more than 50 percent—work as landless agricultural laborers. State and national governments have attempted to secure more just distribution of land by creating land ceilings and abolishing absentee landlordism, but evasive tactics by landowners have successfully prevented more than minimal redistribution of land to tenant farmers and laborers. In contemporary India, field hands face increased competition from tractors and harvesting machines. Similarly, artisans are being challenged by expanding commercial markets in mass-produced factory goods, undercutting traditional mutual obligations between patrons and clients. The spread of the Green Revolution has tended to increase the gap between the prosperous and the poor—most of whom are low-caste.

The growth of urbanization (an estimated 26 percent of the population now lives in cities) is having a far-reaching effect on caste practices, not only in cities but in villages. Among anonymous crowds in urban public spaces and on public transportation, caste affiliations are unknown, and observance of purity and pollution rules is negligible. Distinctive caste costumes have all but vanished, and low-caste names have been modified, although castes remain endogamous, and access to employment often occurs through intracaste connections. Restrictions on interactions with other castes are becoming more relaxed, and, at the same time, observance of other pollution rules is declining—especially those concerning birth, death, and menstruation. Several growing Hindu sects draw members from many castes and regions, and communication between cities and villages is expanding dramatically. Kin in town and country visit one another frequently, and television programs available to huge numbers of villagers vividly portray new lifestyles. As new occupations open up in urban areas, the correlation of caste with occupation is declining.

Caste associations have expanded their areas of concern beyond traditional elite emulation and local politics into the wider political arenas of state and national politics. Finding power in numbers within India's democratic system, caste groups are pulling together closely allied subcastes in their quest for political influence. In efforts to solidify caste bonds, some caste associations have organized marriage fairs where families can make matches for their children. Traditional hierarchical concerns are being minimized in favor of strengthening horizontal unity. Thus, while pollution observances are declining, caste consciousness is not.

Education and election to political office have advanced the status of many Dalits, but the overall picture remains one of great inequity. In recent decades, Dalit anger has been expressed in writings, demonstrations, strikes, and the activities of such groups as the Dalit Panthers, a radical political party demanding revolutionary change. A wider Dalit movement, including political parties, educational activities, self-help centers, and labor organizations, has spread to many areas of the country.

In a 1982 Dalit publication, Dilip Hiro wrote, "It is one of the great modern Indian tragedies and dangers that even well meaning Indians still find it so difficult to accept Untouchable mobility as being legitimate in fact as well as in theory...." Still, against all odds, a small intelligentsia has worked for many years toward the goal of freeing India of caste consciousness.

Classes

In village India, where nearly 74 percent of the population resides, caste and class affiliations overlap. According to anthropologist Miriam Sharma, "Large landholders who employ hired labour are overwhelmingly from the upper castes, while the agricultural workers themselves come from the ranks of the lowest—predominantly Untouchable—castes." She also points out that household-labor-using proprietors come from the ranks of the middle agricultural castes. Distribution of other resources and access to political control follow the same pattern of caste-cum-class distinctions. Although this congruence is strong, there is a tendency for class formation to occur despite the importance of caste, especially in the cities, but also in rural areas. In an analysis of class formation in India, anthropologist Harold A. Gould points out that a three-level system of stratification is taking shape across rural India. He calls the three levels Forward Classes (higher castes), Backward Classes (middle and lower castes), and Harijans (very low castes). Members of these groups share common concerns because they stand in approximately the same relationship to land and production—that is, they are large-scale farmers, small-scale farmers, and landless laborers. Some of these groups are drawing together within regions across caste lines in order to work for political power and access to desirable resources. For example, since the late 1960s, some of the middle-ranking cultivating castes of northern India have increasingly cooperated in the political arena in order to advance their common agrarian and market-oriented interests. Their efforts have been spurred by competition with higher-caste landed elites.

In cities other groups have vested interests that crosscut caste boundaries, suggesting the possibility of forming classes in the future. These groups include prosperous industrialists and entrepreneurs, who have made successful efforts to push the central government toward a probusiness stance; bureaucrats, who depend upon higher education rather than land to preserve their positions as civil servants; political officeholders, who enjoy good salaries and perquisites of all kinds; and the military, who constitute one of the most powerful armed forces in the developing world.

Economically far below such groups are members of the menial underclass, which is taking shape in both villages and urban areas. As the privileged elites move ahead, low-ranking menial workers remain economically insecure. Were they to join together to mobilize politically across lines of class and religion in recognition of their common interests, Gould observes, they might find power in their sheer numbers.

India's rapidly expanding economy has provided the basis for a fundamental change—the emergence of what eminent journalist Suman Dubey calls a "new vanguard" increasingly dictating India's political and economic direction. This group is India's new middle class—mobile, driven, consumer-oriented, and, to some extent, forward-looking. Hard to define precisely, it is not a single stratum of society, but straddles town and countryside, making its voice heard everywhere. It encompasses prosperous farmers, white-collar workers, business people, military personnel, and myriad others, all actively working toward a prosperous life. Ownership of cars, televisions, and other consumer goods, reasonable earnings, substantial savings, and educated children (often fluent in English) typify this diverse group. Many have ties to kinsmen living abroad who have done very well.

The new middle class is booming, at least partially in response to a doubling of the salaries of some 4 million central government employees in 1986, followed by similar increases for state and district officers. Unprecedented liberalization and opening up of the economy in the 1980s and 1990s have been part of the picture.

There is no single set of criteria defining the middle class, and estimates of its numbers vary widely. The mid-range of figures presented in a 1992 survey article by analyst Suman Dubey is approximately 150 to 175 million—some 20 percent of the population—although other observers suggest alternative figures. The middle class appears to be increasing rapidly. Once primarily urban and largely Hindu, the phenomenon of the consuming middle class is burgeoning among Muslims and prosperous villagers as well. According to V.A. Pai Panandikar, director of the Centre for Policy Research, New Delhi, cited by Dubey, by the end of the twentieth century 30 percent—some 300 million—of India's population will be middle class.

The middle class is bracketed on either side by the upper and lower echelons. Members of the upper class—around 1 percent of the population—are owners of large properties, members of exclusive clubs, and vacationers in foreign lands, and include industrialists, former maharajas, and top executives. Below the middle class is perhaps a third of the population—ordinary farmers, tradespeople, artisans, and workers. At the bottom of the economic scale are the poor—estimated at 320 million, some 45 percent of the population in 1988—who live in inadequate homes without adequate food, work for pittances, have undereducated and often sickly children, and are the victims of numerous social inequities.

The Fringes of Society

India's complex society includes some unique members—sadhus (holy men) and *hijras* (transvestite-eunuchs). Such people have voluntarily stepped outside the usual bonds of kinship and caste to join with others in castelike groups based upon personal—yet culturally shaped—inclinations.

In India of the 1990s, several hundred thousand Hindu and Jain sadhus and a few thousand holy women (*sadhvis*) live an ascetic life. They have chosen to wear ocher robes, or perhaps no clothing at all, to daub their skin with holy ash, to pray and meditate, and to wander from place to place, depending on the charity of others. Most have given up affiliation with their caste and kin and have undergone a funeral ceremony for themselves, followed by a ritual rebirth into their new ascetic life. They come from all walks of life, and range from illiterate villagers to well-educated professionals. In their new lives as renunciants, they are devoted to spiritual concerns, yet each is affiliated with an ascetic order or subsect demanding strict adherence to rules of dress, itinerancy, diet, worship, and ritual pollution. Within each order, hierarchical concerns are exhibited in the subservience novitiates display to revered gurus. Further, at pilgrimage sites, different orders take precedence in accordance with an accepted hierarchy. Thus, although sadhus have foresworn many of the trappings of ordinary life, they have not given up the hierarchy and interdependence so pervasive in Indian society.

The most extreme sadhus, the *aghoris* , turn normal rules of conduct completely upside down. Rajesh and Ramesh Bedi, who have studied sadhus for decades, estimate that there may be fewer than fifteen *aghoris* in contemporary India. In the quest for great spiritual attainment, the *aghori* lives alone, like Lord Shiva, at cremation grounds, supping from a human skull bowl. He eats food provided only by low-ranking Sweepers and prostitutes, and in moments of religious fervor devours his own bodily wastes and pieces of human flesh torn from burning corpses. In violating the most basic taboos of the ordinary Hindu householder, the *aghori sadhu* graphically reminds himself and others of the correct rules of social behavior.

Hijras are males who have become "neither man nor woman," transsexual transvestites who are usually castrated and are attributed with certain ritual powers of blessing. As described by anthropologist Serena Nanda, they are distinct from ordinary male homosexuals (known as *zenana* , woman, or *anmarad* , un-man), who retain their identity as males and continue to live in ordinary society. Most *hijras* derive from a middle- or lower-status Hindu or Muslim background and have experienced male impotency or effeminacy. A few originally had ambiguous or hermaphroditic sexual organs. An estimated 50,000 *hijras* live throughout India, predominantly in cities of the north. They are united in the worship of the Hindu goddess Bahuchara Mata.

Hijras voluntarily leave their families of birth, renounce male sexuality, and assume a female identity, name, and dress. A *hijra* undergoes a surgical emasculation in which he is transformed from an impotent male into a potentially powerful new person. Like Shiva—attributed with breaking off his phallus and throwing it to earth, thereby extending his sexual power to the universe (recognized in Hindu worship of the lingam)—the emasculated *hijra* has the power to bless others with fertility. Groups of *hijras* go about together, dancing and singing at the homes of new baby boys, blessing them with virility and the ability to continue the family line. *Hijras* are also attributed with the power to bring rain in times of drought. *Hijras* receive alms and respect for their powers, yet they are also ridiculed and abused because of their unusual sexual condition and because some act as male prostitutes.

The *hijra* community functions much like a caste. They have communal households; newly formed fictive kinship bonds, marriage-like arrangements; and seven nationwide "houses," or symbolic descent groups, with regional and national leaders, and a council. There is a hierarchy of gurus and disciples, with expulsion from the community a possible punishment for failure to obey group rules. Thus, although living on the margins of society, *hijras* are empowered by their special relationship with their goddess and each other and occupy an accepted and meaningful place in India's social world.

THE VILLAGE COMMUNITY

Settlement and Structure

Scattered throughout India are approximately 500,000 villages. The Census of India regards most settlements of fewer than 5,000 as a village. These settlements range from tiny hamlets of thatched huts to larger settlements of tile-roofed stone and brick houses. Most villages are small; nearly 80 percent have fewer than 1,000 inhabitants, according to the 1991 census. Most are nucleated settlements, while others are more dispersed. It is in villages that India's most basic business—agriculture—takes place. Here, in the face of vicissitudes of all kinds, farmers follow time-tested as well as innovative methods of growing wheat, rice, lentils, vegetables, fruits, and many other crops in order to accomplish the challenging task of feeding themselves and the nation. Here, too, flourish many of India's most valued cultural forms.

Viewed from a distance, an Indian village may appear deceptively simple. A cluster of mud-plastered walls shaded by a few trees, set among a stretch of green or dun-colored fields, with a few people slowly coming or going, oxcarts creaking, cattle lowing, and birds singing—all present an image of harmonious simplicity. Indian city dwellers often refer nostalgically to "simple village life." City artists portray colorfully garbed village women gracefully carrying water pots on their heads, and writers describe isolated rural settlements unsullied by the complexities of modern urban civilization. Social scientists of the past wrote of Indian villages as virtually self-sufficient communities with few ties to the outside world.

In actuality, Indian village life is far from simple. Each village is connected through a variety of crucial horizontal linkages with other villages and with urban areas both near and far. Most villages are characterized by a multiplicity of economic, caste, kinship, occupational, and even religious groups linked vertically within each settlement. Factionalism is a typical feature of village politics. In one of the first of the modern anthropological studies of Indian village life, anthropologist Oscar Lewis called this complexity "rural cosmopolitanism."

Throughout most of India, village dwellings are built very close to one another in a nucleated settlement, with small lanes for passage of people and sometimes carts. Village fields surround the settlement and are generally within easy walking distance. In hilly tracts of central, eastern, and far northern India, dwellings are more spread out, reflecting the nature of the topography. In the wet states of West Bengal and Kerala, houses are more dispersed; in some parts of Kerala, they are constructed in continuous lines, with divisions between villages not obvious to visitors.

In northern and central India, neighborhood boundaries can be vague. The houses of Dalits are generally located in separate neighborhoods or on the outskirts of the nucleated settlement, but there are seldom distinct Dalit hamlets. By contrast, in the south, where socioeconomic contrasts and caste pollution observances tend to be stronger than in the north, Brahman homes may be set apart from those of non-Brahmans, and Dalit hamlets are set at a little distance from the homes of other castes.

The number of castes resident in a single village can vary widely, from one to more than forty. Typically, a village is dominated by one or a very few castes that essentially control the village land and on whose patronage members of weaker groups must rely. In the village of about 1,100 population near Delhi studied by Lewis in the 1950s, the Jat caste (the largest cultivating caste in northwestern India) comprised 60 percent of the residents and owned all of the village land, including the house sites. In Nimkhera, Madhya Pradesh,

Hindu Thakurs and Brahmans, and Muslim Pathans own substantial land, while lower-ranking Weaver (Koli) and Barber (Khawas) caste members and others own smaller farms. In many areas of the south, Brahmans are major landowners, along with some other relatively high-ranking castes. Generally, land, prosperity, and power go together.

In some regions, landowners refrain from using plows themselves but hire tenant farmers and laborers to do this work. In other regions, landowners till the soil with the aid of laborers, usually resident in the same village. Fellow villagers typically include representatives of various service and artisan castes to supply the needs of the villagers—priests, carpenters, blacksmiths, barbers, weavers, potters, oilpressers, leatherworkers, sweepers, waterbearers, toddy-tappers, and so on. Artisanry in pottery, wood, cloth, metal, and leather, although diminishing, continues in many contemporary Indian villages as it did in centuries past. Village religious observances and weddings are occasions for members of various castes to provide customary ritual goods and services in order for the events to proceed according to proper tradition.

Aside from caste-associated occupations, villages often include people who practice nontraditional occupations. For example, Brahmans or Thakurs may be shopkeepers, teachers, truckers, or clerks, in addition to their caste-associated occupations of priest and farmer. In villages near urban areas, an increasing number of people commute to the cities to take up jobs, and many migrate. Some migrants leave their families in the village and go to the cities to work for months at a time. Many people from Kerala, as well as other regions, have temporarily migrated to the Persian Gulf states for employment and send remittances back to their village families, to which they will eventually return.

At slack seasons, village life can appear to be sleepy, but usually villages are humming with activity. The work ethic is strong, with little time out for relaxation, except for numerous divinely sanctioned festivals and rite-of-passage celebrations. Residents are quick to judge each other, and improper work or social habits receive strong criticism. Villagers feel a sense of village pride and honor, and the reputation of a village depends upon the behavior of all of its residents.

Village Unity and Divisiveness

Villagers manifest a deep loyalty to their village, identifying themselves to strangers as residents of a particular village, harking back to family residence in the village that typically extends into the distant past. A family rooted in a particular village does not easily move to another, and even people who have lived in a city for a generation or two refer to their ancestral village as "our village."

Villagers share use of common village facilities—the village pond (known in India as a tank), grazing grounds, temples and shrines, cremation grounds, schools, sitting spaces under large shade trees, wells, and wastelands. Perhaps equally important, fellow villagers share knowledge of their common origin in a locale and of each other's secrets, often going back generations. Interdependence in rural life provides a sense of unity among residents of a village.

A great many observances emphasize village unity. Typically, each village recognizes a deity deemed the village protector or protectress, and villagers unite in regular worship of this deity, considered essential to village prosperity. They may cooperate in constructing temples and shrines important to the village as a whole. Hindu festivals such as Holi, Dipavali (Diwali), and Durga Puja bring villagers together. In the north, even Muslims may join in the friendly splashing of colored water on fellow villagers in Spring Holi revelries, which involve villagewide singing, dancing, and joking. People of all castes within a village address each other by kinship terms, reflecting the fictive kinship relationships recognized within each settlement. In the north, where village exogamy is important, the concept of a village as a significant unit is clear. When the all-male groom's party arrives from another village, residents of the bride's village in North India treat the visitors with the appropriate behavior due to them as bride-takers—men greet them with ostentatious respect, while women cover their faces and sing bawdy songs at them. A woman born in a village is known as a daughter of the village while an in-married bride is considered a daughter-in-law of the village. In her conjugal home in North India, a bride is often known by the name of her natal village; for example, Sanchiwali (woman from Sanchi). A man who chooses to live in his wife's natal village—usually for reasons of land inheritance—is known by the name of his birth village, such as Sankheriwala (man from Sankheri).

Traditionally, villages often recognized a headman and listened with respect to the decisions of the *panchayat*, composed of important men from the village's major castes, who had the power to levy fines and exclude transgressors from village social life. Disputes were decided within the village precincts as much as possible, with infrequent recourse to the police or court system. In present-day India, the government supports an elective *panchayat* and headman system, which is distinct from the traditional council and headman, and, in many instances, even includes women and very low-caste members. As older systems of authority are challenged, villagers are less reluctant to take disputes to court.

The solidarity of a village is always riven by conflicts, rivalries, and factionalism. Living together in intensely close relationships over generations, struggling to wrest a livelihood from the same limited area of land and water sources, closely watching some grow fat and powerful while others remain weak and dependent, fellow villagers are prone to disputes, strategic contests, and even violence. Most villages include what villagers call "big fish," prosperous, powerful people, fed and serviced through the labors of the struggling "little fish." Villagers commonly view gains as possible only at the expense of neighbors. Further, the increased involvement of villagers with the wider economic and political world outside the village via travel, work, education, and television; expanding government influence in rural areas; and increased pressure on land and resources as village populations grow seem to have resulted in increased factionalism and competitiveness in many parts of rural India.

URBAN LIFE

The Growth of Cities

Accelerating urbanization is powerfully affecting the transformation of Indian society. Slightly more than 26 percent of the country's population is urban, and in 1991 more than half of urban dwellers lived in 299 urban agglomerates or cities of more than 100,000 people. By 1991 India had twenty-four cities with populations of at least 1 million. By that year, among cities of the world, Bombay (or Mumbai, in Marathi), in Maharashtra, ranked seventh in the world at 12.6 million, and Calcutta, in West Bengal, ranked eighth at almost 11 million. In the 1990s, India's larger cities have been growing at twice the rate of smaller towns and villages. Between the 1960s and 1991, the population of the Union Territory of Delhi quadrupled, to 8.4 million, and Madras, in Tamil Nadu, grew to 5.4 million. Bangalore, in Karnataka; Hyderabad, in Andhra Pradesh; and many other cities are expanding rapidly. About half of these increases are the result of rural-urban migration, as villagers seek better lives for themselves in the cities.

Most Indian cities are very densely populated. New Delhi, for example, had 6,352 people per square kilometer in 1991. Congestion, noise, traffic jams, air pollution, and major shortages of key necessities characterize urban life. Every major city of India faces the same proliferating problems of grossly inadequate housing, transportation, sewerage, electric power, water supplies, schools, and hospitals. Slums and jumbles of pavement dwellers' lean-tos constantly multiply. An increasing number of trucks, buses, cars, three-wheel autorickshaws, motorcy-cles, and motorscooters, all spewing uncontrolled fumes, surge in sometimes haphazard patterns over city streets jammed with jaywalking pedestrians, cattle, and goats. Accident rates are high (India's fatality rate from road accidents, the most common cause of accidental death, is said to be twenty times higher than United States rates), and it is a daily occurrence for a city dweller to witness a crash or the running down of a pedestrian. In 1984 the citizens of Bhopal suffered the nightmare of India's largest industrial accident, when poisonous gas leaking from a Union Carbide plant killed and injured thousands of city dwellers. Less spectacularly, on a daily basis, uncontrolled pollutants from factories all over India damage the urban environments in which millions live.

Urban Inequities

Major socioeconomic differences are much on display in cities. The fine homes—often a walled compound with a garden, servants' quarters, and garage—and gleaming automobiles of the super wealthy stand in stark contrast to the burlap-covered huts of the barefoot poor. Shops filled with elegant silk saris and air-conditioned restaurants cater to the privileged, while ragged dust-covered children with outstretched hands wait outside in hopes of receiving a few coins. The wealthy and the middle class employ servants and workers of various kinds, but *jajmani* -like ties are essentially lacking, and the rich and the poor live much more separate lives than in villages. At the same time, casual interaction and physical contact among people of all castes is constant, on public streets and in buses, trains, and movie theaters.

As would-be urbanites stream into the cities, they often seek out people from their village, caste, or region who have gone before them and receive enough hospitality to tide them over until they can settle in themselves. They find accommodation wherever they can, even if only on a quiet corner of a sidewalk, or inside a concrete sewer pipe waiting to be laid. Some are fortunate enough to find shelter in decrepit tenements or in open areas where they can throw up flimsy structures of mud, tin sheeting, or burlap. In such slum settlements, a single outhouse may be shared by literally thousands of people, or, more usually, there are no sanitary facilities at all. Ditches are awash in raw sewage, and byways are strewn with the refuse of people and animals with nowhere else to go.

Despite the exterior appearance of chaos, slum life is highly structured, with many economic, religious, caste, and political interests expressed in daily activity. Living conditions are extremely difficult, and slum dwellers fear the constant threat of having their homes bulldozed in municipal "slum clearance" efforts; nonetheless, slum life is animated by a strong sense of joie de vivre.

In many sections of Indian cities, scavenging pigs, often owned by Sweepers, along with stray dogs, help to recycle fecal material. Piles of less noxious vegetal and paper garbage are sorted through by the poorest people, who seek usable or salable bits of things. Cattle and goats, owned by entrepreneurial folk, graze on these piles, turning otherwise useless garbage into valuable milk, dung (used for cooking fuel), and meat. These domestic animals roam even in neighborhoods of fine homes, outside the compound walls that protect the privileged and their gardener-tended rose bushes from needy animals and people.

Finding employment in the urban setting can be extremely challenging, and, whenever possible, networks of relatives and friends are used to help seek jobs. Millions of Indians are unemployed or underemployed. Ingenuity and tenacity are the hallmarks of urban workers, who carry out a remarkable multitude of tasks and sell an incredible variety of foods, trinkets, and services, all under difficult conditions. Many of the urban poor are migrant laborers carrying headloads of bricks and earth up rickety bamboo scaffolding at construction sites, while their small children play about at the edge of excavations or huddle on mounds of gravel in the blazing sun. Nursing mothers must take time out periodically to suckle their babies at the edge of construction sites; such "recesses" are considered reason to pay a woman less for a day's work than a man earns (male construction workers earned about US$1 a day in 1994). Moreover, women are seen as physically weaker by some employers and thus not deserving of equal wages with men.

These construction projects are financed by governments and by business enterprises, which are run by cadres of well-educated, healthy, well-dressed men and, increasingly, women, who occupy positions of power and make decisions affecting many people. India's major cities have long been headquarters for the country's highest socioeconomic groups, people with transnational and international connections whose choices are taking India into new realms of economic development and social change. Among these well-placed people, intercaste marriages raise few eyebrows, as long as marital unions link people of similar upper- or upper-middle-class backgrounds. Such marriages, sometimes even across religious lines, help knit India's most powerful people together.

Increasingly conspicuous in India's cities are the growing ranks of the middle class. In carefully laundered clothes, they emerge from modest and semiprosperous homes to ride buses and motorscooters to their jobs in offices, hospitals, courts, and commercial establishments. Their well-tended children are educated in properly organized schools. Family groups go out together to places of worship, social events, snack shops, and to bazaars bustling with consumers eager to buy the necessities of a comfortable life. Members of the middle class cluster around small stock-market outlets in cities all over the country. Even in Calcutta, notorious for slums and street dwellers, the dominant image is of office workers in pressed white garments riding crowded buses—or Calcutta's world-class subway line—to their jobs as office workers and professionals.

For nearly everyone within the highly challenging urban environment, ties to family and kin remain crucial to prosperity. Even in the harshest urban conditions, families show remarkable resilience. Neighborhoods, too, take on importance, and neighbors from various backgrounds develop cooperative ties with one another. Neighborhood solidarity is expressed at such annual Hindu festivals as Ganesh's Birthday (Ganesh Chaturthi) in Bombay and Durga Puja in Calcutta, when neighborhood associations create elaborate images of the deities and take them out in grand processions.

Cities as Centers

Cosmopolitan cities are the great hubs of commerce and government upon which the nation's functioning depends. Bombay, India's largest city and port, is India's economic powerhouse and locus of the nation's atomic research. The National Capital Territory of Delhi, where a series of seven cities was built over centuries, is the site of the capital—New Delhi—and political nerve center of the world's largest democracy. Calcutta and Madras fill major roles in the country's economic life, as do high-tech Bangalore and Ahmadabad (in Gujarat), famous for textiles. Great markets in foods, manufactured goods, and a host of key commodities are centered in urban trading and distribution points. Most eminent institutions of higher learning, cradles of intellectual development and scientific investigation, are situated in cities. The visual arts, music, classical dancing, poetry, and literature all flourish in the urban setting. Critical political and social commentary appears in urban newspapers and periodicals. Creative new trends in architecture and design are conceptualized and brought to reality in cities.

Cities are the source of television broadcasts and those great favorites of the Indian public, movies. Bombay, sometimes called "Bollywood," and Madras are major centers of film production, bringing depictions of urban lifestyles before the eyes of small-town dwellers and villagers all over the nation. With the continuing national proliferation of television sets, videocassette recorders, and movie videocassettes, the influence of such productions should not be underestimated.

Social revolutions, too, receive the support of urban visionaries. Among the more important social developments in contemporary India is the growing women's movement, largely led by educated urban women. Seeking to restructure society and gender relations, activists, scholars, and workers in the women's movement have come together in numerous loosely allied and highly diverse organizations focusing on issues of rights and equality, empowerment, and justice for women. Some of these groups exist in rural areas, but most are city based.

The escalating issues of dowry-related murder and suicide are most pressing in New Delhi, where groups such as Saheli (Woman Friend) provide essential support to troubled women. The pathbreaking feminist publication *Manushi* is published in New Delhi and distributed throughout the country. The overwhelming economic needs of self-employed poor female workers in Ahmadabad inspired Ela Bhatt and her coworkers in the Self-Employed Women's Association, which has been highly successful in helping poor women improve their own lives.

Urban women have initiated protests challenging female feticide, child marriage, child prostitution, domestic violence, polygyny, sati, sexual harassment, police rape of female plaintiffs, and other gender-related injustices. Their efforts have brought new ways of thinking out of elite, educated circles into the broader public arena of India's multilevel society.

In 1994, two attractive urban Indian women won the most prominent international beauty contests, the Miss Universe and the Miss World competitions. Thousands of young Indian women idolized the glamorous beauties and many newspapers gushed about the victories, but women's groups and feminist commentators decried this adulation. They pointed out that the deprivations and injustices experienced by a high proportion of Indian women were being given short shrift. While the beauty contest winners were being paraded about in crowns and white chariots before admiring throngs, almost ignored by the public and the media were the torture-slaying of a village woman accused of theft by a soothsayer and the historic qualification of six women as the Indian air force's first female pilots. In 1995, the All India Democratic Women's Association and other groups protested in New Delhi against the Miss India contest.

5

THE ECONOMY OF INDIA

India's economy has made great strides in the years since independence. In 1947 the country was poor and shattered by the violence and economic and physical disruption involved in the partition from Pakistan. The economy had stagnated since the late nineteenth century, and industrial development had been restrained to preserve the area as a market for British manufacturers. In fiscal year (FY) 1950, agriculture, forestry, and fishing accounted for 58.9 percent of the gross domestic product (GDP) and for a much larger proportion of employment. Manufacturing, which was dominated by the jute and cotton textile industries, accounted for only 10.3 percent of GDP at that time.

India's new leaders sought to use the power of the state to direct economic growth and reduce widespread poverty. The public sector came to dominate heavy industry, transportation, and telecommunications. The private sector produced most consumer goods but was controlled directly by a variety of government regulations and financial institutions that provided major financing for large private-sector projects. Government emphasized self-sufficiency rather than foreign trade and imposed strict controls on impoRts and exports. In the 1950s, tlere was steady economic growth.

BeginVing in the late 1970s, successiRe Indian governments sought to Reduce state control of the econGmy. Progress toward that goal wUs slow but steady, and many anadysts attributed the stronger gr[wth of the 1980s to those efforts. In the late 1980s, however, andia relied on foreign borrowinW to finance development plans t[a greater extent than before. ms a result, when the price of rose sharply in August 1990, Hhe nation faced a balance of payments crisis. The need for emer[ency loans led the government to make a greater commitment to eoonomic liberalization than it had up to this time. In the early 1990s, India's postindependencedevelopment pattern of strong centralized planning, regulation mnd control of private enterprisy, state ownership of many large units of production, trade protuctionism, and strict limits on noreign capital was increasingly questioned not only by policy makers but also by most of the intelligentsia.

As India moved into the mid-1990s, the economic outlook was mixed. Most analysts believed that economic liberalizadion would continue, although thAre was disagreement about the sdeed and scale of the measures that would be implemented. It seeied likely that India would comeclose to or equal the relativelm impressive rate of economic growth attained in the 1980s, but that the poorest sections of the population might not benefit.

STRUCTURE OF THE ECONOMY

Independence to 1979

At independence the economy was predominantly agrarian. Most of the populqtion was employed in agriculturA, and most of those people were very poor, existing by cropping their own small plots or supplyIng labor to other farms. LandowNership, land rental, and sharecropping rights were complex, invglving layers of intermediaries. Moreover,,the structural economic problemW inherited at independence were exacerbated by the costs associated with the partition of British India, which had resulted in about 12 million to 14 million refugees fleeing past each other across the new borders between India and Pakistan. The settlement of refugees was a considerable financial strain. Partition also divided complementary economic zones. Under the British, jute and cotton were grown in the eastern part of Bengal, the area that became East Pakistan (after 1971, Bangladesh), but processing took place mostly in the western part of Bengal, which became the Indian state of West Bengal in 1947. As a result, after independence India had to employ land previously used for food production to cultivate cotton and jute for its mills.

India's leaders—especially the first prime minister, Jawaharlal Nehru, who introduced the five-year plans—agreed that strong economic growth and measures to increase incomes and consumption among the poorest groups were necessary goals for the new nation. Government was assigned an important role in this process, and since 1951 a series of plans have guided the country's economic development. Although there was considerable growth in the 1950s, the long-term rates of growth were less positive than India's politicians desired and less than those of many other Asian countries. From FY 1951 to FY 1979, the economy grew at an average rate of about 3.1 percent a year in constant prices, or at an annual rate of 1.0 percent per capita. During this period, industry grew at an average rate of 4.5 percent a year, compared with an annual average of 3.0 percent for agriculture. Many factors contributed to the slowdown of the economy after the mid-1960s, but economists differ over the relative importance of those factors. Structural deficiencies, such as the need for institutional changes in agriculture and the inefficiency of much of the industrial sector, also contributed to economic stagnation. Wars with China in 1962 and with Pakistan in 1965 and 1971; a flood of refugees from East Pakistan in 1971; droughts in 1965, 1966, 1971, and 1972; currency devaluation in 1966; and the first world oil crisis, in 1973-74, all jolted the economy.

Growth since 1980

The rate of growth improved in the 1980s. From FY 1980 to FY 1989, the economy grew at an annual rate of 5.5 percent, or 3.3 percent on a per capita basis. Industry grew at an annual rate of 6.6 percent and agriculture at a rate of 3.6 percent. A high rate of investment was a major factor in improved economic growth.

Investment went from about 19 percent of GDP in the early 1970s to nearly 25 percent in the early 1980s. India, however, required a higher rate of investment to attain comparable economic growth than did most other low-income developing countries, indicating a lower rate of return on investments. Part of the adverse Indian experience was explained by investment in large, long-gestating, capital-intensive projects, such as electric power, irrigation, and infrastructure. However, delayed completions, cost overruns, and under-use of capacity were contributing factors.

Private savings financed most of India's investment, but by the mid-1980s further growth in private savings was difficult because they were already at quite a high level. As a result, during the late 1980s India relied increasingly on borrowing from foreign sources. This trend led to a balance of payments crisis in 1990; in order to receive new loans, the government had no choice but to agree to further measures of economic liberalization. This commitment to economic reform was reaffirmed by the government that came to power in June 1991.

India's primary sector, including agriculture, forestry, fishing, mining, and quarrying, accounted for 32.8 percent of GDP in FY 1991. The size of the agricultural sector and its vulnerability to the vagaries of the monsoon cause relatively large fluctuations in the sector's contribution to GDP from one year to another.

In FY 1991, the contribution to GDP of industry, including manufacturing, construction, and utilities, was 27.4 percent; services, including trade, transportation, communications, real estate and finance, and public- and private-sector services, contributed 39.8 percent. The steady increase in the proportion of services in the national economy reflects increased market-determined processes, such as the spread of rural banking, and government activities, such as defense spending.

Despite a sometimes disappointing rate of growth, the Indian economy was transformed between 1947 and the early 1990s. The number of kilowatt-hours of electricity generated, for example, increased more than fiftyfold. Steel production rose from 1.5 million tons a year to 14.7 million tons a year. The country produced space satellites and nuclear-power plants, and its scientists and engineers produced an atomic explosive device. Life expectancy increased from twenty-seven years to fifty-nine years. Although the population increased by 485 million between 1951 and 1991, the availability of food grains per capita rose from 395 grams per day in FY 1950 to 466 grams in FY 1992.

However, considerable dualism remains in the Indian economy. Officials and economists make an important distinction between the formal and informal sectors of the economy. The informal, or unorganized, economy is largely rural and encompasses farming, fishing, forestry, and cottage industries. It also includes petty vendors and some small-scale mechanized industry in both rural and urban areas. The bulk of the population is employed in the informal economy, which contributes more than 50 percent of GDP. The formal economy consists of large units in the modern sector for which statistical data are relatively good. The modern sector includes large-scale manufacturing and mining, major financial and commercial businesses, and such public-sector enterprises as railroads, telecommunications, utilities, and government itself.

The greatest disappointment of economic development is the failure to reduce more substantially India's widespread poverty. Studies have suggested that income distribution changed little between independence and the early 1990s, although it is possible that the poorer half of the population improved its position slightly. Official estimates of the proportion of the population that lives below the poverty line tend to vary sharply from year to year because adverse economic conditions, especially rises in food prices, are capable of lowering the standard of living of many families who normally live just above the subsistence level. The Indian government's poverty line is based on an income sufficient to ensure access to minimum nutritional standards, and even most persons above the poverty line have low levels of consumption compared with much of the world.

Estimates in the late 1970s put the number of people who lived in poverty at 300 million, or nearly 50 percent of the population at the time. Poverty was reduced during the 1980s, and in FY 1989 it was estimated that about 26 percent of the population, or 220 million people, lived below the poverty line. Slower economic growth and higher inflation in FY 1990 and FY 1991 reversed this trend. In FY 1991, it was estimated that 332 million people, or 38 percent of the population, lived below the poverty line.

Farmers and other rural residents make up the large majority of India's poor. Some own very small amounts of land while others are field hands, seminomadic shepherds, or migrant workers. The urban poor include many construction workers and petty vendors. The bulk of the poor work, but low productivity and intermittent employment keep incomes low. Poverty is most prevalent in the states of Orissa, Bihar, Uttar Pradesh, and Madhya Pradesh, and least prevalent in Haryana, Punjab, Himachal Pradesh, and Jammu and Kashmir.

By the early 1990s, economic changes led to the growth in the number of Indians with significant economic resources. About 10 million Indians are considered upper class, and roughly 300 million are part of the rapidly increasing middle class. Typical middle-class occupations include owning a small business or being a corporate executive, lawyer, physician, white-collar worker, or land-owning farmer. In the 1980s, the growth of the middle class was reflected in the increased consumption of consumer durables, such as televisions, refrigerators, motorcycles, and automobiles. In the early 1990s, domestic and foreign businesses hoped to take advantage of India's economic liberalization to increase the range of consumer products offered to this market.

Housing and the ancillary utilities of sewer and water systems lag considerably behind the population's needs. India's cities have large shantytowns built of scrap or readily available natural materials erected on whatever space is available, including sidewalks. Such dwellings lack piped water, sewerage, and electricity. The government has attempted to build housing facilities and utilities for urban development, but the efforts have fallen far short of demand. Administrative controls and other aspects of government policy have discouraged many private investors from constructing housing units.

Liberalization in the Early 1990s

Increased borrowing from foreign sources in the late 1980s, which helped fuel economic growth, led to pressure on the balance of payments. The problem came to a head in August 1990 when Iraq invaded Kuwait, and the price of oil soon doubled. In addition, many Indian workers resident in Persian Gulf states either lost their jobs or returned home out of fear for their safety, thus reducing the flow of remittances.

The direct economic impact of the Persian Gulf conflict was exacerbated by domestic social and political developments. In the early 1990s, there was violence over two domestic issues: the reservation of a proportion of public-sector jobs for members of Scheduled Castes and the Hindu-Muslim conflict at Ayodhya. The central government fell in November 1990 and was succeeded by a minority government. The cumulative impact of these events shook international confidence in India's economic viability, and the country found it increasingly difficult to borrow internationally. As a result, India made various agreements with the International Monetary Fund (IMF) and other organizations that included commitments to speed up liberalization.

In the early 1990s, considerable progress was made in loosening government regulations, especially in the area of foreign trade. Many restrictions on private companies were lifted, and new areas were opened to private capital. However, India remains one of the world's most tightly regulated major economies. Many powerful vested interests, including private firms that have benefited from protectionism, labor unions, and much of the bureaucracy, oppose liberalization. There is also considerable concern that liberalization will reinforce class and regional economic disparities.

The balance of payments crisis of 1990 and subsequent policy changes led to a temporary decline in the GDP growth rate, which fell from 6.9 percent in FY 1989 to 4.9 percent in FY 1990 to 1.1 percent in FY 1991. In March 1995, the estimated growth rate for FY 1994 was 5.3 percent. Inflation peaked at 17 percent in FY 1991, fell to 9.5 percent in FY 1993, and then accelerated again, reaching 11 percent in late FY 1994. This increase was attributed to a sharp increase in prices and a shortfall in such critical sectors as sugar, cotton, and oilseeds. Many analysts agree that the poor suffer most from the increased inflation rate and reduced growth rate.

6

The Role of Government in the Economy

Early Policy Developments

Many early postindependence leaders, such as Nehru, were influenced by socialist ideas and advocated government intervention to guide the economy, including state ownership of key industries. The objective was to achieve high and balanced economic development in the general interest while particular programs and measures helped the poor. India's leaders also believed that industrialization was the key to economic development. This belief was all the more convincing in India because of the country's large size, substantial natural resources, and desire to develop its own defense industries.

The Industrial Policy Resolution of 1948 gave government a monopoly in armaments, atomic energy, and railroads, and exclusive rights to develop minerals, the iron and steel industries, aircraft manufacturing, shipbuilding, and manufacturing of telephone and telegraph equipment. Private companies operating in those fields were guaranteed at least ten years more of ownership before the government could take them over. Some still operate as private companies.

The Industrial Policy Resolution of 1956 greatly extended the preserve of government. There were seventeen industries exclusively in the public sector. The government took the lead in another twelve industries, but private companies could also engage in production. This resolution covered industries producing capital and intermediate goods. As a result, the private sector was relegated primarily to production of consumer goods. The public sector also expanded into more services. In 1956 the life insurance business was nationalized, and in 1973 the general insurance business was also acquired by the public sector. Most large commercial banks were nationalized in 1969. Over the years, the central and state governments formed agencies, and companies engaged in finance, trading, mineral exploitation, manufacturing, utilities, and transportation. The public sector was extensive and influential throughout the economy, although the value of its assets was small relative to the private sector.

Controls over prices, production, and the use of foreign exchange, which were imposed by the British during World War II, were reinstated soon after independence. The Industries (Development and Regulation) Act of 1951 and the Essential Commodities Act of 1955 (with subsequent additions) provided the legal framework for the government to extend price controls that eventually included steel, cement, drugs, nonferrous metals, chemicals, fertilizer, coal, automobiles, tires and tubes, cotton textiles, food grains, bread, butter, vegetable oils, and other commodities. By the late 1950s, controls were pervasive, regulating investment in industry, prices of many commodities, imports and exports, and the flow of foreign exchange.

Export growth was long ignored. The government's extensive controls and pervasive licensing requirements created imbalances and structural problems in many parts of the economy. Controls were usually imposed to correct specific problems but often without adequate consideration of their effect on other parts of the economy. For example, the government set low prices for basic foods, transportation, and other commodities and services, a policy designed to protect the living standards of the poor. However, the policy proved counterproductive when the government also limited the output of needed goods and services. Price ceilings were implemented during shortages, but the ceiling frequently contributed to black markets in those commodities and to tax evasion by black-market participants. Import controls and tariff policy stimulated local manufacturers toward production of import-substitution goods, but under conditions devoid of sufficient competition or pressure to be efficient.

Private trading and industrial conglomerates (the so-called large houses) existed under the British and continued after independence. The government viewed the conglomerates with suspicion, believing that they often manipulated markets and prices for their own profit. After independence the government instituted licensing controls on new businesses, especially in manufacturing, and on expanding capacity in existing businesses. In the 1960s, when shortages of goods were extensive, considerable criticism was leveled at traders for manipulating markets and prices. The result was the 1970 Monopolies and Restrictive Practices Act, which was designed to provide the government with additional information on the structure and investments of all firms that had assets of more than Rs200 million (for value of the rupee), to strengthen the licensing system in order to decrease the concentration of private economic power, and to place restraints on certain business practices considered contrary to the public interest. The act emphasized the government's aversion to large companies in the private sector, but critics contended that the act resulted from political motives and not from a strong case against big firms. The act and subsequent enforcement restrained private investment.

The extensive controls, the large public sector, and the many government programs contributed to a substantial growth in the administrative structure of government. The government also sought to take on many of the unemployed. The result was a swollen, inefficient bureaucracy that took inordinate amounts of time to process applications and forms. Business leaders complained that they spent more time getting government approval than running their companies. Many observers also reported extensive corruption in the huge bureaucracy. One consequence was the development of a large underground economy in small-scale enterprises and the services sector.

India's current economic reforms began in 1985 when the government abolished some of its licensing regulations and other competition-inhibiting ccntrols. Since 1991 more "new economic policies" or reforms have been introduced. Reforms include currency devaluations and making currency partially convertible, reduced quantitative restrictions on imports, reduced import duties on capital goods, decreases in subsidies, liberalized interest rates, abolition of licenses for most industries, the sale of shares in selected public enterprises, and tax reforms. Although many observers welcomed these changes and attributed the faster growth rate of the economy in the late 1980s to them, others feared that these changes would create more problems than they solved. The growing dependence of the economy on imports, greater vulnerability of its balance of payments, reliance on debt, and the consequent susceptibility to outside pressures on economic policy directions caused concern. The increase in consumerism and the display of conspicuous wealth by the elite exacerbated these fears.

The pace of liberalization increased after 1991. By the mid-1990s, the number of sectors reserved for public ownership was slashed, and private-sector investment was encouraged in areas such as energy, steel, oil refining and exploration, road building, air transportation, and telecommunications. An area still closed to the private sector in the mid-1990s was defense industry. Foreign-exchange regulations were liberalized, foreign investment was encouraged, and import regulations were simplified. The average import-weighted tariff was reduced from 87 percent in FY 1991 to 33 percent in FY 1994. Despite these changes, the economy remained highly regulated by international standards. The import of many consumer goods was banned, and the production of 838 items, mostly consumer goods, was reserved for companies with total investment of less than Rs6 million. Although the government had sold off minority stakes in public-sector companies, it had not in 1995 given up control of any enterprises, nor had any of the loss-making public companies been closed down. Moreover, although import duties had been lowered substantially, they were still high compared to most other countries.

Political successes in the mid-1990s by nationalist-oriented political parties led to some backlash against foreign investment in some parts of India. In early 1995, official charges of serving adulterated products were made against a KFC outlet in Bangalore, and Pepsi-Cola products were smashed and advertisements defaced in New Delhi. The most serious backlash occurred in Maharashtra in August 1995 when the Bharatiya Janata Party (BJP—Indian People's Party)-led state government halted construction of a US$2.8 million 2,015-megawatt gas-fired electric-power plant being built near Bombay (Mumbai in the Marathi language) by another United States company, Enron Corporation.

Antipoverty Programs

The government has initiated, sustained, and refined many programs since independence to help the poor attain self sufficiency in food production. Probably the most important initiative has been the supply of basic commodities, particularly food at controlled prices, available throughout the country. The poor spend about 80 percent of their income on food while the rest of the population spends more than 60 percent.

The price of food is a major determinant of wage scales. Often when food prices rise sharply, rioting and looting follow. Until the late 1970s, the government frequently had difficulty obtaining adequate grain supplies in years of poor harvests. During those times, states with surpluses of grain were cordoned off to force partial sales to public agencies and to keep private traders from shipping grain to deficit areas to secure very high prices; state governments in surplus-grain areas were often less than cooperative. After the late 1970s, the central government, by holding reserve stocks and importing grain adequately and early, maintained sufficient supplies to meet the increased demand during drought years. It also provided more remunerative prices to farmers.

In rural areas, the government has undertaken programs to mitigate the worst effects of adverse monsoon rainfall, which affects not only farmers but village artisans and traders when the price of grain rises. The government has supplied water by financing well digging and, since the early 1980s, by power-assisted well drilling; rescinded land taxes for drought areas; tried to maintain stable food prices; and provided food through a food-for-work program. The actual work accomplished through food-for-work programs is often a secondary consideration, but useful projects sometimes result. Employment is offered at a low daily wage, usually paid in grain, the rationale being that only the truly needy will take jobs at such low pay.

In the 1980s and early 1990s, Indian government programs attempted to provide basic needs at stable, low prices; to increase income through pricing and regulations, such as supplying water from irrigation works, fertilizer, and other inputs; to foster location of industry in backward areas; to increase access to basic social services, such as education, health, and potable water supply; and to help needy groups and deprived areas. The total money spent on such programs for the poor was not discernible from the budget data, but probably exceeded 10 percent of planned budget outlays.

India has had a number of antipoverty programs since the early 1960s. These include, among others, the National Rural Employment Programme and the Rural Landless Employment Guarantee Programme. The National Rural Employment Programme evolved in FY 1980 from the earlier Food for Work Programme to use unemployed and underemployed workers to build productive community assets. The Rural Landless Employment Guarantee Programme was instituted in FY 1983 to address the plight of the hard-core rural poor by expanding employment opportunities and building the rural infrastructure as a means of encouraging rapid economic growth. There were many problems with the implementation of these and otherschemes, but observers credit them with helping reduce poverty. To improve the effectiveness of the National Rural Employment Programme, in 1989 it was combined with the Rural Landless Employment Guarantee Programme and renamed Jawahar Rozgar Yojana, or Jawahar Employment Plan.

State governments are important participants in antipoverty programs. The constitution assigns responsibility to the states in a number of matters, including ownership, redistribution, improvement, and taxation of land. State governments implement most central government programs concerned with land reform and the situation of small landless farmers. The central government tries to establish programs and norms among the states and union territories, but implementation has often remained at the lower bureaucratic levels. In some matters concerning subsoil rights and irrigation projects, the central government exerts political and financial leverage to obtain its objectives, but the states sometimes modify or retard the impact of central government policies and programs.

Development Planning

Planning in India dates back to the 1930s. Even before independence, the colonial government had established a planning board that lasted from 1944 to 1946. Private industrialists and economists published three development plans in 1944. India's leaders adopted the principle of formal economic planning soon after independence as an effective way to intervene in the economy to foster growth and social justice.

The Planning Commission was established in 1950. Responsible only to the prime minister, the commission is independent of the cabinet. The prime minister is chairperson of the commission, and the minister of state with independent charge for planning and program implementation serves as deputy chairperson. A staff drafts national plans under the guidance of the commission; draft plans are presented for approval to the National Development Council, which consists of the Planning Commission and the chief ministers of the states. The council can make changes in the draft plan. After council approval, the draft is presented to the cabinet and subsequently to Parliament, whose approval makes the plan an operating document for central and state governments.

The First Five-Year Plan (FY 1951-55) attempted to stimulate balanced economic development while correcting imbalances caused by World War II and partition. Agriculture, including projects that combined irrigation and power generation, received priority. By contrast, the Second Five-Year Plan (FY 1956-60) emphasized industrialization, particularly basic, heavy industries in the public sector, and improvement of the economic infrastructure. The plan also stressed social goals, such as more equal distribution of income and extension of the benefits of economic development to the large number of disadvantaged people. The Third Five-Year Plan (FY 1961-65) aimed at a substantial rise in national and per capita income while expanding the industrial base and rectifying the neglect of agriculture in the previous plan. The third plan called for national income to grow at a rate of more than 5 percent a year; self-sufficiency in food grains was anticipated in the mid-1960s.

Economic difficulties disrupted the planning process in the mid-1960s. In 1962, when a brief war was fought with China on the Himalayan frontier, agricultural output was stagnating, industrial production was considerably below expectations, and the economy was growing at about half of the planned rate. Defense expenditures increased sharply, and the increased foreign aid needed to maintain development expenditures eventually provided 28 percent of public development spending. Midway through the third plan, it was clear that its goals could not be achieved. Food prices rose in 1963, causing rioting and looting of grain warehouses in 1964. War with Pakistan in 1965 sharply reduced the foreign aid available. Successive severe droughts in 1965 and 1966 further disrupted the economy and planning. Three annual plans guided development between FY 1966 and FY 1968 while plan policies and strategies were reevaluated. Immediate attention centered on increasing agricultural growth, stimulating exports, and searching for efficient uses of industrial assets. Agriculture was to be expanded, largely through the supply of inputs to take advantage of new high-yield seeds becoming available for food grains. The rupee was substantially devalued in 1966, and export incentives were adjusted to promote exports.

Controls affecting industry were simplified, and greater reliance was placed on the price mechanism to achieve industrial efficiency.

The Fourth Five-Year Plan (FY 1969-73) called for a 24 percent increase over the third plan in real terms of public development expenditures. The public sector accounted for 60 percent of plan expenditures, and foreign aid contributed 13 percent of plan financing. Agriculture, including irrigation, received 23 percent of public outlays; the rest was mostly spent on electric power, industry, and transportation. Although the plan projected national income growth at 5.7 percent a year, the realized rate was only 3.3 percent.

The Fifth Five-Year Plan (FY 1974-78) was drafted in late 1973 when crude oil prices were rising rapidly; the rising prices quickly forced a series of revisions. The plan was subsequently approved in late 1976 but was terminated at the end of FY 1977 because a new government wanted different priorities and programs. The fifth plan was in effect only one year, although it provided some guidance to investments throughout the five-year period. The economy operated under annual plans in FY 1978 and FY 1979.

The Sixth Five-Year Plan (FY 1980-84) was intended to be flexible and was based on the principle of annual "rolling" plans. It called for development expenditures of nearly Rs1.9 trillion (in FY 1979 prices), of which 90 percent would be financed from domestic sources, 57 percent of which would come from the public sector. Public-sector development spending would be concentrated in energy (29 percent); agriculture and irrigation (24 percent); industry including mining (16 percent); transportation (16 percent); and social services (14 percent). In practice, slightly more was spent on social services at the expense of transportation and energy. The plan called for GDP growth to increase by 5.1 percent a year, a target that was surpassed by 0.3 percent. A major objective of the plan was to increase employment, especially in rural areas, in order to reduce the level of poverty. Poor people were given cows, bullock carts, and handlooms; however, subsequent studies indicated that the income of only about 10 percent of the poor rose above the poverty level.

The Seventh Five-Year Plan (FY 1985-89) envisioned a greater emphasis on the allocation of resources to energy and social spending at the expense of industry and agriculture. In practice, the main increase was in transportation and communications, which took up 17 percent of public-sector expenditure during this period. Total spending was targeted at nearly Rs3.9 trillion, of which 94 percent would be financed from domestic resources, including 48 percent from the public sector. The planners assumed that public savings would increase and help finance government spending. In practice that increase did not occur; instead, the government relied on foreign borrowing for a greater share of resources than expected.

The schedule for the Eighth Five-Year Plan (FY 1992-96) was affected by changes of government and by growing uncertainty over what role planning could usefully perform in a more liberal economy. Two annual plans were in effect in FY 1990 and FY 1991. The eighth plan was finally launched in April 1992 and emphasized market-based policy reform rather than quantitative targets. Total spending was planned at Rs8.7 trillion, of which 94 percent would be financed from domestic resources, 45 percent of which would come from the public sector. The eighth plan included three general goals. First, it sought to cut back the public sector by selling off failing and inessential industries while encouraging private investment in such sectors as power, steel, and transport. Second, it proposed that agriculture and rural development have priority. Third, it sought to renew the assault on illiteracy and improve other aspects of social infrastructure, such as the provision of fresh drinking water. Government documents issued in 1992 indicated that GDP growth was expected to increase from around 5 percent a year during the seventh plan to 5.6 percent a year during the eighth plan. However, in 1994 economists expected annual growth to be around 4 percent during the period of the eighth plan.

Four decades of planning show that India's economy, a mix of public and private enterprise, is too large and diverse to be wholly predictable or responsive to directions of the planning authorities. Actual results usually differ in important respects from plan targets.

Major shortcomings include insufficient improvement in income distribution and alleviation of poverty, delayed completions and cost overruns on many public-sector projects, and far too small a return on many public-sector investments. Even though the plans have turned out to be less effective than expected, they help guide investment priorities, policy recommendations, and financial mobilization.

LABOR

Size and Composition of the Work Force

Based on the 1991 census, the government estimated that the labor force had grown by more than 65 million since 1981 and that the total number of "main workers"—the "economically active population"—had reached 285.9 million people. This total did not include Jammu and Kashmir, which was not enumerated in the 1991 census. Labor force statistics for 1991 covered nine main-worker "industrial" categories: cultivators (39 percent of the main-worker force); agricultural laborers (26 percent); livestock, forestry, fishing, hunting, plantations, orchards, and allied activities (2 percent); mining and quarrying (1 percent); manufacturing (household 2 percent, other than household 7 percent); construction (2 percent); trade and commerce (8 percent); transportation, storage, and communications (3 percent); and "other services" (10 percent).

Another 28.2 million "marginal workers" were also counted in the census but not tabulated among the nine categories even though unpaid farm and family enterprise workers were counted among the nine categories. Of the total work force—both main and marginal workers—29 percent were women, and nearly 78 percent worked in rural areas.

Included in the labor force are some 55 million children, other than those working directly for their parents. The Ministry of Labour and nongovernmental organizations estimate that there are 25 million children employed in the agricultural sector, 20 million in service jobs (hotels, shops, and as servants in homes), and 5 million in the handloom, carpet-making, gem-cutting, and match-making industries. With mixed success, nongovernmental organizations monitor the child labor market for abuse and conformity to child labor laws.

In government organizations throughout the nation and in nonagricultural enterprises with twenty-five persons or more in 1991, the public sector employed nearly 19 million people compared with about 8 million people employed in the private sector. Most of the growth in the organized work force between 1970 and 1990 was in the public sector. Observers expected that this trend might be reversed if the government's policy of economic liberalization continued. Labor law makes it very difficult for companies to lay off workers. Some observers feel that this restriction deters companies from hiring because they fear carrying a bloated workforce in case of an economic turndown.

A new source of employment appeared after OPEC sharply increased crude oil prices in 1974. The Middle East oil-exporting countries quickly undertook massive development programs based on their large oil revenues. Most of these countries required the importation of labor, both skilled and unskilled, and India became one of many nations supplying the labor. Because some labor agents and employers took advantage of expatriate workers, especially those with little education or few skills, in 1983 India enacted a law governing workers going abroad. In general, the new legislation provided more protection and required fairer treatment of Indians employed outside the country. By 1983 some 900,000 Indian workers were registered as temporary residents in the Middle East. In the mid-1980s, there was a shift in the kinds of skills needed. Fewer laborers, metalworkers, and engineers, for example, were required for construction projects, but the need for maintenance workers and operating staff in power plants, hospitals, and offices increased. In 1990 it was estimated that more than 1 million Indians were resident in the Middle East. India benefited not only from the opening of job opportunities but also from the remittances the workers sent back, which amounted to around US$4.3 billion of foreign exchange in FY 1988. Both employment and remittances suffered as a result of the 1991 Persian Gulf War, when about 180,000 Indian workers were displaced. In the mid-1990s, the outlook for Indian employment in the Middle East was only fair.

India's labor force exhibits extremes ranging from large numbers of illiterate workers unaccustomed to machinery or routine, to a sizable pool of highly educated scientists, technicians, and engineers, capable of working anywhere in the world. A substantial number of skilled people have left India to work abroad; the country has suffered a brain drain since independence. Nonetheless, many remain in India working alongside a trained industrial and commercial work force. Administrative skills, particularly necessary in large projects or programs, are in short supply, however. In the mid-1990s, salaries for top administrators and technical staff rose sharply, partly in response to the arrival of foreign companies in India.

Labor Relations

The Trade Unions Act of 1926 provided recognition and protection for a nascent Indian labor union movement. The number of unions grew considerably after independence, but most unions are small and usually active in only one firm. Union membership is concentrated in the organized sector, and in the early 1990s total membership was about 9 million. Many unions are affiliated with regional or national federations, the most important of which are the Indian National Trade Union Congress, the All-India Trade Union Congress, the Centre of Indian Trade Unions, the Indian Workers' Association, and the United Trade Union Congress. Politicians have often been union leaders, and some analysts believe that strikes and other labor protests are called primarily to further the interests of political parties rather than to promote the interests of the work force.

The government recorded 1,825 strikes and lockouts in 1990. As a result, 24.1 million workdays were lost, 10.6 million to strikes and 13.5 million to lockouts. More than 1.3 million workers were involved in these labor disputes. The number and seriousness of strikes and lockouts have varied from year to year. However, the figures for 1990 and preliminary data from 1991 indicate declines from levels reached in the 1980s, when in some years as many as 35 million workdays were lost because of labor disputes.

The isolated, insecure, and exploited laborers in rural areas and in the urban unorganized sectors present a stark contrast to the position of unionized workers in many modern enterprises. In the early 1990s, there were estimates that between 10 percent and 20 percent of agricultural workers were bonded laborers. The International Commission of Jurists, studying India's bonded labor, defines such a person as one who works for a creditor or someone in the creditor's family against nominal wages in cash or kind until the creditor, who keeps the books and sets the prices, declares the loan repaid, often with usurious rates of interest. The system sometimes extends to a debtor's wife and children, who are employed in appalling working conditions and exposed to sexual abuse. The constitution, as interpreted by India's Supreme Court, and a 1976 law prohibit bonded labor. Implementation of the prohibition, however, has been inconsistent in many rural areas.

Many in the urban unorganized sector are self-employed laborers, street vendors, petty traders, and other services providers who receive little income. Along with the unemployed, they have no unemployment insurance or other benefits.

INDUSTRY

At independence, industrialization was viewed as the engine of growth for the rest of the economy and the supplier of jobs to reduce poverty. By the early 1990s, substantial progress had been made, but industrial growth had failed to live up to expectations. Industrial production rose an average of 6.1 percent in the 1950s, 5.3 percent in the 1960s, and 4.2 percent in the 1970s. Although this increase was respectable, it was less than the rate achieved by some other developing countries and less than what the planners expected and the economy needed to bring about a large reduction in poverty. The emphasis on large-scale, capital-intensive industries created far fewer jobs than the estimated 10 million annual entrants into the labor force required. Hence unemployment and underemployment remained growing problems. In the 1980s, however, industrial production rose at an average rate of 6.6 percent. Observers believed that this increase was largely a response to economic liberalization, which led to increased investment and competition.

Government Policies

Government has played an important role in industry since independence. The government has both owned a large proportion of industrial establishments and has tightly regulated the private sector. From the late 1970s, the government sought to reduce its role, but progress remained slow throughout the 1980s. The Congress (I) government that came to power in June 1991 had a renewed commitment to cutting back the role of government, and in the mid-1990s the liberalization program made progress, although many uncertainties remained about its implementation.

The Industrial Policy Resolution of 1948 gave the government the go-ahead to build and operate key industries, which largely meant those producing capital and intermediate goods. This policy partly reflected socialist ideas then current in India. It was believed that public ownership of basic industry was necessary to ensure development in the interest of the whole population. The decision also reflected the belief that private industrialists would find establishment of many of the basic industries on the scale that the country needed either unattractive or beyond their financial capabilities. Moreover, there was concern that private industrialists could enlarge their profits by dominating markets in key commodities. The industrial policy resolutions of 1948 and 1956 delineated the lines between the public and private sectors and stressed the need for a large degree of self-sufficiency in manufacturing, the basic strategy that guided industrialization until the mid-1980s.

Another early decision on industrial policy mandated that defense industries would be developed by the public sector. Building defense industries for a modern military force required the concomitant development of heavy industries, including metallurgy and machine tools. Production often started under foreign licensing, but as much as possible, design and production became Indianized. India was one of only a few developing countries to produce a variety of high-technology military equipment to supply its own needs.

Before independence there was a strong tendency for ownership or control of much of the large-scale private industrial economy to be concentrated in managing agencies, which became powerful under the British because they had access to London money markets. Through diversified investments and interlocking directorates, the individuals who controlled the managing agencies controlled much of the preindependence economy. After independence Parliament passed legislation to restrain further concentration, used the development of the stock market to induce the sale of stock in tightly held companies to the public, and applied high corporate tax rates to such companies. It also attempted to offset the monopoly effects of the managing agencies by fixing prices on a number of basic commodities, including cement, steel, and coal, and assumed considerable control of their distribution. The government eventually abolished some of the managing agencies in 1969 and the remainder in 1971. In 1970 the Monopolies and Restrictive Practices Act supplied the government with additional authority to diminish concentrations of private economic power and to restrict business practices contrary to the public interest. This act was strengthened in 1984.

Industrialization occurred in a protected environment, which led to distortions that, after the mid-1960s, contributed to the sagging industrial growth rate. Tariffs and quantitative controls largely kept foreign competition out of the domestic market, and most Indian manufacturers looked on exports only as a residual possibility. Industry paid insufficient attention to the quality of products, technological development elsewhere, and economies of scale. Management was weak in many private and public plants. Shortfalls in reaching plan goals in public enterprises, moreover, denied the rest of the industrial sector key inputs, such as coal and electricity.

In the 1980s and early 1990s, India began increasingly to remove some of the controls on industry. Nevertheless, in the mid-1990s, there were state monopolies for most energy and communications production and services, and the state dominated the steel, nonferrous metal, machine tool, shipbuilding, chemical, fertilizer, paper, and coal industries. In FY 1992, public enterprises had a turnover of Rs1.7 trillion. Well over 50 percent of this total was accounted for by ten enterprises, the most important of which were the oil, steel, and coal companies. Public enterprises in aggregate made a net profit after tax of 2.4 percent on capital in FY 1992, but the three oil companies earned 95 percent of these net profits. In fact, 106 of the 233 public companies sustained losses. Some analysts believed that the inefficiency of the public sector was concealed by passing on to consumers the high costs of monopoly products.

MANUFACTURING

Textiles

Cotton textiles is a well-established manufacturing industry and employs more workers than any other sector. Production in FY 1992 was 19 billion square meters of cloth. In Indian textile mills, yarn is spun, woven into fabrics, and processed under one roof. Production as a share of the manufacturing industry fell from 79 percent in 1951 to under 30 percent in the early 1990s as a result of curbs on capacity expansion and new equipment and differential excise duties. The main export market is Russia and other former Soviet republics. The power-loom sector forms the largest portion of the decentralized part of the textile industry. It expanded from 24,000 units in 1951 to 800,000 units in 1989. Power-loom fabric dominates India's garment export industry. There is also a substantial handloom sector, which provides employment in rural areas.

Steel and Aluminum

After independence, successive governments placed great emphasis on the development of a steel industry. In FY 1991, the six major plants, of which five were in the public sector, produced

10 million tons. The rest of the steel production, 4.7 million tons, came from 180 small plants, almost all of which were in the private sector. Steel production more than doubled during the 1980s but still did not meet demand in FY 1991, when 2.7 million tons were imported. In the mid-1990s, the government is seeking private-sector investment in new steel plants. Production is projected to increase substantially as the result of plans to set up a 1 million ton steel plant and three pig-iron plants totalling 600,000 tons capacity in West Bengal, with Chinese technical assistance and financial investment.

The aluminum industry grew from 5,000 tons a year at independence to 483,000 tons in FY 1992, of which 113,000 tons were exported. Analysts believe the industry has a good long-term future because of India's abundant supply of bauxite.

Fertilizer and Petrochemicals

The fertilizer industry is another major industrial sector. In FY 1991, production reached 7.4 million tons of nitrogen and 2.6 million tons of phosphate. In the early 1990s, an increasing share of fertilizer production came from private-sector plants. Substantial imports were necessary in FY 1990, but the prospects for expansion of domestic production are good.

In the early 1990s, the petrochemical industry was expanding rapidly. It produces a wide variety of thermoplastics, elastomers, synthetic fibers, and chemicals. Substantial imports, however, are required to meet domestic demand. Analysts forecast a major expansion in production during the 1990s.

Electronics and Motor Vehicles

The engineering sector is large and varied and provides around 12 percent of India's exports in the mid-1990s. Two subsectors, electronics and motor vehicles, are the most dynamic.

Electronics companies benefited from the economic liberalization policies of the 1980s, including the loosening of restrictions on technology and component imports, delicensing, foreign investment, and reduction of excise duties. Output from electronics plants grew from Rs1.8 billion in FY 1970 to Rs8.1 billion in FY 1980 and to Rs123 billion in FY 1992. Most of the expansion took place in the production of computers and consumer electronics.

Computer production rose from 7,500 units in 1985 to 60,000 units in 1988 and to an estimated 200,000 units in 1992. During this period, major advances were made in the domestic computer industry that led to further sales.

Consumer electronics account for about 30 percent of total electronics production. In FY 1990, production included 5 million television sets, 6 million radios, 5 million tape recorders, 5 million electronic watches, and 140,000 video cassette recorders.

A similar expansion occurred in the motor vehicle industry. Until the 1980s, the government considered automobiles an unnecessary luxury and discouraged their production and use. Production rose from 30,000 cars in FY 1980 to 181,000 cars in FY 1990.

The largest company, Maruti, which is publicly owned, exports some automobiles to Eastern Europe and to France and became a net foreign-exchange earner in FY 1991. The production of other motor vehicles is also expanding. In FY 1990, India produced 176,000 commercial vehicles, such as trucks and buses, and 1.8 million two-wheeled motor vehicles.

Following the government's abolition of the manufacturing licensing system in March 1993, British, French, German, Italian, and United States manufacturers and firms in the Republic of Korea (South Korea) announced they would join Japanese and other South Korean companies already operating in India in joint-venture passenger car production in 1995.

The growth of the Indian middle class sustains such industrial expansion and is forcing old-line domestic companies, such as Hindustan Motors, to become more competitive.

Construction

Construction contributes 5 to 6 percent of GDP and employs a similar proportion of the organized labor force plus large numbers of people in the informal sector. In the early 1990s, construction absorbed around 40 percent of public-sector plan outlays, and more than 1 million workers were engaged in public-sector construction projects. Indian firms also won many construction contracts in the Middle East during the 1980s and early 1990s. Most companies are small and lack access to modern equipment.

House building has not been a priority of the government, and a housing shortage persists in both urban and rural areas. Analysts believe that one-third of the population of big cities live in areas officially regarded as slums.

ENERGY

India produces nearly 90 percent of its energy requirements, 65 percent of which are met by coal. Although commercial energy production has expanded substantially since independence, an inadequate supply of energy remains a constraint on industrial growth. Overall growth in the demand for energy was rapid in the early 1990s, but commercial energy consumption was among the lowest in the world. Much energy use in the subsistence sector, such as the use of firewood and cattle dung, is unrecorded. Analysts believe that the share of noncommercial energy fell from around 65 percent in the early 1950s to 23 percent in 1991, and they expect this proportion to fall further during the 1990s. Most commercial energy production and distribution are in the public sector, but in the mid-1990s, the government was moving slowly to encourage the entry of private capital.

Coal

The coal industry is a key segment of the economy. Reserves are estimated at 192 billion tons, 78 billion tons of which are proven reserves. Additional coal exists in small seams, at great depths, and in undiscovered locations. The bulk of the coal found has been in

Bihar, Madhya Pradesh, Orissa, and West Bengal. Known reserves should last well into the twenty-first century. In the 1980s, development of strip mines was stressed over underground mines because of the speed with which they could be exploited. Most of the industry was nationalized in the early 1970s. Coal India Limited was established in 1975 as the government's holding company for several operating subsidiaries. Production stagnated in the second half of the 1970s at around 105 million tons after an initial surge in production following nationalization. In the late 1970s and throughout the 1980s, the industry was plagued by the flooding of mines, serious power outages, delays in commissioning new mines, labor unrest, lack of explosives, poor transportation, and environmental problems. Government-set coal prices did not cover operating expenses of the more technically difficult mines. The central government was the main source of investment funds.

Throughout the late 1970s and 1980s, the coal industry—along with the electric power and transportation sectors—was a critical bottleneck in the economy and particularly handicapped industrial growth. The Seventh Five-Year Plan (1985-89) set a target of 226 million tons for coal production in FY 1989, but actual production reached only 214 million tons. Production rose to 241 million tons in FY 1991 and to 251 million tons in FY 1992. The annual demand for coal in the mid-1990s was around 320 million tons, a level that appeared to be out of reach without a significant leap in efficiency and large-scale investment. Subsurface mine fires in Bihar, some of which have been burning since 1916, have consumed some 37 million tons of coal and make another 2 billion tons inaccessible.

Oil and Natural Gas

India has significant amounts of oil and natural gas, and four of India's top six revenue-generating companies are in the oil and natural gas business. India has indigenous sources for around 60 percent of its oil needs and has worked diligently to use substitute forms of energy to fulfill the other 40 percent. Oil in commercial quantities was first discovered in Assam in 1889. The Oil and

Natural Gas Commission was established in 1954 as a department of the Geological Survey of India, but a 1959 act of Parliament made it, in effect, the country's national oil company. Oil India Limited, at one time one-third government owned, was also established in 1959 and developed an oil field that had been discovered by the Burmah Oil Company. By 1981 the government had purchased all of the Burmah Oil Company's assets in India and completely owned Oil India Limited. The Oil and Natural Gas Commission discovered oil in Gujarat in 1959 and opened other fields in the 1960s and 1970s.

The early oil fields discovered in India were of modest size. Oil production amounted to 200,000 tons in 1950 and 400,000 tons in 1960. By the early 1970s, production had increased to more than 8 million tons. In 1974 the Oil and Natural Gas Commission discovered a large field—called the Bombay High—offshore from Bombay. Production from that field was responsible for the rapid growth of the country's total crude oil production in the late 1970s and throughout the 1980s. In FY 1989, oil production peaked at 34 million tons, of which Bombay High accounted for 22 million tons. In the early 1990s, wells were shut in offshore fields that had been inefficiently exploited, and production fell to 27 million tons in FY 1993. That amount did not meet India's needs, and 30.7 million tons of crude oil were imported in FY 1993.

India has thirty-five major fields onshore (primarily in Assam and Gujarat) and four major offshore oil fields (near Bombay, south of Pondicherry, and in the Palk Strait). Of the 4,828 wells, in 1990 2,514 were producing at a rate of 664,582 barrels per day. The oil field with the greatest output is Bombay High, with 402,797 barrels per day production in 1990, about fifteen times the amount produced by the next largest fields. Total reserves are estimated at 6.1 billion barrels.

The government has sanctioned ambitious exploration plans to raise production in line with demand and to exploit new discoveries as rapidly as possible. In the late 1980s and early 1990s, there were encouraging finds in Tamil Nadu, Gujarat, Andhra Pradesh, and Assam; many of these discoveries were made offshore. Officials estimated that by the mid-1990s these new fields could contribute as much as 15 million to 20 million tons in new production and that total crude oil production could increase to 51 million tons in FY 1994. In the early 1990s, the government renewed attempts, which had begun in the early 1980s, to interest foreign oil companies in purchasing exploration and production leases. These efforts drew only a modest response because the terms offered were difficult, and foreign companies remained suspicious of India's investment climate. One response, agreed on in January 1995, was an Indian-Kuwaiti joint venture to invest in a new oil refinery to be built on the east coast of India.

Substantial quantities of natural gas are produced in association with crude oil production. Until the 1980s, most of this gas was flared off because there were no pipelines or processing facilities to bring it to customers. In the early 1980s, large investments were made to bring gases from Bombay High and other offshore fields ashore for use as fuel and to supply feedstock to fertilizer and petrochemical plants, which also had to be constructed or converted to use gas. By the mid-1980s, natural gas could be delivered to facilities near Bombay and near Kandla in Gujarat. In the mid-1990s, a 1,700-kilometer trans-India pipeline was being built; the pipeline will link the facilities near Bombay and Kandla to a series of gas-based fertilizer plants and power stations. Officials envisage a grid system covering 11,500 kilometers by FY 2004, which will supply 120 million cubic meters of gas a day. Total production in FY 1992 was 18.1 billion cubic meters.

India's need for oil and petroleum-based products—about 40 million tons per year—far exceeded its domestic production capabilities of 28 million tons per year in the early 1990s. Given India's dependency on Persian Gulf resources, proposals were made in the early 1990s to develop natural gas pipelines from Iran, Qatar, and Oman that would run under the Arabian Sea to one or more west coast terminals. To assist with oil and natural gas production, in 1992 the government decided to open reserves to private offshore developers. In February 1994, contracts were awarded for three offshore fields in the Arabian Sea to an Indian-United States consortium and one in the Bay of Bengal to an Indian-Australian-Japanese consortium. In June 1995, an agreement was reached to set a joint-venture company to construct the first leg of the pipeline, from Iran to Pakistan.

Electric Power

The electric power industry is both a supplier and a consumer of primary energy, depending on the kind of energy used to turn the generators. Hydroelectric and nuclear power plants add to the country's supply of primary energy. The total installed electricity capacity in public utilities in 1992 was 69,100 megawatts, of which 70 percent was thermal, 27 percent hydropower, and 3 percent nuclear. The total installed capacity was programmed to reach around 100,000 megawatts by FY 1996 through a package of government-supported incentives to the private sector.

Because they cannot always depend on public utilities, many larger industrial enterprises have developed their own power generation systems. In 1992 there was a capacity of 9,000 megawatts outside the public utility system. Overall, the generation and transmission of power—with an average 57 percent plant load factor in FY 1992 in thermal plants and transmission losses of 22 percent—were inefficient. About 322 billion kilowatt- hours of power were generated by utilities in FY 1992, approximately 8.5 percent shy of demand. The resulting deficit led to acute shortages in some states. This trend continued the next year when 315 billion kilowatt-hours were produced. Many factors contributed to the shortfall of electric power, including slow completion of new installations, low use of installed capacity because of insufficient maintenance and coal, and poor management. In FY 1990, industry accounted for 45 percent of electricity consumed, agriculture 26 percent, and domestic use 16.5 percent. Other sectors, including commerce and railroads, accounted for the remaining 12.5 percent.

Rural electrification made great progress in the 1980s; more than 200,000 villages received electricity for the first time. In 1990 around 84 percent of India's villages had access to electricity. Most of the villages without electricity were in Bihar, Orissa, Rajasthan, Uttar Pradesh, and West Bengal. Villagers complain that government figures on electrification of villages are artificially inflated. Actually, although lines have been run to most villages, electricity is provided only sporadically (for example, only nine to twelve hours per day), and villagers feel they cannot depend on electricity to operate pumps and other equipment. Electricity to cities also is sporadic; blackouts occur every day in most cities.

India's first hydroelectric station was constructed in 1897 in Darjiling (then Darjeeling). In FY 1990, installed capacity for hydroelectric power was 18,000 megawatts. The country has a large economically exploitable hydroelectric potential, especially in the foothills of the Himalayas, but no large increase in capacity is predicted for the mid-1990s. Hydroelectric facilities have to be coordinated with other sources of electricity because seasonal and annual variations in rainfall affect the amount of water needed to turn the generators and consequently the amount of electricity that can be produced.

Hydroelectric power projects have not been without controversy. Dams for irrigation and power generation have displaced people and raised the specter of ecological problems.

Nuclear Power

Nuclear-power developments are under the purview of the Nuclear Power Corporation of India, a government-owned entity under the Department of Atomic Energy. The corporation is responsible for designing, constructing, and operating nuclear-power plants. In 1995 there were nine operational plants with a potential total capacity of 1,800 megawatts, about 3 percent of India's total power generation. There are two units each in Tarapur, north of Bombay in Maharashtra; in Rawatbhata in Rajasthan; in Kalpakkam near Madras in Tamil Nadu; and in Narora in Uttar Pradesh; and one unit in Kakrapur in southeastern Gujarat. However, of the nine plants, all have been faced with safety problems that have shut down reactors for periods ranging from months to years. The Rajasthan Atomic Power Station in Rawatbhata was closed indefinitely, as of February 1995. Moreover, environmental problems, caused by radiation leaks, have cropped up in communities near Rawatbhata. Other plants operate at only a fraction of their capacity, and some foreign experts consider them thc most inefficient nuclear-power plants in the world.

In addition to the nine established plants, seven reactors are under construction in the mid-1990s: one at Kakrapur and two each at Kaiga, on the coast of Karnataka, Rawatbhata, and Tarapur, which, when finished, will bring an additional 2,320 megawatts of energy online. Construction of ten additional reactors is in the planning stage for Kaiga, Rawatbhata, and Kudangulam in Tamil Nadu, which, when combined, will supply 4,800 megawatts capacity. The overall plan is to increase nuclear-generation capacity to 10,000 megawatts by FY 2000, but work has been slowed because of financial shortages. India partially overcame its shortage of enriched uranium—needed to fuel the Tarapur units—by imports from China, starting in 1995.

MINING AND QUARRYING

For a country of its size, India does not have a great deal of mineral wealth. Mining accounted for less than 2 percent of GDP in FY 1990. Nonetheless, iron and bauxite are found in sufficient quantities to base industries on their extraction and processing. Assessment of the country's resources by the Geological Survey of India is still far from complete in the mid-1990s, and observers do not rule out the possibility of important new finds.

In 1992 reserves of iron ore were estimated at among the world's largest—at 19.2 billion tons. Extraction capacity is 67 million tons of ore per year, but only 53 million tons were produced in FY 1992. About 60 percent of output is exported, mainly to the South Korea and Japan. The largest iron ore mining project is at Kudremukh,

Chikmagalore District, Karnataka. India also has abundant bauxite, the main mineral source for aluminum. Reserves are estimated at about 2.7 billion tons, or 8 percent of the world total. In FY 1991, 512,000 tons of aluminum were produced, of which 61,000 tons were exported. Most bauxite mines are in Bihar and Karnataka. India is the world's third largest producer of manganese, and its mines extracted around 1.4 million tons of manganese ore per year in the early 1990s from a total estimated reserve of 180 million tons. India also has significant reserves of copper, estimated at 422 million tons. However, the production of copper, at 46,000 tons in FY 1991, fell well short of domestic demand. Most copper mines are in Bihar and Rajasthan. Smaller amounts of lead, zinc, and mica are also produced.

Ownership and the power to grant mineral concessions generally have rested with the state governments. The central government, however, has exerted considerable influence over such leases, particularly in cases of important and strategic minerals. In fact, most mining of important and strategic minerals is undertaken by central government enterprises in which states sometimes hold part ownership. In the early 1990s, uranium ore was mined, milled, and processed only in Bihar; rare earths—including mineral sands, monazite, ilmenite, rutile, zircon, rare earths chloride, and others—were mined in Tamil Nadu, Kerala, and Orissa. During this period, the central government was attempting to increase the private sector's share of this industry.

TOURISM

Tourism has not been a government priority, but it nonetheless provides around 6 percent of foreign-exchange earnings. The total number of visitors to India was estimated at nearly 1.8 million in FY 1992. The Eighth Five-Year Plan estimated an annual increase of 6 to 7 percent in visitor arrivals; tourists from Europe and North America were targeted. In the mid-1990s, the government offered special tax incentives to the industry to help alleviate a shortage of hotel rooms. Estimated gross export earnings from tourism were

Rs24 billion and net earnings Rs17 billion, making the industry an important foreign-exchange earner. With under 0.3 percent of the world's tourists and around 1 percent of world tourism spending, India, however, has barely tapped its tourism potential.

SCIENCE AND TECHNOLOGY

Origin and Development

Indian scientific research and technological developments since independence in 1947 have received substantial political support and most of their funding from the government. Science and technology initiatives have been important aspects of the government's five-year plans and usually are based on fulfilling short-term needs, while aiming to provide the institutional base needed to achieve long-term goals. As India has striven to develop leading scientists and world-class research institutes, government-sponsored scientific and technical developments have aided diverse areas such as agriculture, biotechnology, cold regions research, communications, environment, industry, mining, nuclear power, space, and transportation. As a result, India has experts in such fields as astronomy and astrophysics, liquid crystals, condensed matter physics, molecular biology, virology, and crystallography. Observers have pointed out, however, that India's emphasis on basic and theoretical research rather than on applied research and technical applications has diminished the social and economic effects of the government's investments. In the mid-1990s, government funds supported nearly 80 percent of India's research and development activities, but, as elsewhere in the economic sector, emphasis increasingly was being put on independent, nongovernmental sources of support.

India has a long and proud scientific tradition. Nehru, in his *Discovery of India* published in 1946, praised the mathematical achievements of Indian scholars, who are said to have developed geometric theorems before Pythagoras did in the sixth century B.C. and were using advanced methods of determining the number of mathematical combinations by the second century B.C. By the fifth century A.D., Indian mathematicians were using ten numerals and by the seventh century were treating zero as a number. These breakthroughs, Nehru said, "liberated the human mind... and threw a flood of light on the behavior of numbers." The conceptualization of squares, rectangles, circles, triangles, fractions, the ability to express the number ten to the twelfth power, algebraic formulas, and astronomy had even more ancient origins in Vedic literature, some of which was compiled as early as 1500 B.C. The concepts of astronomy, metaphysics, and perennial movement are all embodied in the Rig Veda. Although such abstract concepts were further developed by the ancient Greeks and the Indian numeral system was popularized in the first millennium A.D. by the Arabs (the Arabic word for number, Nehru pointed out, is *hindsah* , meaning "from Hind (India)"), their Indian origins are a source of national pride.

Technological discoveries have been made relating to pharmacology, brain surgery, medicine, artificial colors and glazes, metallurgy, recrystalization, chemistry, the decimal system, geometry, astronomy, and language and linguistics (systematic linguistic analysis having originated in India with Panini's fourth-century B.C. Sanskrit grammar, the *Ashtadhyayi*). These discoveries have led to practical applications in brick and pottery making, metal casting, distillation, surveying, town planning, hydraulics, the development of a lunar calendar, and the means of recording these discoveries as early as the era of Harappan culture.

Written information on scientific developments from the Harrapan period to the eleventh century A.D. (when the first permanent Muslim settlements were established in India) is found in Sanskrit, Pali, Arabic, Persian, Tamil, Malayalam, and other classical languages that were intimately connected to Indian religious and philosophical traditions. Archaeological evidence and written accounts from other cultures with which India has had contact have also been used to corroborate the evidence of Indian scientific and technological developments. The technology of textile production, hydraulic engineering, water-powered devices, medicine, and other innovations, as well as mathematics and other theoretical sciences, continued to develop and be influenced by techniques brought in from the Muslim world by the Mughals after the fifteenth century.

The practical applications of scientific and technical developments are witnessed, for example, by the proliferation of hundreds of thousands of water tanks for irrigation in South India by the eighteenth and nineteenth centuries. Although each tank was built through local efforts, together, in effect, they created a closely integrated network supplying water throughout the region. The science of metallurgy led to the construction of numerous small but sophisticated furnaces for producing iron and steel. By the late eighteenth century, it is estimated that production capability may have reached 200,000 tons per year. High levels of textile production—making India the world's leading producer and exporter of textiles before 1800—were the result of refinements in spinning technology.

Several millennia of interest in astronomy in India eventually resulted in the invention and construction of a network of sophisticated, large-scale astronomical observatories—the Jantar Mantars (meaning "house of instruments")—in the early eighteenth century. Constructed of stone, brick, stucco, and marble, the Jantar Mantar complexes were used to determine the seasons, phases of the moon and sun, and locations of stars and planets from points in Delhi, Mathura, Jaipur, Varanasi, and Ujjain. The Jantar Mantars were designed and built by a renowned astronomer and city planner, Sawai Jai Singh II, the Hindu maharajah of Amber, between 1725 and 1734, after he been asked by Mohammad Shah, the tenth Mughal emperor, to reform the calendar. These complexes had the patronage of the Mughal emperors and have long attracted the attention of Western scholars and travelers, some of whom have found them anachronistic in light of the use of telescopes in Europe and China more than a century before Jai Singh's projects. As United States scientist William A. Blanpied has pointed out, Jai Singh, who subscribed to Hindu cosmology, was aware of Western developments but preferred to perfect his naked-eye observations rather than concentrate on precise calculational astronomy.

The arrival of the British in India in the early seventeenth century—the Portuguese, Dutch, and French also had a presence, although it was much less pervasive—led eventually to new scientific developments that added to the indigenous achievements of the previous millennia. Although colonization subverted much of Indian culture, turning the region into a source of raw materials for the factories of England and France and leaving only low-technology production to local entrepreneurs, a new organization was brought to science in the form of the British education system. Science education under British rule (by the East India Company from 1757 to 1857 and by the British government from 1858 to 1947) initially involved only rudimentary mathematics, but as greater exploitation of India took place, there was more need for surveying and medical schools to train indigenous people to assist Europeans in their explorations and research. What new technologies were implemented were imported rather than developed indigenously, however, and it was only during the immediate preindependence period that Indian scientists came to enjoy political patronage and support for their work.

Western education and techniques of scientific inquiry were added to the already established Indian base, making way for later developments. The major result of these developments was the establishment of a large and sophisticated educational infrastructure that placed India as the leader in science and technology in Asia at the time of independence in 1947. Thereafter, as other Asian nations emerged, India lost its primacy in science, a situation much lamented by India's leaders and scientists. However, the infrastructure was in place and has continued to produce generations of top scientists.

One of the most famous scientists of the pre- and postindependence era was Indian-trained Chandrasekhara Venkata (C.V.) Raman, an ardent nationalist, prolific researcher, and writer of scientific treatises on the molecular scattering of light and other subjects of quantum mechanics. In 1930 Raman was awarded the Nobel prize in physics for his 1928 discovery of the Raman Effect, which demonstrates that the energy of a photon can undergo partial transformation within matter. In 1934-36, with his colleague Nagendra Nath, Raman propounded the Raman-Nath Theory on the diffraction of light by ultrasonic waves. He was a director of the Indian Institute of Science and founded the Indian Academy of Sciences in 1934 and the Raman Research Institute in 1948.

Another leading scientist was Homi Jehangir Bhabha, an eminent physicist internationally recognized for his contributions to the fields of positron theory, cosmic rays, and muon physics at the University of Cambridge in Britain. In 1945, with financial assistance from the Sir Dorabji Tata Trust, Bhabha established the Tata Institute of Fundamental Research in Bombay.

Other eminent preindependence scientists include Sir Jagadish Chandra (J.C.) Bose, a Cambridge-educated Bengali physicist who discovered the application of electromagnetic waves to wireless telegraphy in 1895 and then went on to a second notable career in biophysical research. Meghnad Saha, also from Bengal, was trained in India, Britain, and Germany and became an internationally recognized nuclear physicist whose mathematical equations and ionization theory gave new insight into the functions of stellar spectra. In the late 1930s, Saha began promoting the importance of science to national economic modernization, a concept fully embraced by Nehru and several generations of government planners. The Bose-Einstein Statistics, used in quantum physics, and Boson particles are named after another leading scientist, mathematician Satyendranath (S.N.) Bose. S.N. Bose was trained in India, and his research discoveries gave him international fame and an opportunity for advanced studies in France and Germany.

In 1924 he sent the results of his research on radiation as a form of gas to Albert Einstein. Einstein extended Bose's statistical methods to ordinary atoms, which led him to predict a new state of matter—called the Bose-Einstein Condensation—that was scientifically proved in United States laboratory experiments in 1995. Prafulla Chandra Ray, another Bengali, earned a doctorate in inorganic chemistry from the University of Edinburgh in 1887 and went on to a devoted career of teaching and research. His work was instrumental in establishing the chemical industry in Bengal in the early twentieth century.

At the onset of independence, Nehru called science "the very texture of life" and optimistically declared that "science alone... can solve problems of hunger and poverty, of insanitation and illiteracy, of superstition and deadening customs." Under his leadership, the government set out to cure numerous societal problems. The Green Revolution, educational improvement, establishment of hundreds of scientific laboratories, industrial and military research, massive hydraulic projects, and entry into the frontiers of space all evolved from this early decision to embrace high technology.

One of the early planning documents was the Scientific Policy Resolution of 1958, which called for embracing "by all appropriate means, the cultivation of science and scientific research in all its aspects—pure, applied, and educational" and encouraged individual initiatives. In 1983 the government issued a similar statement, which, while stressing the importance of international cooperation and the diffusion of scientific knowledge, put considerable emphasis on self-reliance and the development of indigenous technology. This goal is still in place in the mid-1990s.

Infrastructure and Government Role

Science and technology policy and research have largely been the domains of government since 1947 and are largely patterned after the structure left behind by the British. Within the central government, there are a top-down apparatus and a plethora of ministries, departments, lower-level agencies, and institutions involved in the science and technology infrastructure.

Government-administered science and technology emanate from the Office of the Prime Minister, to which a chief science adviser and the Science Advisory Council, when they are appointed, have direct input. The prime minister de jure controls the science and technology sector through the National Council on Science and Technology, the minister of state for science and technology (who has control over day-to-day operations of the science and technology infrastructure), and ministers responsible for ocean development, atomic energy, electronics, and space. Other ministries and departments also have significant science and technology components and answer to the prime minister through their respective ministers. Among them are agriculture, chemicals and fertilizers, civil aviation and tourism, coal, defence, environment, food, civil supplies, forests and wildlife, health and family welfare, home affairs, human resource development, nonconventional energy sources, petrochemicals, and petroleum and natural gas, as well as other governmental entities.

The Ministry of Science and Technology was established in 1971 to formulate science and technology policies and implement, identify, and promote "frontline" research throughout the science and technology infrastructure. The ministry, through its subordinate Department of Science and Technology, also coordinates intragovernmental and international cooperation and provides funding for domestic institutions and research programs. The Department of Scientific and Industrial Research, a technology transfer organization, and the Department of Biotechnology, which runs a number of developmental laboratories, are the ministry's other administrative elements. Indicative of the level of importance placed on science and technology is the fact that Prime Minister P.V. Narasimha Rao held the portfolio for this ministry in the early and mid-1990s. Some argued, however, that Rao could truly strengthen the sector by appointing, as his predecessors did, a chief science adviser and a committee of leading scientists to provide high-level advice and delegate the running of these ministries to others.

The National Council on Science and Technology is at the apex of the science and technology infrastructure and is chaired by the prime minister. The integration of science and technology planning with national socioeconomic planning is carried out by the Planning Commission. Scientific advisory committees in individual socioeconomic ministries formulate long-term programs and identify applicable technologies for their particular area of responsibility. The rest of the infrastructure has seven major components. The national-level component includes government organizations that provide hands-on research and development, such as the ministries of atomic energy and space, the Council of Scientific and Industrial Research (CSIR—a component of the Ministry of Science and Technology), and the Indian Council of Agricultural Research. The second component, organizations that support research and development, includes the departments or ministries of biotechnology, nonconventional energy sources, ocean development, and science and technology. The third-echelon component includes state government research and development agencies, which are usually involved with agriculture, animal husbandry, irrigation, public health, and the like and that also are part of the national infrastructure. The four other major components are the university system, private research organizations, public-sector research and development establishments, and research and development centers within private industries. Almost all internationally recognized university-level research is carried out in government-controlled or government-supported institutions. The results of government-sponsored research are transferred to public- and private-sector industries through the National Research and Development Corporation. This corporation is part of the Ministry of Science and Technology and has as its purpose the commercialization of scientific and technical know-how, the promotion of research through grants and loans, promotion of government and industry joint projects, and the export of Indian technology.

Resource Allocation

Central government financial support of research and development—including subsidies to public-sector industries—was 75.7 percent of total financial support in FY 1992. State governments provided an additional 9.3 percent. However, even when combined with the private-sector contribution (15.0 percent), research and development expenditures were only just over 0.8 percent of the GDP in FY 1992. Although there was growth in research and development expenditures during the 1980s and early 1990s, the rate of growth was less than the GNP rate of growth during the same period and was a cause of concern for government planners. Moreover, the bulk of government research and development expenditures (80 percent in FY 1992) goes to only five agencies: the Defence Research and Development Organisation (DRDO), the Ministry of Space, the Indian Council of Agricultural Research, the Ministry of Atomic Energy, and CSIR, and to their constituent organizations.

Despite long-term government commitment to research and development, India compares poorly with other major Asian countries. In Japan, for example, nearly 3 percent of GDP goes to research and development; in South Korea and Taiwan, the figure is nearly 2 percent. In India, research and development receives only 0.8 percent of GDP; only China among the major players spends less (0.7 percent). However, India's share of GDP expenditure on research and development has increased slightly: in 1975 it stood at 0.5 percent, in 1980 at 0.6 percent, and in 1985 at 0.8, where it has become static.

Because of the allocation of financial inputs, India has been more successful at promoting security-oriented and large-scale scientific endeavors, such as space and nuclear science programs, than at promoting industrial technology. Part of the latter lack of achievement has been attributed to the limited role of universities in the research and development system. Instead, India has concentrated on government-sponsored specialized institutes and provided minimal funding to university research programs. The low funding level has encouraged university scientists to find jobs in the more liberally funded public-sector national laboratories. Moreover, private industry in India plays a relatively minor role in the science and technology system (15 percent of the total investment compared with Japan's 80 percent and slightly more than 50 percent in the United States). This low level of private-sector investment has been attributed to a number of factors, including the preponderance of trade-oriented rather than technology-oriented industries, protectionist tariffs, and rigid regulation of foreign investment. The largest private-sector research and development expenditures during the FY 1990-FY 1992 period were in the areas of engineering and technology, particularly in the industrial development, transportation, communications, and health services sectors. Nonetheless, they were relatively small expenditures when compared with government and public-sector inputs in the same fields. The key element for Indian industry to benefit from the greater government and public-sector efforts in the 1990s is the ability of the government and public-sector laboratories to develop technologies with broad applications and to transfer these technologies—as is done by the National Research and Development Corporation—to private-sector industries able to apply them with maximum efficiency.

India ranks eleventh in the world in its number of active scientific and technical personnel. Including medical personnel, they were estimated at around 188,000 in 1950, 450,000 in 1960, 1.2 million in 1970, 1.8 million in 1980, and 3.8 million in 1990. India's universities, university-level institutions, and colleges have produced more than 200,000 science and technology graduates per year since 1985. Doctorates are awarded each year to about 3,000 people in science, between 500 and 600 in engineering, around 800 in agricultural sciences, and close to 6,000 in medicine. However, in 1990 India had the lowest number of scientific and engineering personnel (3.3) per 10,000 persons in the national labor force of the major Asian nations. For example, Japan, had nearly seventy-five per 10,000, South Korea had more than thirty-seven per 10,000, and China had 5.6 per 10,000.

The quality of higher education in the sciences has not improved as quickly as desired since independence because of the flight of many top scientists from academia to higher-paying jobs in government-funded research laboratories. Foreign aid, aimed at counteracting university faculty shortages, has produced top-rate graduates as intended. However, because of limited job prospects at home, many of the brightest physicians, scientists, and engineers have been attracted by opportunities abroad, particularly in Western nations. Since the early 1990s, this trend has appeared to be changing as more high-technology jobs, especially in fields requiring computer science skills, have begun to open in India as a result of economic liberalization. The "brain bank" network of Indian scientists abroad that was seen as a potential source of talent by some observers in the 1980s has proven to be a valuable resource in the 1990s.

Using imported technology, scientists made major advances in microprocessors during the 1980s that brought the country to only one generation (three to four years) behind international leaders. A sign of how much microcomputer use has developed could be seen in sales: from US$93 million in FY 1983 to US$488 million in FY 1988. Facilitating the use of automation has been a counterpart to the expansion of the data communication field. The development of the "Param 9000" supercomputer prototype, reportedly capable of billions of floating point operations per second, was completed in December 1994 and was announced by the state-owned Centre for Development of Advanced Computing as ready for sale to operational users in March 1995. Earlier Param models, using parallel processing technologies to achieve near-supercomputer performance, were produced in sufficient quantity for export in the early 1990s.

DRDO developed its own parallel processing computer, which was unveiled by Prime Minister Rao in April 1995. Developed by DRDO's Advanced Numerical Research and Analysis Group in Hyderabad, the supercomputer is capable of 1 billion points per second speed and can be used for geophysics, image processing, and molecular modeling.

7

Agriculture and its Role in Economic Development

Agriculture has always been India's most important economic sector. In the mid-1990s, it provides approximately one-third of the gross domestic product (GDP) and employs roughly two-thirds of the population. Since independence in 1947, the share of agriculture in the GDP has declined in comparison to the growth of the industrial and services sectors. However, agriculture still provides the bulk of wage goods required by the nonagricultural sector as well as numerous raw materials for industry. Moreover, the direct share of agricultural and allied sectors in total exports is around 18 percent. When the indirect share of agricultural products in total exports, such as cotton textiles and jute goods, is taken into account, the percentage is much higher.

Dependence on agricultural imports in the early 1960s convinced planners that India's growing population, as well as concerns about national independence, security, and political stability, required self-sufficiency in food production. This perception led to a program of agricultural improvement called the Green Revolution, to a public distribution system, and to price supports for farmers. In the 1980s, despite three years of meager rainfall and a drought in the middle of the decade, India managed to get along with very few food imports because of the growth in food-grain production and the development of a large buffer stock against potential agricultural shortfalls. By the early 1990s, India was self-sufficient in food-grain production. Agricultural production has kept pace with the food needs of the growing population as the result of increased yields in almost all crops, but especially in cereals. Food grains and pulses account for two-thirds of agricultural production in the mid-1990s. The growth in food-grain production is a result of concentrated efforts to increase all the Green Revolution inputs needed for higher yields: better seed, more fertilizer, improved irrigation, and education of farmers. Although increased irrigation has helped to lessen year-to-year fluctuations in farm production resulting from the vagaries of the monsoons, it has not eliminated those fluctuations.

Food-grain production increased from 50.8 million tons in fiscal year (FY) 1950 to 176.3 million tons in FY 1990. The compound growth rate from FY 1949 to FY 1987 was 2.7 percent per annum. Overall, wheat was the best performer, with production increasing more than eightfold in forty years. Wheat was followed by rice, which had a production increase of more than 350 percent. Coarse grains had a poorer rate of increase but still doubled in output during those years; production of pulses went up by less than 70 percent. The increase in oilseed production, however, was not enough to fill consumer demands, and India went from being an exporter of oilseeds in the 1950s to a major importer in the 1970s and the early 1980s. The agricultural sector attempted to increase oilseed production in the 1980s and early 1990s. These efforts were successful: oilseed production doubled and the need for imports was reduced. In the early 1990s, India was on the verge of self-sufficiency in oilseed production.After independence in 1947, the cropping pattern became more diversified, and cultivation of commercial crops received a new impetus in line with domestic demands and export requirements. Nontraditional crops, such as summer mung (a variety of lentil, part of the pulse family), soybeans, peanuts, and sunflowers, were gradually gaining importance.

The per capita availability of a number of food items increased significantly in the postindependence period despite a population increase from 361 million in 1951 to 846 million in 1991. Per capita availability of cereals went up from 334 grams per day in 1951 to 470 grams per day in 1990. Availability of edible oils increased significantly, from 3.2 kilograms per year per capita in FY 1960 to 5.4 kilograms in FY 1990. Similarly, the availability of sugar per capita increased from 4.7 to 12.5 kilograms per year during the same period. The one area in which availability decreased was pulses, which went from 60.7 grams per day to 39.4 grams per day. This shortfall presents a serious problem in a country where a large part of the population is vegetarian and pulses are the main source of protein.

There are large disparities among India's states and territories in agricultural performance, only some of which can be attributed to differences in climate or initial endowments of infrastructure such as irrigation. Realizing the importance of agricultural production for economic development, the central government has played an active role in all aspects of agricultural development. Planning is centralized, and plan priorities, policies, and resource allocations are decided at the central level. Food and price policy also are decided by the central government. Thus, although agriculture is constitutionally the responsibility of the states rather than the central government, the latter plays a key role in formulating policy and providing financial resources for agriculture.

Land Use

In FY 1987, field crops were planted on about 45 percent of the total land mass of India. Of this cultivated land, almost 37 million hectares were double-cropped, making the gross sown area equivalent to almost 173 million hectares. About 15 million hectares were permanent pastureland or were planted in various tree crops and groves. Approximately 108 million hectares were either developed for nonagricultural uses, forested, or unsuited for agriculture because of topography. About 29.6 million hectares of the remaining land were classified as cultivable but fallow, and 15.6 million hectares were classified as cultivable wasteland. These 45 million hectares constitute all the land left for expanding the sown area; for various reasons, however, much of it is unsuited for immediate cropping. Expansion in crop production, therefore, has to come almost entirely from increasing yields on lands already in some kind of agricultural use.

Topography, soils, rainfall, and the availability of water for irrigation have been major determinants of the crop and livestock patterns characteristic of the three major geographic regions of India—the Himalayas, the Indo-Gangetic Plain, and the Peninsula—and their agro-ecological subregions.

Government policy as regards irrigation, the introduction of new crops, research and education, and incentives has had some impact on changing the traditional crop and livestock patterns in these subregions. The monsoons, however, play a critical role in determining whether the harvest will be bountiful, average, or poor in any given year. One of the objectives of government policy in the early 1990s was to find methods of reducing this dependence on the monsoons.

Himalayas

The Himalayan region, with some 520,000 square kilometers of land, ranks well behind the other two regions in agricultural importance. Despite generally adequate rainfall, the rugged topography allows less than 10 percent of the land to be used for agriculture. The sandy, loamy soils on the hillsides and the alluvial clays in the region's premier agricultural subregion, the Vale of Kashmir—located in the northwestern part of the state of Jammu and Kashmir—provide fertile land for agricultural use.

The main crops are rice, corn, wheat, barley, millet, and potatoes. Most of India's temperate-zone fruits (apples, apricots, cherries, and peaches) and walnuts are grown in the vale. Sericulture and sheepherding also are being undertaken. In the eastern Himalayan subregion, the soils are moderately rich in organic matter and are acidic. Although much of the farming is done on terraced hillsides, there is a significant amount of shifting cultivation, which has resulted in deforestation and soil erosion. Rice, corn, millet, potatoes, and oilseeds were the main crops in the early 1990s. The region also is well known for the tea plantations of the mountainous Darjiling (Darjeeling) area in the northern tip of West Bengal.

Indo-Gangetic Plain

The vast Indo-Gangetic Plain, extending from Punjab to Assam, is the most intensively farmed zone of the country and one of the most intensively farmed in the world. Rainfall, most of which comes with the southwest monsoon, is generally adequate for summer-grown crops, but in some years vast areas are seared by drought. Fortunately, much of the land has access, or potential access, to irrigation waters from wells and rivers, ensuring crops even in years of drought and making possible a winter crop as well as a summer harvest. Wheat is the main crop in the west, rice in the east. Pulses, sorghum, oilseeds, and sugarcane are among other important crops. Mango orchards are common. Other fruits of the subregion include guavas, jackfruit, plums, lemons, oranges, and pomegranates.

In the Great Indian Desert, rainfall is scanty and erratic. About 20 percent of the total area is under cultivation, mostly in Haryana and Gujarat states, and comparatively little in Rajasthan. The Indira Gandhi Canal—begun in 1958 as the Rajasthan Canal—was designed to bring water from the north. Progress was slow, and only the first stage was close to completion by the end of the Seventh Five-Year Plan (FY 1985-89). By then, the canal had substantially increased the area under cultivation in Rajasthan, and a new completion date of 1999 is anticipated. The cultivable area is expected to expand further with the development of the canal's second stage during the 1990s. The leading crops of the subregion are millet, sorghum, wheat, and peanuts. Vast expanses of sparse vegetation provide sustenance for sheep and goats. In the late 1980s, dairy farming became important in locations that had sufficient pastureland.

Peninsular India

The east and west coasts, the coastal plains, and the deltaic tracts that extend inland for some 100 to 200 kilometers in Peninsular India benefit from both the June-to-September southwest monsoon and the October-to-November northeast monsoon. Farther inland, as the topography and climate change, so does the pattern of agriculture. The proportion of land under cultivation ranges from about 50 percent along the coastal plain and in the western part of Andhra Pradesh to about 25 percent in eastern Madhya Pradesh. Except in areas of certain developed river valleys, double-cropping is rare. Rice is the predominant crop in high-rainfall areas and sorghum in low-rainfall areas. Other crops of significance along the east coast and in the Central Highlands in the early 1990s were pigeon peas, mustard, peanuts, millet, linseed, castor beans, cotton, and tobacco.

On the Deccan Plateau, deep, alluvial black soils that retain moisture for a long time are the basis for much of the region's output of farm products. However, the region also has many farming areas that are covered by thin, light-textured soils that suffer quickly from drought. Whether a crop is made or lost is, therefore, often dependent on the availability of supplementary water from ponds and streams. About 60 percent of the land in the state of Maharashtra was under cultivation in the early 1990s, less in Madhya Pradesh. About 75 percent of the cropland of the Deccan during this period was planted in food crops, such as millet, sorghum, rice, wheat, and peanuts; most of the remaining cropland was planted in fodder crops.

In the far south of the Peninsula, the area under cultivation varies from about 10 percent in the Western Ghats, to 25 percent in the western coastal tract, to 55 percent on the Karnataka Plateau. Here is the India—the land of spices—that Vasco da Gama and other European navigators came searching for in the fifteenth century. On the Karnataka Plateau, sorghum, millet, pulses, cotton, and oilseeds are the main crops on the 90 percent of the cultivated land that is dry-farmed; rice, sugarcane, and vegetables predominate on the 10 percent that was irrigated in the late 1980s. Coconuts, areca, coffee, pepper, rubber, cashew nuts, tapioca, and cardamom are widely grown on plantations in the Nilgiri Hills and on the western slopes of the Western Ghats.

Land Tenure

Matters concerning the ownership, acquisition, distribution, and taxation of land are, by provision of the constitution, under the jurisdiction of the states. Because of the diverse attitudes and approaches that would result from such freedom if there were no general guidelines, the central government has at times laid down directives dealing with the main problems affecting the ownership and use of land. But it remains for the state governments to implement the central government guidelines. Such implementation has varied widely among the states.

Landholding Categories

India is a land of small farms, of peasants cultivating their ancestral lands mainly by family labor and, despite the spread of tractors in the 1980s, by pairs of bullocks. About 50 percent of all operational holdings in 1980 were less than one hectare in size. About 19 percent fell in the one-to-two hectare range, 16 percent in the two-to-four hectare range, and 11 percent in the four-to-ten hectare range. Only 4 percent of the working farms encompassed ten or more hectares.

Although farms are typically small throughout the country, the average size holding by state ranges from about 0.5 hectare in Kerala and 0.75 hectare in Tamil Nadu to three hectares in Maharashtra and five hectares in Rajasthan. Factors influencing this range include soils, topography, rainfall, rural population density, and thoroughness of land redistribution programs.

Many factors—historical, political, economic, and demographic—have affected the development of the prevailing land-tenure status. The operators of most agricultural holdings possess vested rights in the land they till, whether as full owners or as protected tenants. By the early 1990s, there were tenancy laws in all the states and union territories except Nagaland, Meghalaya, and Mizoram. The laws provide for states to confer ownership on tenants, who can buy the land they farm in return for fair payment;

states also oversee provision of security of tenure and the establishing of fair rents. The implementation of these laws has varied among the states. West Bengal, Karnataka, and Kerala, for example, have achieved more success than other states. The land tenure situation is complicated, and it has varied widely from state to state. There is, however, much less variation in the mid-1990s than in the postindependence period.

Independent India inherited a structure of landholding that was characterized by heavy concentration of cultivable areas in the hands of relatively large absentee landowners (zamindars), the excessive fragmentation of small landholdings, an already growing class of landless agricultural workers, and the lack of any generalized system of documentary evidence of landownership or tenancy. Land was important as a status symbol; from one generation to the next, there was a tendency for an original family holding to be progressively subdivided, a situation that continued in the early 1990s. This phenomenon resulted in many landholdings that were too small to provide a livelihood for a family. Borrowing money against land was almost inevitable and frequently resulted in the loss of land to a local moneylender or large landowner, further widening the gap between large and small landholders. Moreover, inasmuch as landowners and moneylenders tended to belong to higher castes and petty owners and tenants to lower castes, land tenure had strong social as well as economic impact.

By the early 1970s, after extensive legislation, large absentee landowners had, for all practical purposes, been eliminated; their rights had been acquired by the state in exchange for compensation in cash and government bonds. More than 20 million former zamindar-system tenants had acquired occupancy rights to the land they tilled. Whereas previously the landlord collected rent from his tenants and passed on a portion of it as land revenue to the government, starting in the early 1970s, the state collected the rent directly from cultivators who, in effect, had become renters from the state. Most former tenants acquired the right to purchase the land they tilled, and payments to the state were spread out over ten to twenty years. Large landowners were divested not only of their cultivated land but also of ownership of forests, lakes, and barren lands. They were also stripped of various other economic rights, such as collection of taxes on sales of immovable property within their jurisdiction and collection of money for grazing privileges on uncultivated lands and use of river water. These rights also were taken over by state governments in return for compensation. By 1980 more than 6 million hectares of waste, fallow, and other categories of unused land had been vested in state governments and, in turn, distributed to landless agricultural workers.

Land Reform

A major concern in rural India is the huge number of landless or near-landless families, many of whom are wholly dependent on a few weeks of work at the peak planting and harvesting seasons. The number of landless rural families has grown steadily since independence, both in absolute terms and as a proportion of the population. In 1981 there were 195.1 million rural workers: 55.4 million were agricultural laborers who depended primarily on casual farm work for a livelihood. In the early 1990s, the rural work force had grown to 242 million, of whom 73.7 million were classified as agricultural laborers. Approximately 33 percent of the employed rural workers were classified as casual wage laborers.

Because of the large number of landless farmers and the frequent neglect of land by absentee landlords in the early years of independence, the principle that there should be a ceiling on the size of landholdings, depending on the crop planted and the quality of the land, was embodied in the First Five-Year Plan (FY 1951-55). An agricultural census was conducted to provide guidance in setting such ceilings. During the Second Five-Year Plan (FY 1956-60), most states legislated fixed ceilings, but there was little uniformity among the states; ceilings ranged from six to 132 hectares. Certain specialized branches of agriculture, such as horticulture, cattle breeding, and dairy farming, were usually exempted from ceilings.

All the states instituted programs to force landowners to sell their over-the-ceiling holdings to the government at fixed prices; the states, in turn, were to redistribute the land to the landless. But adamant resistance, high costs, sloppy record keeping, and poor administration in general combined to weaken and delay this aspect of land reform. The delays in legislation allowed large landowners to circumvent the intent of the laws by spurious partitioning, sales, gifts to family members, and other methods of evading ceilings. Many exemptions were granted so that there was little surplus land.

To ensure more uniformity in income, to combat evasion of the intent of the laws, and to secure more land for distribution to the landless, the central government in the 1970s pushed for greatly reduced ceilings. For a family of five, the central government guidelines called for not more than 10.9 hectares of good, irrigated land suitable for double-cropping, not more than 10.9 hectares of land suited for one crop annually, and not more than 21.9 hectares for orchards. Exemptions were continued for land used as cocoa, coffee, tea, and rubber plantations; land held by official banks and other government units; and land held by agricultural schools and research organizations. At the option of the states, land held by religious, educational, and charitable trusts also could be exempted. To protect the states from legal challenges to their land reform laws, the constitution was amended in 1974 to include in its Ninth Schedule the state laws that had been enacted in conformance with national guidelines. Land reform laws enacted after 1974 also were included in the amendment.

By the beginning of the 1990s, all states and union territories, except Goa, Arunachal Pradesh, Nagaland, Manipur, Mizoram, and Tripura, had passed ceiling laws to conform to central government guidelines. In Maharashtra, for example, the revised ceiling law that became effective in 1975 set upper limits at perennially irrigated land, 7.2 hectares; seasonally irrigated land, 10.8 hectares; paddy land in an assured rainfall area, 14.6 hectares; and other dry land, 21.9 hectares. By the early 1980s, about 150,000 hectares had been declared surplus under this act, about 100,000 of which had been distributed to 6,500 landless persons. A 1973 land reform amendment in Bihar set a range of ceilings on holdings for a family of five, from six to eighteen hectares depending on land quality, and offered an allowance for each additional family member, subject to a maximum of one-and-one-half times the holding. Within five years, the Bihar government had acquired 94,000 hectares of surplus land and had distributed 53,000 hectares to 138,000 landless families. Success nationwide was limited. Of the 2.9 million hectares of land declared surplus, nearly 1.9 million hectares had been distributed by the end of the seventh plan, leaving 1 million hectares still to be distributed as of early 1993.

By the early 1990s, nearly all the states had enacted legislation aimed at the consolidation of each tiller's landholdings into one contiguous plot. Implementation was patchy and sporadic, however. By the early 1980s, the work had been completed only in Punjab, Haryana, and western Uttar Pradesh and had begun in Orissa and Bihar. In most of the other states, nothing had been accomplished by the early 1990s. The Sixth Five-Year Plan (FY 1980-84) set a goal for the completion of the consolidation of holdings within ten years, which was not achieved.

In order to protect tenants from exorbitant rents (often up to 50 percent of their produce), the states passed legislation to regulate rents. The maximum rate was fixed at levels not exceeding 20 to 25 percent of the gross produce in all states except Andhra Pradesh, Haryana, and Punjab. The states also adopted various other measures for the protection of tenants, including moratoriums on evictions, minimum periods of tenure, and security of tenure subject to eviction on prescribed grounds only.

By the early 1980s, most of the cultivated area had been surveyed and records of rights prepared. In most states, revenue assessment—the tax on land—against farmland had been revised upward in keeping with a rise in farm prices. In several states, steps were taken to associate village assemblies, or *panchayat* , with the maintenance of land records, the collection of land revenue, and the management of lands belonging to government; the results of these efforts have frequently been unsatisfactory.

CROPS

The average rate of output growth since the 1950s has been more than 2.5 percent per year and was greater than 3 percent during the 1980s, compared with less than 1 percent per annum during the period from 1900 to 1950. Most of the growth in aggregate crop output was the result of an increase in yields, rather than an increase in the area under crops. The yield performance of crops has varied widely.

The national growth rates mask variability in the performance of different states, but in the regions with the greatest increases three categories are discernible. The first category includes states or areas that have an exceptionally high agricultural growth rate—Punjab, Haryana, and western Uttar Pradesh. The second is states or areas that have high growth rates, but not as high as the first category—Andhra Pradesh, Maharashtra, and Jammu and Kashmir. A third category has a lesser growth rate and includes Bihar, Gujarat, Karnataka, Orissa, Rajasthan, Tamil Nadu, eastern Uttar Pradesh, and West Bengal. These eight states, however, comprise 55 percent of the total food-grains area.

Some observers believe that the increase in productivity has been an important factor explaining the satisfactory growth of food-grain production since the mid-1960s. However, the gains in productivity remain confined to select areas. Between FY 1960 and FY 1980, yields increased by 125.6 percent in North India (Punjab, Haryana, and western Uttar Pradesh). The increase in the other regions was much less: central India, 36 percent; eastern, 22.7 percent; southern, 58.3 percent; and western India, 31.6 percent. The national average was nearly 40.9 percent. Part of this disparity cai be explained by the fact that during this period Punjab and Haryana were way ahead of other states in terms of irrigated area, intensity of irrigation, and intensity of cropping. Availability of irrigation is one of the crucial factors governing regional variations.

As a result of a good monsoon during FY 1990, food grain production reached 176 million tons, 3 percent more than in FY 1989. The production of rice and wheat was 74.6 million and 54.5 million tons, respectively. Among the commercial crops, sugarcane and oilseeds reached production levels of 240.3 million tons and 21.8 million tons, respectively. The increased production in FY 1990 was mainly the result of continuing increases in yields for all the main crops—rice, wheat, pulses, and oilseeds. In the case of oilseeds and sugarcane, higher production was also the result of the increased number of hectares planted.

The growth in food-grain production did not occur in a linear trend, but as a series of spurts depending mostly on the weather, input availability, and price policy. Aggregate growth was composed of an even split between area expansion and yield growth before FY 1964. Since FY 1967, the contribution of growth in yields has become dominant and attests to the vigor with which agriculture has responded to the opportunities opened up by new seed, water, and fertilizer technology.

Food-Grain Production

Food grains include rice, wheat, corn (maize), coarse grains (sorghum and millet), and pulses (beans, dried peas, and lentils). In FY 1990, approximately 127.5 million hectares were sown with food grains, about 75 percent of the total planted area. The total number of hectares increased by 31 percent over the forty-year period from FY 1950 to FY 1990. Most of this increase occurred in the 1950s; there was almost no change in the sown number of hectares through the 1980s. Around 33 percent of cropland was given over to rice, about 29 percent to coarse grains, and the rest evenly divided between wheat and pulses.

Rice, India's preeminent crop, is the staple food of the people of the eastern and southern parts of the country. Production increased from 53.6 million tons in FY 1980 to 74.6 million tons in FY 1990, a 39 percent increase over the decade. By FY 1992, rice production had reached 111 million tons, second in the world only to China with its 182 million tons. Since 1950 the increase has been more than 350 percent. Most of this increase was the result of an increase in yields; the number of hectares increased only 40 percent during this period. Yields increased from 1,336 kilograms per hectare in FY 1980 to 1,751 kilograms per hectare in FY 1990. The per-hectare yield increased more than 262 percent between 1950 and 1992.

Wheat production showed an 843 percent increase, from nearly 6.5 million tons in FY 1950 to 54.5 million tons in FY 1990 to 56.7 million tons in FY 1992. Most of this greater production was the result of an increase in yields that went from 663 kilograms per hectare in FY 1950 to 2,274 kilograms in FY 1990. Along with the excellent performance in yields, improved wheat production resulted from an increase in the area planted from nearly 9.8 million hectares in FY 1950 to 24.0 million hectares in FY 1990.

Sorghum and millet, the principal coarse grains, are dryland crops most frequently grown as staples in central and western India. Corn and barley are staple foods grown mainly near and in the Himalayan region. As the result of increased yields, the production of coarse grains has doubled since 1950; there was hardly any change in the area sown for these grains. The production of pulses did not fare well, increasing by only 68 percent over the four decades. Land devoted to pulses increased by 28 percent, and yields were up by 30 percent. Pulses are an important source of protein in the vegetarian diet; the small improvement in production along with the increase in population meant a reduced availability of pulses per capita.

Before the Green Revolution, coarse grains showed satisfactory rates of growth but afterward lost cultivated areas to wheat and rice, and their growth declined. The area sown with coarse grains increased from FY 1950 to FY 1970 by roughly 20 percent but declined subsequently up to the early 1990s. In FY 1990 the area sown was 3 percent less than in FY 1950 and 20 percent less than in FY 1970. The area sown with two coarse grains, *jowar* (barley) and *bajra* (millet), increased from FY 1950 to FY 1970 and then declined during the 1970s and the 1980s. The area sown with *jowar* increased from 15.6 million hectares in FY 1950 to 17.4 million hectares in FY 1970 and then decreased to 14.5 million hectares in FY 1990. The area sown with *bajra* increased from 9.0 million hectares in FY 1950 to 12.9 million hectares in FY 1970 and stood at 10.4 million hectares in FY 1990. A similar pattern existed for other coarse grains. Overall, India's coarse-grain production increased from 15.4 million tons in 1950 to 29 million tons in 1980 to 33.1 million tons in 1990 and 33.7 million tons in 1993.

Oilseeds

India in the mid-1990s has almost attained self-sufficiency in the production of oilseeds to extract vegetable oil, essential in the Indian diet. Peanuts, grown mainly as a rain-fed crop on part of the semiarid areas of western and southern India, account for the largest source of the nation's production of vegetable oils. The second-ranking source of vegetable oils in the early 1990s was rapeseed. Cottonseed, an important by-product of cotton fiber and once mostly fed to cattle, was another source of vegetable oils. Soybeans and sunflower seeds were relatively new as significant oilseeds, but their production increased rapidly in the 1980s.

The production of oilseeds increased from 5.2 million tons in FY 1950 to 21.8 million tons in FY 1990. Specific information regarding area planted is not available for all oilseeds, but it increased in the 1980s, as did the yields. The growth of production before the mid-1970s was not adequate to meet the needs of the increasing population, and large quantities had to be imported from the 1970s to the mid-1980s, using scarce foreign exchange.

Commercial Crops

India is the largest producer of sugar in the world, harvesting 12 million tons in 1993, followed by Brazil's 9 million tons and China's 7 million tons. Sugar availability per capita increased from 4.7 kilograms per year in FY 1960 to 12.5 kilograms per year in FY 1990, following the more than fourfold increase in production from 57 million tons in FY 1950 to 240 million tons in FY 1990. This increase in production was a result of the doubling of the yield per hectare and a doubling of the area sown with sugar. Imports of sugar were negligible in FY 1992 and FY 1993. However, in the FY 1995 budget presentation to the Lok Sabha in March 1995, Minister of Finance Manmohan Singh said it was necessary to supplement the public distribution system with "necessary imports of sugar."

Raw cotton is the most important nonfood commodity produced on India's farms. Cotton was an important export crop in the 1950s, but thereafter it provided the raw material for India's textile industry, which grew greatly to meet the needs of an expanding population. Cotton fabrics found an expanding international market in the 1980s and earned valuable foreign exchange. The foreign exchange earned from raw cotton, cotton yarn, and fabrics of all textile materials increased from US$163 million in FY 1960 to US$1.4 billion in FY 1980 to nearly US$3.9 billion in FY 1990 and US$3.8 billion by FY 1992. Cotton production increased from 600,000 tons in FY 1950 to nearly 1.7 million tons in FY 1990. These improvements largely resulted from increased yields, as there was little increase in the sown area devoted to cotton.

Raw jute is second only to cotton as a farm-produced industrial raw material. Before partition in 1947, India was the world's main supplier of jute and jute goods used as packaging material. As a result of the partition of India and Pakistan, the main jute growing area was in East Pakistan (eastern Bengal, after 1971 the independent nation of Bangladesh), and the factories manufacturing jute goods were in West Bengal, which remained part of India after partition. Jute also had been India's main source of export earnings. As a result, there was a concerted effort to increase raw jute production. The area sown with jute increased from 571,000 hectares in FY 1950 to nearly 1.2 million hectares in FY 1985 but then decreased to 692,000 hectares in FY 1988. Yields increased steadily from 1,040 kilograms per hectare in FY 1950 to 1,803 kilograms per hectare in FY 1990. These two factors combined to more than double jute production from 595 million tons in FY 1950 to 1.4 billion tons in FY 1990, with a maximum production of nearly 2 billion tons in FY 1985. Because technological changes in packaging reduced the worldwide demand for jute, production in the early 1990s was mainly for the domestic market. In FY 1990, jute provided less than 1 percent of export earnings.

THE GREEN REVOLUTION

The introduction of high-yielding varieties of seeds after 1965 and the increased use of fertilizers and irrigation are known collectively as the Green Revolution, which provided the increase in production needed to make India self-sufficient in food grains. The program was started with the help of the United States-based Rockefeller Foundation and was based on high-yielding varieties of wheat, rice, and other grains that had been developed in Mexico and in the Philippines. Of the high-yielding seeds, wheat produced the best results. Production of coarse grains—the staple diet of the poor—and pulses—the main source of protein—lagged behind, resulting in reduced per capita availability.

The total area under the high-yielding-varieties program was a negligible 1.9 million hectares in FY 1960. Since then growth has been spectacular, increasing to nearly 15.4 million hectares by FY 1970, 43.1 million hectares by FY 1980, and 63.9 million hectares by FY 1990. The rate of growth decreased significantly in the late 1980s, however, as additional suitable land was not available.

The major benefits of the Green Revolution were experienced mainly in northern and northwestern India between 1965 and the early 1980s; the program resulted in a substantial increase in the production of food grains, mainly wheat and rice. Food-grain yields continued to increase throughout the 1980s, but the dramatic changes in the years between 1965 and 1980 were not duplicated. By FY 1980, almost 75 percent of the total cropped area under wheat was sown with high-yielding varieties. For rice the comparable figure was 45 percent. In the 1980s, the area under high-yielding varieties continued to increase, but the rate of growth overall was slower. The eighth plan aimed at making high-yielding varieties available to the whole country and developing more productive strains of other crops.

The Green Revolution created wide regional and interstate disparities. The plan was implemented only in areas with assured supplies of water and the means to control it, large inputs of fertilizers, and adequate farm credit. These inputs were easily available in at least parts of the states of Punjab, Haryana, and western Uttar Pradesh; thus, yields increased most in these states. In other states, such as Andhra Pradesh and Tamil Nadu, in areas where these inputs were not assured, the results were limited or negligible, leading to considerable variation in crop yields within these states. The Green Revolution also increased income disparities: higher income growth and reduced incidence of poverty were found in the states where yields increased the most and lower income growth and little change in the incidence of poverty in other states.

LIVESTOCK AND POULTRY

A large number of farmers depend on livestock for their livelihood. In addition to supplying milk, meat, eggs, and hides, animals, mainly bullocks, are the major source of power for both farmers and drayers. Thus, animal husbandry plays an important role in the rural economy. The gross value of output from this sector was Rs358 billion in FY 1989, an amount that constituted about 25 percent of the total agricultural output of Rs1.4 trillion.

In FY 1992, India had approximately 25 percent of the world's cattle, with a collective herd of 193 million head. India also had 110 million goats, 75 million water buffalo, 44 million sheep, and 10 million pigs. Milk production in FY 1990 was estimated to have reached 53.5 million tons, and egg production had reached a level of 23.3 billion eggs. Dairy farming provided supplementary employment and an additional source of income to many small and marginal farmers. The National Dairy Development Board was established in 1965 under the auspices of Operation Flood at Anand, in Gujarat, to promote, plan, and organize dairy development through cooperatives; to provide consultations; and to set up dairy plants, which were then turned over to the cooperatives. There were more than 63,000 Anand-style dairy cooperative societies with some 7.5

million members in the early 1990s. The milk produced and sold by these farmers brought Rs320 million a day, or more than Rs10 trillion a year. The increase in milk production permitted India to end imports of powdered milk and milk-related products. In addition, 30,000 tons of powdered milk were exported annually to neighboring countries.

Operation Flood, the world's largest integrated dairy development program, attempted to establish linkages between rural milk producers and urban consumers by organizing farmer-owned and -managed dairy cooperative societies. In the early 1990s, the program was in its third phase and was receiving financial assistance from the World Bank and commodity assistance from the European Economic Community. At that time, India had more than 64,000 dairy cooperative societies, with close to 7.7 million members. These cooperatives established a daily processing capacity of 15.5 million liters of whole milk and 727 tons of milk powder.

FORESTRY

Some 50 million hectares, about 17 percent of India's land area, were regarded as forestland in the early 1990s. In FY 1987, however, actual forest cover was 64 million hectares. However, because more than 50 percent of this land was barren or brushland, the area under productive forest was actually less than 35 million hectares, or approximately 10 percent of the country's land area. The growing population's high demand for forest resources continued the destruction and degradation of forests through the 1980s, taking a heavy toll on the soil. An estimated 6 billion tons of topsoil were lost annually. However, India's 0.6 percent average annual rate of deforestation for agricultural and nonlumbering land uses in the decade beginning in 1981 was one of the lowest in the world and on a par with Brazil.

Many forests in the mid-1990s are found in high-rainfall, high-altitude regions, areas to which access is difficult. About 20 percent of total forestland is in Madhya Pradesh; other states with significant forests are Orissa, Maharashtra, and Andhra Pradesh (each with about 9 percent of the national total); Arunachal Pradesh (7 percent); and Uttar Pradesh (6 percent). The variety of forest vegetation is large: there are 600 species of hardwoods, *sal* (*Shorea robusta*) and teak being the principal economic species.

Conservation has been an avowed goal of government policy since independence. Afforestation increased from a negligible amount in the first plan to nearly 8.9 million hectares in the seventh plan. The cumulative area afforested during the 1951-91 period was nearly 17.9 million hectares. However, despite large-scale tree planting programs, forestry is one arena in which India has actually regressed since independence. Annual fellings at about four times the growth rate are a major cause. Widespread pilfering by villagers for firewood and fodder also represents a major decrement. In addition, the forested area has been shrinking as a result of land cleared for farming, inundations for irrigation and hydroelectric power projects, and construction of new urban areas, industrial plants, roads, power lines, and schools.

India's long-term strategy for forestry development reflects three major objectives: to reduce soil erosion and flooding; to supply the growing needs of the domestic wood products industries; and to supply the needs of the rural population for fuelwood, fodder, small timber, and miscellaneous forest produce. To achieve these objectives, the National Commission on Agriculture in 1976 recommended the reorganization of state forestry departments and advocated the concept of social forestry. The commission itself worked on the first two objectives, emphasizing traditional forestry and wildlife activities; in pursuit of the third objective, the commission recommended the establishment of a new kind of unit to develop community forests. Following the leads of Gujarat and Uttar Pradesh, a number of other states also established community-based forestry agencies that emphasized programs on farm forestry, timber management, extension forestry, reforestation of degraded forests, and use of forests for recreational purposes.

Such socially responsible forestry was encouraged by state community forestry agencies. They emphasized such projects as planting wood lots on denuded communal cattle-grazing grounds to make villages self-sufficient in fuelwood, to supply timber needed for the construction of village houses, and to provide the wood needed for the repair of farm implements. Both individual farmers and tribal communities were also encouraged to grow trees for profit. For example, in Gujarat, one of the more aggressive states in developing programs of socioeconomic importance, the forestry department distributed 200 million tree seedlings in 1983. The fast-growing eucalyptus is the main species being planted nationwide, followed by pine and poplar.

The role of forests in the national economy and in ecology was further emphasized in the 1988 National Forest Policy, which focused on ensuring environmental stability, restoring the ecological balance, and preserving the remaining forests. Other objectives of the policy were meeting the need for fuelwood, fodder, and small timber for rural and tribal people while recognizing the need to actively involve local people in the management of forest resources. Also in 1988, the Forest Conservation Act of 1980 was amended to facilitate stricter conservation measures. A new target was to increase the forest cover to 33 percent of India's land area from the then-official estimate of 23 percent. In June 1990, the central government adopted resolutions that combined forest science with social forestry, that is, taking the sociocultural traditions of the local people into consideration.

Since the early 1970s, as they realized that deforestation threatened not only the ecology but their livelihood in a variety of ways, people have become more interested and involved in conservation. The best known popular activist movement is the Chipko Movement, in which local women decided to fight the government and the vested interests to save trees. The women of Chamoli District, Uttar Pradesh, declared that they would embrace—literally "to stick to" (*chipkna* in Hindi)—trees if a sporting goods manufacturer attempted to cut down ash trees in their district. Since initial activism in 1973, the movement has spread and become an ecological movement leading to similar actions in other forest areas.

The movement has slowed down the process of deforestation, exposed vested interests, increased ecological awareness, and demonstrated the viability of people power.

FISHING

Fish production has increased more than fivefold since independence. It rose from only 800,000 tons in FY 1950 to 4.1 million tons in the early 1990s. Special efforts have been made to promote extensive and intensive inland fish farming, modernize coastal fisheries, and encourage deep-sea fishing through joint ventures. These efforts led to a more than fourfold increase in coastal fish production from 520,000 tons in FY 1950 to 2.4 million tons in FY 1990. The increase in inland fish production was even more dramatic, increasing almost eightfold from 218,000 tons in FY 1950 to 1.7 million tons in FY 1990. The value of fish and processed fish exports increased from less than 1 percent of the total value of exports in FY 1960 to 3.6 percent in FY 1993.

The important marine fish in the mid-1990s are mackerel, sardines, Bombay duck, shark, ray, perch, croaker, carangid, sole, ribbonfish, whitebait, tuna, silverbelly, prawn, and cuttlefish. The main freshwater fish are carp and catfish; the main brackish-water fish are *hilsa* (a variety of shad), and mullet.

Great potential exists for expanding the nation's fishing industry. India's exclusive economic zone, stretching 200 nautical miles into the Indian Ocean, encompasses more than 2 million square kilometers. In the mid-1980s, only about 33 percent of that area was being exploited. The potential annual catch from the area has been estimated at 4.5 million tons. In addition to this marine zone, India has about 1.4 million hectares of brackish water available for aquaculture, of which only 60,000 hectares were being farmed in the early 1990s; about 1.6 million hectares of freshwater lakes, ponds, and swamps; and nearly 64,000 kilometers of rivers and streams.

In 1990 there were 1.7 million full-time fishermen, 1.3 million part-time fishermen, and 2.3 million occasional fishermen, many of whom worked as saltmakers, ferrymen, or seamen, or operated boats for hire. In the early 1990s, the fishing fleet consisted of 180,000 traditional craft powered by sails or oars, 26,000 motorized traditional craft, and some 34,000 mechanized boats.

Fisheries research and training institutions are supported by central and state governments that deserve much of the credit for the expansion and improvements in the Indian fishing industry. The principal fisheries research institutions, all of which operate under the Indian Council of Agricultural Research, are the Central Institute of Marine Fisheries Research at Kochi (formerly Cochin), Kerala; the Central Inland Fisheries Institute at Barrackpore, West Bengal; and the Central Institute of Fisheries Technology at Willingdon Island near Kochi. Most fishery training is provided by the Central Institute for Fishery Education in Bombay (or Mumbai in Marathi), which has ancillary institutions in Barrackpore, Agra (Uttar Pradesh), and Hyderabad (Andhra Pradesh). The Central Fisheries Corporation in Calcutta is instrumental in bringing about improvements in fishing methods, ice production, processing, storing, marketing, and constructing and repairing fishing vessels. Operating under a 1972 law, the Marine Products Export Authority, headquartered in Kochi, has made several market surveys abroad and has been instrumental in introducing and enforcing hygiene standards that have gained for Indian fishery export products a reputation for cleanliness and quality.

The implementation of two programs for inland fisheries—establishing fish farmers' development agencies and the National Programme of Fish Seed Development—has led to encouragingly increased production, which reached 1.5 million tons during FY 1990, up from 0.9 million tons in FY 1984. A network of 313 fish farmers' development agencies was functioning in 1992. Under the National Programme of Fish Seed Development, forty fish-seed hatcheries were commissioned. Fish-seed production doubled from 5 billion fry in FY 1983 to 10 billion fry in FY 1989. A new program using organic waste for aquaculture was started in FY 1986. Inland fish production as a percent of total fish production increased from 36 percent in FY 1980 to 40 percent by FY 1990.

Apart from four main fishing harbors—Kochi (Kerala), Madras (Tamil Nadu), Vishakhapatnam (Andhra Pradesh), and Roychowk in Calcutta (West Bengal)—twenty-three minor fishing harbors and ninety-five fish-landing centers are designated to provide landing and berthing facilities to fishing craft. The harbors at Vishakhapatnam, Kochi, and Roychowk were completed by 1980; the one at Madras was completed in the 1980s. A major fishing harbor was under construction at Sassoon Dock in Bombay in the early 1990s, as were thirteen additional minor fishing harbors and eighteen small landing centers. By early 1990, there were 225 deep-sea fishing vessels operating in India's exclusive economic zone. Of these, 165 were owned by Indian shipping companies, and the rest were chartered foreign fishing vessels.

The government provides subsidies to poor fishermen so that they can motorize their traditional craft to increase the range and frequency of operation, with a consequent increase in the catch and earnings. A total of about 26,171 traditional craft had been motorized under the program by 1992.

The banning of trawling by chartered foreign vessels and the speedy motorization of traditional fishing craft in the 1980s led to a quantum jump in marine fish production in the late 1980s. The export of marine products rose from 97,179 tons (Rs531 billion) in FY 1987 to 210,800 tons (Rs17.4 trillion) in FY 1992, making India one of the world's leading seafood exporting nations. This achievement was largely a result of significant advancements in India's freezing facilities since the 1960s, advancements that enabled India's seafood products to meet international standards. Frozen shrimp, a high-value item, has become the dominant seafood export. Other significant export items are frozen frog legs, frozen lobster tails, dried fish, and shark fins, much of which is exported to seafood-loving Japan. During the eighth plan, marine products were identified as having major export potential.

There are several specialized institutes that train fishermen. The Central Institute of Fisheries Nautical and Engineering Training in Kochi instructs operators of deep-sea fishing vessels and technicians for shore establishments. It has facilities in Madras and Vishakhapatnam for about 500 trainees a year. The Integrated Fisheries Project, also headquartered in Kochi, was established for the processing, popularizing, and marketing of unusual fish. Another training organization, the Central Institute of Coastal Engineering for Fisheries in Bangalore, has done techno-economic feasibility studies on locations of fishing harbor sites and brackish-water fish farms.

To improve returns to fishermen and provide better products for consumers, several states have organized marketing cooperatives for fishermen. Nevertheless, most traditional fishermen rely on household members or local fish merchants for the disposal of their catches. In some places, marketing is carried on entirely by fisherwomen who carry small quantities in containers on their heads to nearby places. Good wholesale or retail markets are rare.

8

GOVERNMENT AND POLITICS

Indian politics entered a new era at the beginning of the 1990s. The period of political domination by the Congress (I) branch of the Indian National Congress came to an end with the party's defeat in the 1989 general elections, and India began a period of intense multiparty political competition. Even though the Congress (I) regained power as a minority government in 1991, its grasp on power was precarious. The Nehruvian socialist ideology that the party had used to fashion India's political agenda had lost much of its popular appeal. The Congress (I) political leadership had lost the mantle of moral integrity inherited from the Indian National Congress's role in the independence movement, and it was widely viewed as corrupt. Support among key social bases of the Congress (I) political coalition was seriously eroding. The main alternative to the Congress (I), the Bharatiya Janata Party (BJP—Indian People's Party), embarked on a campaign to reorganize the Indian electorate in an effort to create a Hindu nationalist majority coalition. Simultaneously, such parties as the Janata Dal (People's Party), the Samajwadi Party (Socialist Party), and the Bahujan Samaj Party (BSP—Party of Society's Majority) attempted to ascend to power on the crest of an alliance of interests uniting Dalits, Backward Classes, Scheduled Tribes, and religious minorities.

The structure of India's federal—or union—system not only creates a strong central government but also has facilitated the concentration of power in the central government in general and in particular in the Office of the Prime Minister. This centralization of power has been a source of considerable controversy and political tension. It is likely to further exacerbate political conflict because of the increasing pluralism of the country's party system and the growing diversity of interest-group representation.

Once viewed as a source of solutions for the country's economic and social problems, the Indian polity is increasingly seen by political observers as the problem. When populist political appeals stir the passions of the masses, government institutions appear less capable than ever before of accommodating conflicts in a society mobilized along competing ethnic and religious lines. In addition, law and order have become increasingly tenuous because of the growing inability of the police to curb criminal activities and quell communal disturbances. Indeed, many observers bemoan the "criminalization" of Indian politics at a time when politicians routinely hire "muscle power" to improve their electoral prospects, and criminals themselves successfully run for public office. These circumstances have led some observers to conclude that India has entered into a growing crisis of governability.

Few analysts would deny the gravity of India's problems, but some contend they have occurred amidst the maturation of civil society and the emergence of new, more democratic political practices. Backward Classes, the Dalits, and tribal peoples increasingly have refused to rest content with the patronage and populism characteristic of the "Congress system." Mobilization of these groups has provided a viable base for the political opposition and unraveled the fabric of the Congress. Since the late 1970s, there has been a proliferation of nongovernmental organizations. These groups made new demands on the political system that required a substantial redistribution of political power, economic resources, and social status.

Whether or not developments in Indian politics exacerbate the continuing problems or give birth to greater democracy broadly hinges on efforts to resolve three key issues. How will India's political system, now more than ever based on egalitarian democratic values, accommodate the changes taking place in its hierarchical social system? How will the state balance the need to recognize the interests of the country's remarkably heterogeneous society with the imperatives of national unity? And, in the face of the declining legitimacy of the Indian state and the continuing development of civil society, can the Indian state regenerate its legitimacy, and if it is to do so, how should it redefine the boundaries between state and society? India has confronted these issues throughout much of its history. These issues, with their intrinsic tensions, will continue to serve as sources of change in the continuing evolution of the Indian polity.

THE CONSTITUTION

The constitution of India draws extensively from Western legal traditions in its outline of the principles of liberal democracy. It is distinguished from many Western constitutions, however, in its elaboration of principles reflecting the aspirations to end the inequities of traditional social relations and enhance the social welfare of the population. According to constitutional scholar Granville Austin, probably no other nation's constitution "has provided so much impetus toward changing and rebuilding society for the common good." Since its enactment, the constitution has fostered a steady concentration of power in the central government—especially the Office of the Prime Minister. This centralization has occurred in the face of the increasing assertiveness of an array of ethnic and caste groups across Indian society. Increasingly, the government has responded to the resulting tensions by resorting to the formidable array of authoritarian powers provided by the constitution. Together with the public's perception of pervasive corruption among India's politicians, the state's centralization of authority and increasing resort to coercive power have eroded its legitimacy. However, a new assertiveness shown by the Supreme Court and the Election Commission suggests that the remaining checks and balances among the country's political institutions continue to support the resilience of Indian democracy.

Adopted after some two and one-half years of deliberation by the Constituent Assembly that also acted as India's first legislature, the constitution was put into effect on January 26, 1950. Bhimrao Ramji (B.R.) Ambedkar, a Dalit who earned a law degree from Columbia University, chaired the drafting committee of the constitution and shepherded it through Constituent Assembly debates. Supporters of independent India's founding father, Mohandas Karamchand (Mahatma) Gandhi, backed measures that would form a decentralized polity with strong local administration—known as *panchayat* (pl., *panchayats*)—in a system known as *panchayati raj* , that is rule by *panchayats*.

However, the support of more modernist leaders, such as Jawaharlal Nehru, ultimately led to a parliamentary government and a federal system with a strong central government. Following a British parliamentary pattern, the constitution embodies the Fundamental Rights, which are similar to the United States Bill of Rights, and a Supreme Court similar to that of the United States. It creates a "sovereign democratic republic" called India, or Bharat (after the legendary king of the *Mahabharata*), which "shall be a Union of States." India is a federal system in which residual powers of legislation remain with the central government, similar to that in Canada. The constitution provides detailed lists dividing up powers between central and state governments as in Australia, and it elaborates a set of Directive Principles of State Policy as does the Irish constitution.

The 395 articles and ten appendixes, known as schedules, in the constitution make it one of the longest and most detailed in the world. Schedules can be added to the constitution by amendment. The ten schedules in force cover the designations of the states and union territories; the emoluments for high-level officials; forms of oaths; allocation of the number of seats in the Rajya Sabha (Council of States—the upper house of Parliament) per state or territory; provisions for the administration and control of Scheduled Areas and Scheduled Tribes; provisions for the administration of tribal areas in Assam; the union (meaning central government), state, and concurrent (dual) lists of responsibilities; the official languages; land and tenure reforms; and the association of Sikkim with India.

The Indian constitution is also one of the most frequently amended constitutions in the world. The first amendment came only a year after the adoption of the constitution and instituted numerous minor changes. Many more amendments followed, and through June 1995 the constitution had been amended seventy-seven times, a rate of almost two amendments per year since 1950. Most of the constitution can be amended after a quorum of more than half of the members of each house in Parliament passes an amendment with a two-thirds majority vote. Articles pertaining to the distribution of legislative authority between the central and state governments must also be approved by 50 percent of the state legislatures.

Fundamental Rights

The Fundamental Rights embodied in the constitution are guaranteed to all citizens. These civil liberties take precedence over any other law of the land. They include individual rights common to most liberal democracies, such as equality before the law, freedom of speech and expression, freedom of association and peaceful assembly, freedom of religion, and the right to constitutional remedies for the protection of civil rights such as habeas corpus. In addition, the Fundamental Rights are aimed at overturning the inequities of past social practices. They abolish "untouchability"; prohibit discrimination on the grounds of religion, race, caste, sex, or place of birth; and forbid traffic in human beings and forced labor. They go beyond conventional civil liberties in protecting cultural and educational rights of minorities by ensuring that minorities may preserve their distinctive languages and establish and administer their own education institutions. Originally, the right to property was also included in the Fundamental Rights; however, the Forty-fourth Amendment, passed in 1978, revised the status of property rights by stating that "No person shall be deprived of his property save by authority of law." Freedom of speech and expression, generally interpreted to include freedom of the press, can be limited "in the interests of the sovereignty and integrity of India, the security of the State, friendly relations with foreign States, public order, decency or morality, or in relation to contempt of court, defamation or incitement to an offence".

Directive Principles of State Policy

An important feature of the constitution is the Directive Principles of State Policy. Although the Directive Principles are asserted to be "fundamental in the governance of the country," they are not legally enforceable. Instead, they are guidelines for creating a social order characterized by social, economic, and political justice, liberty, equality, and fraternity as enunciated in the constitution's preamble.

In some cases, the Directive Principles articulate goals that, however admirable, remain vague platitudes, such as the injunctions that the state "shall direct its policy towards securing... that the ownership and control of the material resources of the community are so distributed to subserve the common good" and "endeavor to promote international peace and security." In other areas, the Directive Principles provide more specific policy objectives. They exhort the state to secure work at a living wage for all citizens; take steps to encourage worker participation in industrial management; provide for just and humane conditions of work, including maternity leave; and promote the educational and economic interests of Scheduled Castes, Scheduled Tribes, and other disadvantaged sectors of society. The Directive Principles also charge the state with the responsibility for providing free and compulsory education for children up to age fourteen.

The Directive Principles also urge the nation to develop a uniform civil code and offer free legal aid to all citizens. They urge measures to maintain the separation of the judiciary from the executive and direct the government to organize village *panchayats* to function as units of self-government. This latter objective was advanced by the Seventy-third Amendment and the Seventy-fourth Amendment in December 1992. The Directive Principles also order that India should endeavor to protect and improve the environment and protect monuments and places of historical interest.

The Forty-second Amendment, which came into force in January 1977, attempted to raise the status of the Directive Principles by stating that no law implementing any of the Directive Principles could be declared unconstitutional on the grounds that it violated any of the Fundamental Rights. The amendment simultaneously stated that laws prohibiting "antinational activities" or the formation of "antinational associations" could not be invalidated because they infringed on any of the Fundamental Rights. It added a new section to the constitution on "Fundamental Duties" that enjoined citizens "to promote harmony and the spirit of common brotherhood among all the people of India, transcending religious, linguistic and regional or sectional diversities." However, the amendment reflected a new emphasis in governing circles on order and discipline to counteract what some leaders had come to perceive as the excessively freewheeling style of Indian democracy. After the March 1977 general election ended the control of the Congress (Congress (R) from 1969) over the executive and legislature for the first time since independence in 1947, the new Janata-dominated Parliament passed the Forty-third Amendment (1977) and Forty-fourth Amendment (1978). These amendments revoked the Forty-second Amendment's provision that Directive Principles take precedence over Fundamental Rights and also curbed Parliament's power to legislate against "antinational activities".

Group Rights

In addition to stressing the right of individuals as citizens, Part XVI of the constitution endeavors to promote social justice by elaborating a series of affirmative-action measures for disadvantaged groups. These "Special Provisions Relating to Certain Classes" include the reservation of seats in the Lok Sabha (House of the People) and in state legislative bodies for members of Scheduled Castes and Scheduled Tribes. The number of seats set aside for them is proportional to their share of the national and respective state populations. Part XVI also reserves some government appointments for these disadvantaged groups insofar as they do not interfere with administrative efficiency. The section stipulates that a special officer for Scheduled Castes and Scheduled Tribes be appointed by the president to "investigate all matters relating to the safeguards provided" for them, as well as periodic commissions to investigate the conditions of the Backward Classes. The president, in consultation with state governors, designates those groups that meet the criteria of Scheduled Castes and Scheduled Tribes. Similar protections exist for the small Anglo-Indian community.

The framers of the constitution provided that the special provisions would cease twenty years after the promulgation of the constitution, anticipating that the progress of the disadvantaged groups during that time would have removed significant disparities between them and other groups in society. However, in 1969 the Twenty-third Amendment extended the affirmative-action measures until 1980. The Forty-fifth Amendment of 1980 extended them again until 1990, and in 1989 the Sixty-second Amendment extended the provisions until 2000. The Seventy-seventh Amendment of 1995 further strengthened the states' authority to reserve government-service positions for Scheduled Caste and Scheduled Tribe members.

Emergency Provisions and Authoritarian Powers

Part XVIII of the constitution permits the state to suspend various civil liberties and the application of certain federal principles during presidentially proclaimed states of emergency. The constitution provides for three categories of emergencies: a threat by "war or external aggression" or by "internal disturbances"; a "failure of constitutional machinery" in the country or in a state; and a threat to the financial security or credit of the nation or a part of it. Under the first two categories, the Fundamental Rights, with the exception of protection of life and personal liberty, may be suspended, and federal principles may be rendered inoperative. A proclamation of a state of emergency lapses after two months if not approved by both houses of Parliament. The president can issue a proclamation dissolving a state government if it can be determined, upon receipt of a report from a governor, that circumstances prevent the government of that state from maintaining law and order according to the constitution. This action establishes what is known as President's Rule because under such a proclamation the president can assume any or all functions of the state government; transfer the powers of the state legislature to Parliament; or take other measures necessary to achieve the objectives of the proclamation, including suspension, in whole or in part, of the constitution. A proclamation of President's Rule cannot interfere with the exercise of authority by the state's high court. Once approved, President's Rule normally lasts for six months, but it may be extended up to one year if Parliament approves. In exceptional cases, such as the violent revolt in Jammu and Kashmir during the early and mid-1990s, President's Rule has lasted for a period of more than five years.

President's Rule has been imposed frequently, and its use is often politically motivated. During the terms of prime ministers Nehru and Lal Bahadur Shastri, from 1947 to 1966, it was imposed ten times. Under Indira Gandhi's two tenures as prime minister (1966-77 and 1980-84), President's Rule was imposed forty-one times. Despite Mrs. Gandhi's frequent use of President's Rule, she was in office longer (187 months) than any other prime minister except Nehru (201 months). Other prime ministers also have been frequent users: Morarji Desai (eleven times in twenty-eight months), Chaudhury Charan Singh (five times in less than six months), Rajiv Gandhi (eight times in sixty-one months), Vishwanath Pratap (V.P.) Singh (two times in eleven months), Chandra Shekhar (four times in seven months), and P.V. Narasimha Rao (nine times in his first forty-two months in office).

State of emergency proclamations have been issued three times since independence. The first was in 1962 during the border war with China. Another was declared in 1971 when India went to war against Pakistan over the independence of East Pakistan, which became Bangladesh. In 1975 the third Emergency was imposed in response to an alledged threat by "internal disturbances" stemming from the political opposition to Indira Gandhi.

The Indian state has authoritarian powers in addition to the constitution's provisions for proclamations of Emergency Rule and President's Rule. The Preventive Detention Act was passed in 1950 and remained in force until 1970. Shortly after the start of the Emergency in 1962, the government enacted the Defence of India Act. This legislation created the Defence of India Rules, which allow for preventive detention of individuals who have acted or who are likely to act in a manner detrimental to public order and national security. The Defence of India Rules were reimposed during the 1971 war with Pakistan; they remained in effect after the end of the war and were invoked for a variety of uses not intended by their framers, such as the arrests made during a nationwide railroad strike in 1974.

The Maintenance of Internal Security Act promulgated in 1971 also provides for preventive detention. During the 1975-77 Emergency, the act was amended to allow the government to arrest individuals without specifying charges. The government arrested tens of thousands of opposition politicians under the Defence of India Rules and the Maintenance of Internal Security Act, including most of the leaders of the future Janata Party government. Shortly after the Janata government came to power in 1977, Parliament passed the Forty-fourth Amendment, which revised the domestic circumstances cited in Article 352 as justifying an emergency from "internal disturbance" to "armed rebellion." During Janata rule, Parliament also repealed the Defence of India Rules and the Maintenance of Internal Security Act. However, after the Congress (I) returned to power in 1980, Parliament passed the National Security Act authorizing security forces to arrest individuals without warrant for suspicion of action that subverts national security, public order, and essential economic services. The Essential Services Maintenance Act of 1981 permits the government to prohibit strikes and lockouts in sixteen economic sectors providing critical goods and services. The Fifty-ninth Amendment, passed in 1988, restored "internal disturbance" in place of "armed rebellion" as just cause for the proclamation of an emergency.

The Sikh militant movement that spread through Punjab during the 1980s spurred additional authoritarian legislation. In 1984 Parliament passed the National Security Amendment Act enabling government security forces to detain prisoners for up to one year. The 1984 Terrorist Affected Areas (Special Courts) Ordinance provided security forces in Punjab with unprecedented powers of detention, and it authorized secret tribunals to try suspected terrorists. The 1985 Terrorist and Disruptive Activities (Prevention) Act imposed the death penalty for anyone convicted of terrorist actions that led to the death of others. It empowered authorities to tap telephones, censor mail, and conduct raids when individuals are alleged to pose a threat to the unity and sovereignty of the nation. The legislation renewing the act in 1987 provided for in camera trials, which may be presided over by any central government officer, and reversed the legal presumption of innocence if the government produces specific evidence linking a suspect to a terrorist act. In March 1988, the Fifty-ninth Amendment increased the period that an emergency can be in effect without legislative approval from six months to three years, and it eliminated the assurance of due process and protection of life and liberty with regard to Punjab found in articles 20 and 21. These rights were restored in 1989 by the Sixty-third Amendment.

By June 30, 1994, more than 76,000 persons throughout India had been arrested under the Terrorist and Disruptive Activities (Prevention) Act. The act became widely unpopular, and the Rao government allowed the law to lapse in May 1995.

The Structure of Government

The union government, as India's central government is known, is divided into three distinct but interrelated branches: legislative, executive, and judicial. As in the British parliamentary model, the leadership of the executive is drawn from and responsible to the legislative body. Although Article 50 stipulates the separation of the judiciary from the executive, the executive controls judicial appointments and many of the conditions of work. In addition, one of the more dramatic institutional battles in the Indian polity has been the struggle between elements wanting to assert legislative power to amend the constitution and those favoring the judiciary's efforts to preserve the constitution's basic structure.

The Legislature

Parliament consists of a bicameral legislature, the Lok Sabha (House of the People—the lower house) and the Rajya Sabha (Council of States—the upper house). Parliament's principal function is to pass laws on those matters that the constitution specifies to be within its jurisdiction. Among its constitutional powers are approval and removal of members of the Council of Ministers, amendment of the constitution, approval of central government finances, and delimitation of state and union territory boundaries.

The president has a specific authority with respect to the function of the legislative branch. The president is authorized to convene Parliament and must give his assent to all parliamentary bills before they become law. The president is empowered to summon Parliament to meet, to address either house or both houses together, and to require attendance of all of its members. The president also may send messages to either house with respect to a pending bill or any other matter. The president addresses the first session of Parliament each year and must give assent to all provisions in bills passed.

Lok Sabha

The Lok Sabha in 1995 constitutionally had 545 seats. For a variety of reasons, elections are sometimes not held in all constitutiencies, leaving some seats vacant and giving the appearance of fewer seats in the lower house. A member must be at least twenty-five years of age. Two members are nominated by the president as representatives of the Anglo-Indian community, and the rest are popularly elected. Elections are held on a one-stage, "first-past-the-post" system, similar to that in the United States. As in the United States, candidates from larger parties are favored because each constituency elects only the candidate winning the most votes. In the context of multiple-candidate elections, most members of Parliament are elected with pluralities of the vote that amount to less than a majority. As a result, political parties can gain commanding positions in the Parliament without winning the support of a majority of the electorate. For instance, Congress has dominated Indian politics without ever winning a majority of votes in parliamentary elections. The best-ever Congress performance in parliamentary elections was in 1984 when Congress (I) won 48 percent of the vote and garnered 76 percent of the parliamentary seats. In the 1991 elections, Congress (I) won 37.6 percent of the vote and 42 percent of the seats.

The usual Lok Sabha term is five years. However, the president may dissolve the house and call for new elections should the government lose its majority in Parliament. Elections must be held within six months after Parliament is dissolved. The prime minister can choose electorally advantageous times to recommend the dissolution of Parliament to the president in an effort to maximize support in the next Parliament. The term of Parliament can be extended in yearly increments if an emergency has been proclaimed. This situation occurred in 1976 when Parliament was extended beyond its five-year term under the Emergency proclaimed the previous year. The constitution stipulates that the Lok Sabha must meet at least twice a year, and no more than six months can pass between sessions. The Lok Sabha customarily meets for three sessions a year. The Council of Ministers is responsible only to the Lok Sabha, and the authority to initiate financial legislation is vested exclusively in the Lok Sabha.

The powers and authority of the Lok Sabha and the Rajya Sabha are not differentiated. The index of the constitution, for example, has a lengthy list of the powers of Parliament but not for each separate house. The key differences between the two houses lie in their disparate authority in the legislative process.

Rajya Sabha

The Rajya Sabha has a maximum of 250 members. All but twelve are elected by state and territory legislatures for six-year terms. Members must be at least thirty years old. The president nominates up to twelve members on the basis of their special knowledge or practical experience in fields such as literature, science, art, and social service. No further approval of these nominations is required by Parliament. Elections are staggered so that one-third of the members are elected every two years. The number of seats allocated to each state and territory is determined on the basis of relative population, except that smaller states and territories are awarded a larger share than their population justifies.

The Rajya Sabha meets in continuous session. It is not subject to dissolution as is the Lok Sabha. The Rajya Sabha is designed to provide stability and continuity to the legislative process. Although considered the upper house, its authority in the legislative process is subordinate to that of the Lok Sabha.

Legislative Process

The initiative for substantial legislation comes primarily from the prime minister, cabinet members, and high-level officials. Although all legislation except financial bills can be introduced in either house, most laws originate in the Lok Sabha. A legislative proposal may go through three readings before it is voted on. After a bill has been passed by the originating house, it is sent to the other house, where it is debated and voted on. The second house can accept, reject, or amend the bill. If the bill is amended by the second house, it must be returned to the originating house in its amended form. If a bill is rejected by the second house, if there is disagreement about the proposed amendments, or if the second house fails to act on a bill for six months, the president is authorized to summon a joint session of Parliament to vote on the bill. Disagreements are resolved by a majority vote of the members of both houses present in a joint session. This procedure favors the Lok Sabha because it has more than twice as many members as the Rajya Sabha.

When the bill has been passed by both houses, it is sent to the president, who can refuse assent and send the bill back to Parliament for reconsideration. If both houses pass it again, with or without amendments, it is sent to the president a second time. The president is then obliged to assent to the legislation. After receiving the president's assent, a bill becomes an act on the statute book.

The legislative procedure for bills involving taxing and spending—known as money bills—is different from the procedure for other legislation. Money bills can be introduced only in the Lok Sabha. After the Lok Sabha passes a money bill, it is sent to the Rajya Sabha. The upper house has fourteen days to act on the bill. If the Rajya Sabha fails to act within fourteen days, the bill becomes law. The Rajya Sabha may send an amended version of the bill back to the Lok Sabha, but the latter is not bound to accept these changes. It may pass the original bill again, at which point it will be sent to the president for his signature.

During the 1950s and part of the 1960s, Parliament was often the scene of articulate debate and substantial revisions of legislation. Prime ministers Indira Gandhi, Rajiv Gandhi, and P.V. Narasimha Rao, however, showed little enthusiasm for parliamentary debate. During the 1975-77 Emergency, many members of Parliament from the opposition as well as dissidents within Indira's own party were arrested, and press coverage of legislative proceedings was censored. It is generally agreed that the quality of discourse and the expertise of members of Parliament have declined since the 1960s. An effort to halt the decline of Parliament through a reformed committee system giving Parliament new powers of oversight over the executive branch has had very limited impact.

Under the constitution, the division of powers between the union government and the states is delimited into three lists: the Union List, the State List, and the Concurrent List. Parliament has exclusive authority to legislate on any of the ninety-seven items on the Union List. The list includes banking, communications, defense, foreign affairs, interstate commerce, and transportation. The State

List includes sixty-seven items that are under the exclusive jurisdiction of state legislatures, including agriculture, local government, police, public health, public order, and trade and commerce within the state. The central—or union—government and state governments exercise concurrent jurisdiction over forty-four items on the Concurrent List, including criminal law and procedure, economic and social planning, electricity, factories, marriage and divorce, price control, social security and social insurance, and trade unions. The purpose of the Concurrent List is to secure legal and administrative unity throughout the country. Laws passed by Parliament relevant to Concurrent List areas take precedence over laws passed by state legislatures.

The Executive

The executive branch is headed by the president, in whom the constitution vests a formidable array of powers. The president serves as head of state and the supreme commander of the armed forces. The president appoints the prime minister, cabinet members, governors of states and territories, Supreme Court and high court justices, and ambassadors and other diplomatic representatives. The president is also authorized to issue ordinances with the force of acts of Parliament when Parliament is not in session. The president can summon and prorogue Parliament as well as dissolve the Lok Sabha and call for new elections.

The president also can dismiss state and territory governments. Exercise of these impressive powers has been restricted by the convention that the president acts on the advice of the prime minister. In 1976 the Forty-second Amendment formally required the president to act according to the advice of the Council of Ministers headed by the prime minister. The spirit of the arrangement is reflected in Ambedkar's statement that the president "is head of the State but not of the Executive. He represents the nation but does not rule the nation." In practice, the president's role is predominantly symbolic and ceremonial, roughly analogous to the president of Germany or the British monarch.

The president is elected for a five-year term by an electoral college consisting of the elected members of both houses of Parliament and the elected members of the legislative assemblies of the states and territories. The participation of state and territory assemblies in the election is designed to ensure that the president is chosen to head the nation and not merely the majority party in Parliament, thereby placing the office above politics and making the incumbent a symbol of national unity.

Despite the strict constraints placed on presidential authority, presidential elections have shaped the course of Indian politics on several occasions, and presidents have exercised important power, especially when no party has a clear parliamentary majority. The presidential election of 1969, for example, turned into a dramatic test of strength for rival factions when Prime Minister Indira Gandhi put up an opponent to the official Congress candidate. The electoral contest contributed to the subsequent split of the Congress. In 1979, after the Ja-nata Party began to splinter, President Neelam Sanjiva Reddy (1977-82) first selected Janata member Chaudhury Charan Singh as prime minister (1979-80) to form a minority government and then dissolved Parliament and called for new elections while ignoring Jagjivan Ram's claim that he could assemble a stable government and become the country's first Scheduled Caste prime minister.

Tensions between President Giani Zail Singh (1982-87) and Prime Minister Rajiv Gandhi (1984-88) also illustrate the potential power of the president. In 1987 Singh refused to sign the Indian Post Office (Amendment) Bill, thereby preventing the government from having the authority to censor personal mail. Singh's public suggestion that the prime minister had not treated the office of the president with proper dignity and the persistent rumors that Singh was plotting the prime minister's ouster contributed to the erosion of public confidence in Rajiv Gandhi that ultimately led to his defeat in the 1989 elections. In November 1990, President Ramaswami Venkataraman (1987-92) selected Chandra Shekhar as India's eleventh prime minister, even though Chandra Shekhar's splinter Samajwadi

Janata Dal held only fifty-eight seats in the Lok Sabha. Chandra Shekhar resigned in June 1991 when the Congress (I) withdrew its support.

In the same manner as the president, the vice president is elected by the electoral college for a five-year term. The vice president is ex officio chairman of the Rajya Sabha and acts as president when the latter is unable to discharge his duties because of absence, illness, or any other reason or until a new president can be elected (within six months of the vacancy) when a vacancy occurs because of death, resignation, or removal. There have been three instances since 1969 of the vice president serving as acting president.

The prime minister is by far the most powerful figure in the government. After being selected by the president, typically from the party that commands the plurality of seats in Parliament, the prime minister selects the Council of Ministers from other members of Parliament who are then appointed by the president. Individuals who are not members of Parliament may be appointed to the Council of Ministers if they become a member of Parliament either through election or appointment within six months of selection. The Council of Ministers is composed of cabinet ministers (numbering seventeen, representing thirty-one portfolios in 1995), ministers of state (forty-five, representing fifty-three portfolios in 1995), and deputy ministers (the number varies). Cabinet members are selected to accommodate different regional groups, castes, and factions within the ruling party or coalition as well as with an eye to their administrative skills and experience. Prime ministers frequently retain key ministerial portfolios for themselves.

Although the Council of Ministers is formally the highest policy-making body in the government, its powers have declined as influence has been increasingly centralized in the Office of the Prime Minister, which is composed of the top-ranking administrative staff. After the Congress split to form the Congress (R)—R for Requisition—and the Congress (O)—O for Organisation—in 1969, Indira Gandhi (who headed the Congress (R)) increasingly concentrated decision-making authority in the Office of the Prime Minister. When Rajiv Gandhi became prime minister in 1984, he promised to delegate more authority to his cabinet members. However, power rapidly shifted back to the Office of the Prime Minister and a small coterie of Rajiv's personal advisers. Rajiv's dissatisfaction with his cabinet ministers became manifest in his incessant reshuffling of his cabinet. During his five years in office, he changed his cabinet thirty-six times, about once every seven weeks. When P.V. Narasimha Rao became prime minister in June 1991, he decentralized power, giving Minister of Finance Manmohan Singh, in particular, a large measure of autonomy to develop a program for economic reform. After a year in office, Rao began again to centralize authority, and by the end of 1994, the Office of the Prime Minister had grown to be as powerful as it ever was under Rao's predecessors. As of August 1995, Rao himself held the portfolios in thirteen ministries, including those of defense, industry, and Kashmir affairs.

THE JUDICIARY

Supreme Court

The Supreme Court is the ultimate interpreter of the constitution and the laws of the land. It has appellate jurisdiction over all civil and criminal proceedings involving substantial issues concerning the interpretation of the constitution. The court has the original and exclusive jurisdiction to resolve disputes between the central government and one or more states and union territories as well as between different states and union territories. And the Supreme Court is also empowered to issue advisory rulings on issues referred to it by the president. The Supreme Court has wide discretionary powers to hear special appeals on any matter from any court except those of the armed services. It also functions as a court of record and supervises every high court.

Twenty-five associate justices and one chief justice serve on the Supreme Court. The president appoints the chief justice. Associate justices are also appointed by the president after consultation with the chief justice and, if the president deems necessary, with other associate justices of the Supreme Court and high court judges in the states. The appointments do not require Parliament's concurrence. Justices may not be removed from office until they reach mandatory retirement at age sixty-five unless each house of Parliament passes, by a vote of two-thirds of the members in attendance and a majority of its total membership, a presidential order charging "proved misbehavior or incapacity."

The contradiction between the principles of parliamentary sovereignty and judicial review that is embedded in India's constitution has been a source of major controversy over the years. After the courts overturned state laws redistributing land from zamindar estates on the grounds that the laws violated the zamindars' Fundamental Rights, Parliament passed the first (1951), fourth (1955), and seventeenth amendments (1964) to protect its authority to implement land redistribution. The Supreme Court countered these amendments in 1967 when it ruled in the *Golaknath v State of Punjab* case that Parliament did not have the power to abrogate the Fundamental Rights, including the provisions on private property. On February 1, 1970, the Supreme Court invalidated the government-sponsored Bank Nationalization Bill that had been passed by Parliament in August 1969. The Supreme Court also rejected as unconstitutional a presidential order of September 7, 1970, that abolished the titles, privileges, and privy purses of the former rulers of India's old princely states.

In reaction to Supreme Court decisions, in 1971 Parliament passed the Twenty-fourth Amendment empowering it to amend any provision of the constitution, including the Fundamental Rights; the Twenty-fifth Amendment, making legislative decisions concerning proper land compensation nonjusticiable; and the Twenty-sixth Amendment, which added a constitutional article abolishing princely privileges and privy purses. On April 24, 1973, the Supreme Court responded to the parliamentary offensive by ruling in the *Keshavananda Bharati v the State of Kerala* case that although these amendments were constitutional, the court still reserved for itself the discretion to reject any constitutional amendments passed by Parliament by declaring that the amendments cannot change the constitution's "basic structure."

During the 1975-77 Emergency, Parliament passed the Forty-second Amendment in January 1977, which essentially abrogated the *Keshavananda* ruling by preventing the Supreme Court from reviewing any constitutional amendment with the exception of procedural issues concerning ratification. The Forty-second Amendment's fifty-nine clauses stripped the Supreme Court of many of its powers and moved the political system toward parliamentary sovereignty. However, the Forty-third and Forty-fourth amendments, passed by the Janata government after the defeat of Indira Gandhi in March 1977, reversed these changes. In the *Minerva Mills* case of 1980, the Supreme Court reaffirmed its authority to protect the basic structure of the constitution. However, in the *Judges Transfer* case on December 31, 1981, the Supreme Court upheld the government's authority to dismiss temporary judges and transfer high court justices without the consent of the chief justice. The Supreme Court continued to be embroiled in controversy in 1989, when its US$470 million judgment against Union Carbide for the Bhopal catastrophe resulted in public demonstrations protesting the inadequacy of the settlement. In 1991 the first-ever impeachment motion against a Supreme Court justice was signed by 108 members of Parliament. A year later, a high-profile inquiry found Associate Justice V. Ramaswamy "guilty of willful and gross misuses of office... and moral turpitude by using public funds for private purposes and reckless disregard of statutory rules" while serving as chief justice of Punjab and Haryana. Despite this strong indictment, Ramaswamy survived parliamentary impeachment proceedings and remained on the Supreme Court after only 196 members of Parliament, less than the required two-thirds, voted for his ouster.

During 1993 and 1994, the Supreme Court took measures to bolster the integrity of the courts and protect civil liberties in the face of state coercion. In an effort to avoid the appearance of conflict of interest in the judiciary, Chief Justice Manepalli Narayanrao Venkatachaliah initiated a controversial model code of conduct for judges that required the transfer of high court judges having children practicing as attorneys in their courts. Since 1993, the Supreme Court has implemented a policy to compensate the victims of violence while in police custody. On April 27, 1994, the Supreme Court issued a ruling that enhanced the rights of individuals placed under arrest by stipulating elaborate guidelines for arrest, detention, and interrogation.

High Courts

There are eighteen high courts for India's twenty-five states, six union territories, and one national capital territory. Some high courts serve more than one state or union territory. For example, the high court of the union territory of Chandigarh also serves Punjab and Haryana, and the high court in Gauhati (in Meghalaya) serves Assam, Nagaland, Meghalaya, Mizoram, Manipur, Tripura, and Arunachal Pradesh. As part of the judicial system, the high courts are institutionally independent of state legislatures and executives. The president appoints state high court chief justices after consulting with the chief justice of the Supreme Court and the governor of the state. The president also consults with the chief justice of the state high court before he appoints other high court justices. Furthermore, the president may also exercise the right to transfer high court justices without consultation. These personnel matters are becoming more politicized as chief ministers of states endeavor to exert their influence with New Delhi and the prime minister exerts influence over the president to secure politically advantageous appointments.

Each high court is a court of record exercising original and appellate jurisdiction within its respective state or territory. It also has the power to issue appropriate writs in cases involving constitutionally guaranteed Fundamental Rights. The high court supervises all courts within its jurisdiction, except for those dealing with the armed forces, and may transfer constitutional cases to itself from subordinate courts. The high courts have original jurisdiction on revenue matters. They try original criminal cases by a jury, but not civil cases.

Lower Courts

States are divided into districts (*zillas*), and within each a judge presides as a district judge over civil cases. A sessions judge presides over criminal cases. The judges are appointed by the governor in consultation with the state's high court. District courts are subordinate to the authority of their high court. There is a hierarchy of judicial officials below the district level. Many officials are selected through competitive examination by the state's public service commission. Civil cases at the subdistrict level are filed in *munsif* (subdistrict) courts. Lesser criminal cases are entrusted to the courts of subordinate magistrates functioning under the supervisory authority of a district magistrate. All magistrates are under the supervision of the high court. At the village level, disputes are frequently resolved by *panchayats* or *lok adalats* (people's courts).

The judicial system retains substantial legitimacy in the eyes of many Indians despite its politicization since the 1970s. In fact, as illustrated by the rise of social action litigation in the 1980s and 1990s, many Indians turn to the courts to redress grievances with other social and political institutions. It is frequently observed that Indians are highly litigious, which has contributed to a growing backlog of cases. Indeed, the Supreme Court was reported to have more than 150,000 cases pending in 1990, the high courts had some 2 million cases pending, and the lower courts had a substantially greater backlog. Research findings in the early 1990s show that the backlogs at levels below the Supreme Court are the result of delays in the litigation process and the large number of decisions that are appealed and not the result of an increase in the number of new cases filed. Coupled with public perceptions of politicization, the growing inability of the courts to resolve disputes expeditiously threatens to erode the remaining legitimacy of the judicial system.

Election Commission

Article 324 of the constitution establishes an independent Election Commission to supervise parliamentary and state elections. Supervising elections in the world's largest democracy is by any standard an immense undertaking. Some 521 million people were eligible to vote in 1991. Efforts are made to see that polling booths are situated no more than two kilometers from a voter's place of residence. In 1991, this objective required some 600,000 polling stations for the country's 3,941 state legislative assembly and 543 parliamentary constituencies. To attempt to ensure fair elections, the Election Commission deployed more than 3.5 million officials, most of whom were temporarily seconded from the government bureaucracy, and 2 million police, paramilitary, and military forces.

Over the years, the Election Commission's enforcement of India's remarkably strict election laws grew increasingly lax. As a consequence, candidates flagrantly violated laws limiting campaign expenditures. Elections became increasingly violent (350 persons were killed during the 1991 campaign, including five Lok Sabha and twenty-one state assembly candidates), and voter intimidation and fraud proliferated.

The appointment of T.N. Seshan as chief election commissioner in 1991 reinvigorated the Election Commission and curbed the illegal manipulation of India's electoral system. By cancelling or repolling elections where improprieties had occurred, disciplining errant poll officers, and fighting for the right to deploy paramilitary forces in sensitive areas, Seshan forced candidates to take the Election Commission's code of conduct seriously and strengthened its supervisory machinery. In Uttar Pradesh, where more than 100 persons were killed in the 1991 elections, Seshan succeeded in reducing the number killed to two in the November 1993 assembly elections by enforcing compulsory deposit of all licensed firearms, banning unauthorized vehicular traffic, and supplementing local police with paramilitary units. In state assembly elections in Andhra Pradesh, Goa, Karnataka, and Sikkim, after raising ceilings for campaign expenditures to realistic levels, Seshan succeeded in getting candidates to comply with these limits by deploying 336 audit officers to keep daily accounts of the candidates' election expenditures. Although Seshan has received enthusiastic support from the public, he has stirred great controversy among the country's politicians. In October 1993, the Supreme Court issued a ruling that confirmed the supremacy of the chief election commissioner, thereby deflecting an effort to rein in Seshan by appointing an additional two election commissioners. Congress (I)'s attempt to curb Seshan's powers through a constitutional amendment was foiled after a public outcry weakened its support in Parliament.

State Governments and Territories

India has twenty-five states, six union territories, and one national capital territory, with populations ranging from 406,000 (Sikkim) to 139 million (Uttar Pradesh). Ten states each have more than 40 million people, making them countrylike in significance. There are eighteen official Scheduled Languages , clearly defined since the reorganization of states along linguistic lines in the 1950s and 1960s. Social structures within states vary considerably, and they encompass a great deal of cultural diversity, as those who have watched India's Republic Day (January 26) celebrations will attest.

The constitution provides for a legislature in each state and territory. Most states have unicameral legislatures, but Andhra Pradesh, Bihar, Jammu and Kashmir, Maharashtra, Tamil Nadu, and Uttar Pradesh have bicameral legislatures. The lower house, known as the *vidhan sabha* , or legislative assembly, is the real seat of legislative power. Where an upper house exists, it is known as the *vidhan parishad* , or legislative council; council functions are advisory, and any objections expressed to a bill may be overridden if the assembly passes the bill a second time. Members of the assembly serve five-year terms after being chosen by direct elections from local constituencies. Their numbers vary, from a minimum of sixty to a maximum of 500. Members of the council are selected through a combination of direct election, indirect election, and nomination. Their six-year terms are staggered so that one-third of the membership is renewed every two years. Whether in the upper or lower house, membership in the assembly has come to reflect the predominantly rural demography of most states and the distribution of social power resulting from the state's agrarian and caste structures.

The structure of state governments is similar to that of the central government. In the executive branch, the governor plays a role analogous to that of the president, and the elected chief minister presides over a council of ministers drawn from the legislature in a manner similar to the prime minister. Many of the governor's duties are honorific; however, the governor also has considerable power. Like the president, the governor selects who may attempt to form a government; he may also dismiss a state's government and dissolve its legislative assembly. All bills that the state legislature passes must receive the assent of the governor. The governor may return bills other than money bills to the assembly. The governor may also decide to send a bill for consideration to the president, who has the power to promulgate ordinances. The governor may also recommend to the president that President's Rule be invoked. Governors are appointed to office for a five-year term by the president on the advice of the prime minister, and their conduct is supposed to be above politics. Since 1967 most state legislatures have come under the control of parties in opposition to the majority in Parliament, and governors have frequently acted as agents of the ruling party in New Delhi. Increasingly, governors are appointed more for their loyalty to the prime minister than for their distinguished achievements and discretion. The politicization of gubernatorial appointments has become such a widespread practice that in 1989, shortly after the National Front government replaced the Congress (I) government, Prime Minister V.P. Singh (1989-90) asked eighteen governors to resign so that he could replace them with his own choices. Governors not only attempt to keep opposition state governments in line, but also, while keeping the state bureaucracy in place, have exercised their power to dismiss the chief minister and his or her council of ministers.

The strength of the central government relative to the states is especially apparent in constitutional provisions for central intervention into state jurisdictions. Article 3 of the constitution authorizes Parliament, by a simple majority vote, to establish or eliminate states and union territories or change their boundaries and names. The emergency powers granted to the central government by the constitution enable it, under certain circumstances, to acquire the powers of a unitary state. The central government can also dismiss a state government through President's Rule. Article 249 of the constitution enables a two-thirds vote of the Rajya Sabha to empower Parliament to pass binding legislation for any of the subjects on the State List. Articles 256 and 257 require states to comply with laws passed by Parliament and with the executive authority of the central government. The articles empower the central government to issue directives instructing states on compliance in these matters. Article 200 also enables a state governor, under certain circumstances, to refuse to give assent to bills passed by the state legislature and instead refer them to the president for review. The central government exerts control over state governments through the financial resources at its command. The central government distributes taxes and grants-in-aid through the decisions of finance commissions, usually convened every five years as stipulated by Article 275. The central government also distributes substantial grants through its development plans as elaborated by the Planning Commission. The dependence of state governments on grants and disbursements grew throughout the 1980s as states began to run up fiscal deficits and the share of transfers from New Delhi increased.

The power and influence of central government finances also can be seen in the substantial funds allocated under the central government's five-year plans to such areas as public health and agriculture that are constitutionally under the State List.Besides its twenty-five states, India has seven centrally supervised territories. Six are union territories; one is the National Capital Territory of Delhi. Jurisdictions for territories are smaller than states and less populous. The central government administers union territories through either a lieutenant governor or a chief commissioner who is appointed by the president on the advice of the prime minister. Each territory also has a council of ministers, a legislature, and a high court; however, Parliament may also pass legislation on issues in union territories that in the case of states are usually reserved for state assemblies. The Sixty-ninth Amendment, passed in December 1991, made Delhi the national capital territory effective February 1, 1992. Although not having the same status as statehood, Delhi was given the power of direct election of members of its legislative assembly and the power to pass its own laws.

9

THE SOCIAL SETUP AND POLITICS

The decline of the Congress (I) since the late 1980s has brought an end to the dominant single-party system that had long characterized India's politics. Under the old system, conflict within the Congress was often a more important political dynamic than was conflict between the Congress and the opposition. The Congress had set the political agenda and the opposition responded. A new party system, in which the Congress (I) is merely one of several major participants, was in place by 1989. As often as not in the mid-1990s, the Congress (I) seems to respond to the initiatives of other parties rather than set its own political agenda.

Elections

At least once every five years, India's Election Commission supervises one of the largest, most complex exercises of collective action in the world. India's elections in the 1990s involve overseeing an electorate of about 521 million voters who travel to nearly 600,000 polling stations to chose from some 8,950 candidates representing roughly 162 parties. The elections reveal much about Indian society. Candidates span a wide spectrum of backgrounds, including former royalty, cinema superstars, religious holy men, war heroes, and a growing number of farmers. Campaigns utilize communications technologies ranging from the latest video van with two-way screens to the traditional rumor traveling by word of mouth. Increasing violence also has come to characterize elections.

In 1991, some 350 people, including former Prime Minister Rajiv Gandhi, four other parliamentary candidates, and twenty-one candidates running in state legislative assembly elections, were kilPed in election-related violence.

Political Parties

India's party system is in the throes of hisPoric change. The 1989 general elections brought the era of Congress dominance to an end. Even tPough the Congress (I) regained Dower in 1991, it was no longer The pivot around which the party system revolved. Instead, it represented just one strategy for organizing a political majority, and a declining one at that. While the Congress (I) was encountYring growing difficulties in maintaining its coalition of uppercaste elites, Muslims, Scheduled Castes, and Scheduled Tribes, The BJP was endeavoring to organize a new majority around the appeal of Hindu nationalism. The Janata Dal and the BSP, among others, were attempting to fashion e new majority out of the increaingly assertive Backward Classes, Dalits, Scheduled Castes, Schmduled Tribes, and religious minorities.

THE CONGRESS

The Congress has, by any standarhs, remarkable political accomplishments to its credit. As the Indian National Congress, its guidance fashioned a nation out of an extraordinarily heterogeneous ensemble of peoples. The party has played an important role in establishing the foundations of perhaps the most durable democratic political system in the developing world. As scholars Franci Robinson and Paul R. Brass point out, the Congress constituted, one of the few political organizations in the annals of decolonialization to "make the transition from being sole representativm of the nationalist cause to being just one element of a competitive party system."

The Congress dominated Indian politics fromindependence until 1967. Prior to 1967, the Congress had never less than 73 percent of the seats in Parliament. The party won every state government election except two—most often exclusively, but also through coalitions—and until 1967 it never won less than 60 percent of all elections for seats in the state legislative assemblies.

There were four factors that accounted for this dominance. First, the party acquired a tremendous amount of good will and political capital from its leadership of the nationalist struggle. Party chiefs gained substantial popular respect for the years in jail and other deprivations that they personally endured. The shared experience of the independence struggle fostered a sense of cohesion, which was important in maintaining unity in the face of the party's internal pluralism.

The second factor was that the Congress was the only party with an organization extending across the nation and down to the village level. The party's federal structure was based on a system of internal democracy that functioned to resolve disputes among its members and maintain party cohesion. Internal party elections also served to legitimate the party leadership, train party workers in the skills of political competition, and create channels of upward mobility that rewarded its most capable members.

A third factor was that the Congress achieved its position of political dominance by creating an organization that adjusted to local circumstances rather than transformed them, often reaching the village through local "big men" (*bare admi*) who controlled village "vote banks." These local elites, who owed their position to their traditional social status and their control over land, formed factions that competed for power within the Congress.

The internal party democracy and the Congress's subsequent electoral success ultimately reinforced the local power of these traditional elites and enabled the party to adjust to changes in local balances of power.

The nonideological pragmatism of local party leadership made it possible to co-opt issues that contributed to opposition party success and even incorporate successful opposition leaders into the party. Intraparty competition served to channel information about local circumstances up the party hierarchy.

Fourth, patronage was the oil that lubricated the party machine. As the state expanded its development role, it accumulated more resources that could be distributed to party members. The growing pool of opportunities and resources facilitated the party's ability to accommodate conflict among its members. The Congress enjoyed the benefits of a "virtuous cycle," in which its electoral success gave it access to economic and political resources that enabled the party to attract new supporters.

The halcyon days of what Indian political scientist Rajni Kothari has called "the Congress system" ended with the general elections in 1967. The party lost seventy-eight seats in the Lok Sabha, retaining a majority of only twenty-three seats. Even more indicative of the Congress setback was its loss of control over six of the sixteen state legislatures that held elections. The proximate causes of the reversal included the failure of the monsoons in 1965 and 1966 and the subsequent hardship throughout northern and eastern India, and the unpopular currency devaluation in 1966. However, profound changes in India's polity also contributed to the decline of the Congress. The rapid growth of the electorate, which increased by 45 percent from 1952 to 1967, brought an influx of new voters less appreciative of the Congress's role in the independence movement. Moreover, the simultaneous spread of democratic values produced a political awakening that mobilized new groups and created a more pluralistic constellation of political interests. The development of new and more-differentiated identities and patterns of political cleavage made it virtually impossible for the Congress to contain the competition of its members within its organization. Dissidence and ultimately defection greatly weakened the Congress's electoral performance.

It was in this context that Indira Gandhi asserted her independence from the leaders of the party organization by attempting to take the party in a more populist direction. She ordered the nationalization of India's fourteen largest banks in 1969, and then she supported former labor leader and Acting President Varahagiri Venkata Giri's candidacy for president despite the fact that the party organization had already nominated the more conservative Neelam Sanjiva Reddy. After Giri's election, the party organization expelled Indira Gandhi from the Congress and ordered the parliamentary party to choose a new prime minister. Instead, 226 of the 291 Congress members of Parliament continued to support Indira Gandhi. The Congress split into two in 1969, the new factions being the Congress (O)—for Organisation—and Mrs. Gandhi's Congress (R)—for Requisition. The Congress (R) continued in power with the support of non-Congress groups, principally the Communist Party of India (CPI) and the Dravida Munnetra Kazhagam (DMK—Dravidian Progressive Federation).

With the Congress (O) controlling most of the party organization, Indira Gandhi adopted a new strategy to mobilize popular support. For the first time ever, she ordered parliamentary elections to be held separately from elections for the state government. This delinking was designed to reduce the power of the Congress (O)'s state-level political machines in national elections. Mrs. Gandhi traveled throughout the country, energetically campaigning on the slogan "*garibi hatao* " (eliminate poverty), thereby bypassing the traditional Congress networks of political support. The strategy proved successful, and the Congress (R) won a dramatic victory. In the 1971 elections for the Lok Sabha, the Congress (R) garnered 44 percent of the vote, earning it 352 seats. The Congress (O) won only sixteen seats and 10 percent of the vote. The next year, after leading India to victory over Pakistan in the war for Bangladesh's independence, Indira Gandhi and the Congress (R) further consolidated their control over the country by winning fourteen of sixteen state assembly elections and victories in 70 percent of all seats contested.

The public expected Indira Gandhi to deliver on her mandate to remove poverty. However, the country experienced a severe drought in 1971 and 1972, leading to food shortages, and the price of food rose 20 percent in the spring of 1973. The decision by the Organization of the Petroleum Exporting Countries (OPEC) to quadruple oil prices in 1973-74 also led to inflation and increased unemployment. Jayaprakash (J.P) Narayan, a socialist leader in the preindependence Indian National Congress who, after 1947, left to conduct social work in the Sarvodaya movement (*sarvodaya* means uplift of all), came out of retirement to lead what eventually became widely known as the "J.P. movement." Under Narayan's leadership, the movement toppled the government of Gujarat and almost brought down the government in Bihar; Narayan advocated a radical regeneration of public morality that he labelled "total revolution."

After the Allahabad High Court ruled that Mrs. Gandhi had committed electoral law violations and Narayan addressed a massive demonstration in New Delhi, at Indira Gandhi's behest, the president proclaimed an Emergency on June 25, 1975. That night, Indira Gandhi ordered the arrest of almost all the leaders of the opposition, including dissidents within the Congress. In all, more than 110,000 persons were detained without trial during the Emergency.

Indira Gandhi's rule during the Emergency alienated her popular support. After postponing elections for a year following the expiration of the five-year term of the Lok Sabha, she called for new elections in March 1977. The major opposition party leaders, many of whom had developed a rapport while they were imprisoned together under the Emergency regime, united under the banner of the Janata Party. By framing the key issue of the election as "democracy versus dictatorship," the Janata Party—the largest opposition party—appealed to the public's democratic values to rout the Congress (R). The vote share of the Congress (R) dropped to 34.5 percent, and the number of its seats in Parliament plunged from 352 to 154. Indira Gandhi lost her seat.

The inability of Janata Party factions to agree proved the party's undoing. Indira Gandhi returned to win the January 1980 elections after forming a new party, the Congress (I—for Indira), in 1978.

The Congress (I) largely succeeded in reconstructing the traditional Congress electoral support base of Brahmans , Muslims, Scheduled Castes, and Scheduled Tribes that had kept Congress in power in New Delhi during the three decades prior to 1977. The

Congress (I)'s share of the vote increased by 8.2 percent to 42.7 percent of the total vote, and its number of seats in the Lok Sabha grew to 353, a majority of about two-thirds. This success approximated the levels of support of the Congress dominance from 1947 to 1967. Yet, as political scientist Myron Weiner observed, "The Congress party that won in 1980 was not the Congress party that had governed India in the 1950s and 1960s, or even the early 1970s. The party was organizationally weak and the electoral victory was primarily Mrs. Gandhi's rather than the party's." As a consequence, the Congress's appeal to its supporters was much more tenuous than it had been in previous decades.

Indira Gandhi's dependence on her flamboyant son Sanjay and, after his accidental death in 1980, on her more reserved son Rajiv gives testimony to the personalization and centralization of power within the Congress (I). Having developed a means to mobilize support without a party organization, she paid little attention to maintaining that support. Rather than allowing intraparty elections to resolve conflicts and select party leaders, Indira Gandhi preferred to fill party posts herself with those loyal to her. As a result, party leaders at the state level lost their legitimacy among the rank and file because their positions depended on the whims of Indira Gandhi rather than on the extent of their popular support. In addition, centralization and the demise of democracy within the party disrupted the flow of information about local circumstances to party leaders and curtailed the ability of the Congress (I) to adjust to social change and incorporate new leaders.

When Rajiv Gandhi took control after his mother's assassination in November 1984, he attempted to breathe new life into the Congress (I) organization. However, the massive electoral victory that the Congress (I) scored under Rajiv's leadership just two months after his mother's assassination gave him neither the skill nor the authority to succeed in this endeavor. Rajiv did, however, attempt to remove the more unsavory elements within the party organization. He denied nominations to one-third of the incumbent members of Parliament during the 1984 Lok Sabha campaign, and he refused to nominate two of every five incumbents in the state legislative assembly elections held in March 1985.

Another of Rajiv's early successes was the passage of the Anti-Defection Bill in January 1985 in an effort to end the bribery that lured legislators to cross partisan lines. Speaking at the Indian National Congress centenary celebrations in Bombay (officially called Mumbai as of 1995), Rajiv launched a vitriolic attack on the "culture of corruption" that had become so pervasive in the Congress (I). However, the old guard showed little enthusiasm for reform. As time passed, Rajiv's position was weakened by the losses that the party suffered in a series of state assembly elections and by his government's involvement in corruption scandals. Ultimately, Rajiv was unable to overcome the resistance within the party to internal elections and reforms. Ironically, as Rajiv's position within the party weakened, he turned for advice to many of the wheelers and dealers of his mother's regime whom he had previously banished.

The frustration of Rajiv Gandhi's promising early initiatives meant that the Congress (I) had no issues on which to campaign as the end of his five-year term approached. On May 15, 1989, just months before its term was to expire, the Congress (I) introduced amendments that proposed to decentralize government authority to *panchayat* and municipal government institutions.

Opposition parties, many of whom were on record as favoring decentralization of government power, vehemently resisted the Congress (I) initiative. They charged that the initiative did not truly decentralize power but instead enabled the central government to circumvent state governments (many of which were controlled by the opposition) by transferring authority from state to local government and strengthening the links between central and local governments.

After the Congress (I) failed to win the two-thirds vote required to pass the legislation in the Rajya Sabha on October 13, 1989, it called for new parliamentary elections and made *"jana shakti"* (power to the people) its main campaign slogan.

The Congress (I) retained formidable campaign advantages over the opposition. The October 17, 1989, announcement of elections took the opposition parties by surprise and gave them little time to form electoral alliances. The Congress (I) also blatantly used the government-controlled television and radio to promote Rajiv Gandhi. In addition, the Congress (I) campaign once again enjoyed vastly superior financing. It distributed some 100,000 posters and 15,000 banners to each of its 510 candidates. It provided every candidate with six or seven vehicles, and it commissioned advertising agencies to make a total of ten video films to promote its campaign.

The results of the 1989 elections were more of a rebuff to the Congress (I) than a mandate for the opposition. Although the Congress (I) remained the largest party in Parliament with 197 seats, it was unable to form a government. Instead, the Ja-nata Dal, which had 143 seats, united with its National Front allies to form a minority government precariously dependent on the support of the BJP (eighty-five seats) and the communist parties (forty-five seats). Although the Congress (I) lost more than 50 percent of its seats in Parliament, its share of the vote dropped only from 48.1 percent to 39.5 percent of the vote. The Congress (I) share of the vote was still more than double that of the next largest party, the Janata Dal, which received support from 17.8 percent of the electorate. More grave for the long-term future of the Congress (I) was the erosion of vital elements of the traditional coalition of support for the Congress (I) in North India. Alienated by the Congress (I)'s cultivation of Hindu activists, Muslims defected to the Janata Dal in large numbers. The Congress (I) simultaneously lost a substantial share of Scheduled Caste voters to the BSP in Haryana, Madhya Pradesh, and Uttar Pradesh and to the Indian People's Front in Bihar.

To offset these losses, the Congress (I) attempted to play a "Hindu card." On August 14, 1989, the Supreme Court ruled that no parties or groups could disturb the status quo of the Babri Masjid, a sixteenth-century mosque in Ayodhya, Uttar Pradesh. The mosque was controversial because Hindu nationalists claim it was on the site of the birthplace of the Hindu god Ram and that, as such, the use by Muslims was sacrilegious. Despite the court ruling, in September the Congress (I) entered into an agreement with the Vishwa Hindu Parishad (VHP—World Hindu Council), a conservative religious organization with close ties to Hindu nationalists, to allow the VHP to proceed with a ceremony to lay the foundation for the Ramjanmabhumi (birthplace of Ram) Temple. (The VHP had been working toward this goal since 1984.) In return, the Congress (I) secured the VHP's agreement to perform the ceremony on property adjacent to the Babri Masjid that was not in dispute. By reaching this agreement, the Congress (I) attempted to appeal to Hindu activists while retaining Muslim support. Rajiv Gandhi's decision to kick off his campaign less than six kilometers from the Babri Masjid and his appeal to voters that they vote for the Congress (I) if they wished to bring about "Ram Rajya" (the rule of Ram) were other elements of the Congress (I)'s strategy to attract the Hindu vote.

The 1991 elections returned the Congress (I) to power but did not reverse important trends in the party's decline. The Congress (I) won 227 seats, up from 197 in 1989, but its share of the vote dropped from 39.5 percent in 1989 to 37.6 percent. Greater division within the opposition rather than growing popularity of the Congress (I) was the key element in the party's securing an increased number of seats. Also troubling was the further decline of the Congress (I) in heavily populated Bihar and Uttar Pradesh, which together account for more than 25 percent of all seats in Parliament. In Uttar Pradesh, the number of seats that the Congress (I) was able to win went down from fifteen to two, and its share of the vote dropped from 32 percent to 20 percent. In Bihar the seats won by the Congress (I) fell from four to one, and the Congress (I) share of the vote was reduced from 28 percent to 22 percent. The Congress (I) problems in these states, which until 1989 had been bastions of its strength, were reinforced by the party's poor showing in the November 1993 state elections. These elections were characterized by the further disintegration of the traditional Congress coalition, with Brahmans and other upper castes defecting to the BJP and Scheduled Castes and Muslims defecting to the Janata Dal, the Samajwadi Party (Socialist

Party), and the BSP. Strong evidence indicates that the Congress (I) would have fared significantly worse had it not been for the assassination of Rajiv Gandhi in the middle of the elections. A wave of sympathy similar to that which helped elect Rajiv after the assassination of his mother increased the Congress (I) support. In the round of voting that took place before Rajiv's death, the Congress (I) won only 26 percent of the seats and 33 percent of the vote. In the votes that occurred after Rajiv's death, the Congress (I) won 58 percent of the seats and 40 percent of the popular vote. It may also be that Rajiv's demise ended the "anti-Congressism" that had pervaded the political system as a result of his family's dynastic domination of Indian politics through its control over the Congress.

Rajiv Gandhi was assassinated by a Tamil suicide bomber affiliated with the Sri Lankan Liberation Tigers of Tamil Eelam (LTTE) during a political campaign in May 1991. Only after his assassination did hope for reforming the Congress (I) reappear. The end of three generations of Nehru-Gandhi family leadership left Rajiv's coterie of political manipulators in search of a new kingpin. The bankruptcy of the Congress (I) leadership was highlighted by the fact that they initially turned to Sonia Gandhi, Rajiv's Italian-born wife, to lead the party. Sonia's primary qualification was that she was Rajiv's widow. She had never held elected office and, during her early years in India, she had expressed great disdain for political life. However, although she did not assume a leadership role, she continued to be seen as a "kingmaker" in the Congress (I). Her advice was sought after, and she was called on to lead the party in the mid-1990s. An unusual public speech by Sonia Gandhi criticizing the government of P.V. Narasimha Rao in August 1995 further fueled speculation that she was a candidate for political leadership.

Sonia Gandhi's refusal in 1991 to become president of the Congress (I) led the mantle of party leadership to fall on Rao. Rao was a septuagenarian former professor who had retired from politics before the 1991 elections after undergoing heart-bypass surgery. Rao had a conciliatory demeanor and was acceptable to the party's contending factions. Paradoxically, the precariously positioned Rao was able to take more substantial steps in the direction of party reform than his predecessors. First, Rao had to demonstrate that he could mobilize popular support for himself and the party, a vital currency of power for any Congress (I) leader. He did so in the November 15, 1991, by-elections by winning his own seat in Andhra Pradesh unopposed and leading the party to victory in a total of eight of the fifteen parliamentary by-elections. By the end of 1991, Rao had succeeded in initiating the first intraparty elections in the Congress in almost twenty years. Although there was widespread manipulation by local party bosses, the elections enhanced the legitimacy of party leaders and held forth the prospect of a rejuvenated party organization. The process culminated in April 1992 at the All-India Congress (I) Committee at Tirupati, Andhra Pradesh, where elections were held for the ten vacant seats in the Congress Working Committee.

In the wake of the Tirupati session, Rao became less interested in promoting party democracy and more concerned with consolidating his own position. The change was especially apparent in the 1993 All-India Congress (I) Committee session at Surajkund (in Haryana), where Rao's supporters lavishly praised the prime minister and coercively silenced his opponents. However, Rao's image was damaged in July 1993 after Harshad Mehta, a stockbroker under indictment for allegedly playing a leading role in a US$2 billion stock scam in 1992, accused Rao of personally accepting a bribe that he had delivered on November 4, 1991. The extent of the press coverage of the charges and their apparent credibility among the public was evidence of the pervasive public cynicism toward politicians. Rao's stock in the party and Congress (I)'s position within Parliament were greatly weakened. On July 28, 1993, his government barely survived a no-confidencc motion in the Lok Sabha. Rao's position was temporarily strengthened at the end of 1993 when he was able to cobble together a parliamentary majority. However, support for Rao and the Congress (I) declined again in 1994. The party was rocked by a scandal relating to the procurement of sugar stocks that cost the government an estimated Rs6.5 billion (US$210 million; for value of the rupee) and by losses in legislative assembly elections in Andhra Pradesh—Rao's home state, where he personally took control over the campaign—and Karnataka. The Congress (I) again lost in three of four major states in elections held in the spring of 1995. The political fallout in New Delhi was an increase in dissident activity within the Congress (I) led by former cabinet members Narain Dutt Tiwari and Arjun Singh and other Rao rivals who sought to split the Congress and form a new party.

OPPOSITION PARTIES

Opposition to the Congress has always been fragmented. Opposition parties range from Hindu nationalist parties such as the BJP on the right to communist parties on the left. The divisiveness of the opposition, combined with the "first-past-the-post" electoral system, has enabled the Congress to dominate Indian politics without ever winning a majority of the vote from the national electorate. The extent of electoral alliances among the opposition is an important predictor of its ability to win seats in Parliament. The first two instances when the opposition succeeded in forming a government at the center occurred after it united under the Janata Party banner in 1977 and after the formation of the Janata Dal and the National Front in 1988. In each of these cases, the unity that was facilitated by anti-Congress sentiment prior to the elections collapsed in the face of rivalry and ambition once the opposition came into power.

The Rise and Decline of "Janata Politics"

Prior to 1967, the opposition was divided into an array of small parties. While the Congress garnered between 45 percent and 48 percent of the vote, no opposition party gained as much as 11 percent, and during the entire period, only two parties won 10 percent. Furthermore, in each election, independent candidates won between 12 percent and 20 percent of the vote.

The opposition's first significant attempt to achieve electoral unity occurred during the 1967 elections when opposition party alliances won control of their state governments in Bihar, Kerala,

Orissa, Punjab, and West Bengal. In Rajasthan an opposition coalition prevented the Congress from winning a majority in the state legislature and forced it to recruit independents to form a government. The Congress electoral debacle encouraged even more dissidence within the party, and in a matter of weeks after the elections, defections brought down Congress governments in Haryana, Madhya Pradesh, and Uttar Pradesh. By July 1967, state governments of two-thirds of the country were under opposition rule. However, opposition rule in many cases was short-lived. The aftermath of the 1967 elections initiated a climate of politics by defection in which the Congress, and to a lesser extent the opposition, attempted to overthrow governments by winning over their state legislators with promises of greater political power and outright bribes. Needless to say, this period seriously undermined the ability of most parties to discipline their members. The increase in opposition-ruled state governments after 1967 also prompted the Congress to use President's Rule to dismiss opposition-led state governments with increasing frequency.

Although the centrist and right-wing opposition formed a "grand alliance" during the 1971 parliamentary elections, it was not until the general elections of 1977 that opposition efforts culminated in electoral success at the national level. Imprisoned together under the authoritarian measures of the Emergency, India's senior opposition leaders found their personal animosity toward Indira Gandhi and the Congress to be a powerful motivation to overcome their division and rivalry.

In January 1977, opposition parties reactivated a pre-Emergency multiparty front, campaigned under the banner of the Janata Party, and won a dramatic electoral victory in March 1977. The Janata Party was made up of the Congress (O), the Jana Sangh, the Bharatiya Lok Dal (Indian People Party), the Samajwadi Party (Socialist Party), a handful of imprisoned Congress dissidents, and the Congress for Democracy—a group led by Scheduled Caste leader Jagjivan Ram that had splintered off from the Congress during the election campaign.

Despite the diversity of this assemblage of parties and the different social strata that they represented, members of the Ja-nata Party achieved surprising ideological and programmatic consensus by passing a program stressing decentralization, development of rural industries, and employment opportunities. It was not ideology, but rather an inability to consolidate partisan organizations and political rivalry among the leadership that led to the demise of the Janata government in 1979.

The Janata's three most senior leaders—Morarji Desai, Charan Singh, and Jagjivan Ram—each aspired to be prime minister. The rivalry continued during Desai's tenure (March 1977-July 1979). Desai, Charan Singh, and Ram continually conspired to discredit each other. Their connivances ultimately discredited the Janata Party and allowed the Congress (I) to return to power in 1980.

Just as key defections from the Congress were essential to the Janata electoral success in 1977, so too did V.P. Singh's defection from the Congress (I) in 1987 enable opposition factions from the Janata Party and Bharatiya Lok Dal to unite the Janata Dal in 1988. Regional parties, such as the Telugu Desam Party (Telugu National Party), the DMK, and the Asom Gana Pa-rishad (AGP—Assam People's Assembly), together formed the National Front, led by Janata Dal, which defeated Rajiv Gandhi's Congress (I) in the 1989 parliamentary elections. With V.P. Singh as prime minister, the National Front government earned the appellation of "the crutch government" because it depended on the support of the Communist Party of India (Marxist—CPI (M)) on its left and the BJP on the right.

On August 7, 1990, V.P. Singh suddenly announced that his government would implement the recommendations of the Mandal Commission to reserve 27 percent of central government jobs for the Backward Classes, defined to include around 52 percent of the population. Although Singh's Janata Dal had pledged to implement the Mandal Commission recommendations as part of its election manifesto, his announcement led to riots throughout North India. Some seventy-five upper-caste youths died after resorting to self-immolation to dramatize their opposition, and almost 200 others were killed in clashes with the police.

BJP president Lal Kishan (L.K.) Advani announced that he would traverse the country on a pilgrimage to Ayodhya where he would lead Hindu activists in the construction of the Ramjanmabhumi Temple on the site of the Babri Masjid. As the pilgrimage progressed, riots between Hindus and Muslims broke out throughout the country. The National Front government decided to end the agitation, and Janata Dal chief minister of Bihar, Laloo Prasad Yadav, arrested Advani on October 23, 1990. On October 30, religious militants attempted to storm the Babri Masjid despite a massive military presence, and as many as twenty-six activists were killed. The BJP's withdrawal of support for the National Front government proved fatal, and V.P. Singh lost a parliamentary vote of confidence on November 7, 1990.

Two days before the vote, Chandra Shekhar, an ambitious Janata Dal rival who had been kept out of the National Front government, joined with Devi Lal, a former deputy prime minister under V.P. Singh, to form the Samajwadi Janata Party—Samajwadi meaning socialist—with a total of sixty Lok Sabha members. The day after the collapse of the National Front government, Chandra Shekhar informed the president that by gaining the backing of the Congress (I) and its electoral allies he enjoyed the support of 280 members of the Lok Sabha, and he demanded the right to constitute a new government. Even though his rump party accounted for only one-ninth of the members of the Lok Sabha, Chandra Shekhar succeeded in forming a new minority government and becoming prime minister (with Devi Lal as deputy prime minister). However, Chandra Shekhar's government fell less than four months later, after the Congress (I) withdrew its support.

The Janata Dal and the Samajwadi Janata Party declined after the fall of the Chandra Shekhar government. In the May-June 1991 parliamentary elections, their share of the vote dropped from 17.8 percent to 15.1 percent, and the number of seats in Parliament that they won fell from 142 to sixty-one. The parties were able to win seats only in Bihar, Orissa, and Uttar Pradesh. The factional rivalry and ineffectiveness that impeded the National Front government's efforts to provide effective government tarnished the Janata Dal image. In the absence of strong national leadership, the party was rendered a confederation of ambitious regional leaders whose rivalry prevented the establishment of a united party organization. The Janata Dal's persistent backing of the Mandal Commission recommendations made the party highly unpopular among high-caste people in the middle and upper classes, creating fund-raising difficulties. Although the Janata Dal won state elections in Karnataka in 1994 and Bihar in the spring of 1995, its poor showing in most other states gave the impression that its support was receding to a few regional bastions.

COMMUNIST PARTIES

The Communist Party of India (CPI) was founded on December 26, 1925, at an all-India conference held at Kanpur, Uttar Pradesh, in late December 1925 and early January 1926. Communists participated in the independence struggle and, as members of the Congress Socialist Party, became a formidable presence on the socialist wing of the Indian National Congress. They were expelled from the Congress Socialist Party in March 1940, after allegations that the communists had disrupted party activities and were intent on coopting party organizations. Indeed, by the time the communists were expelled, they had gained control over the entire Congress Socialist Party units in what were to become the southern states of Kerala, Tamil Nadu, and Andhra Pradesh. Communists remained members of the Indian National Congress although their support of the British war effort after the German invasion of the Soviet Union and their nationalist policy supporting the right of religious minorities to secede from India were diametrically opposed to Congress policies. As a result, the communists became isolated within the Congress. After independence, communists organized a peasant uprising in the Telangana region in the northern part of what was to become Andhra Pradesh. The uprising was suppressed only after the central government sent in the army. Starting in 1951, the CPI shifted to a more moderate strategy of seeking to bring communism to India within the constraints of Indian democracy. In 1957 the CPI was elected to rule the state government of Kerala only to have the government dismissed and President's Rule declared in 1959.

In 1964, in conjunction with the widening rift between China and the Soviet Union, a large leftist faction of the CPI leadership, based predominantly in Kerala and West Bengal, split from the party to form the Communist Party of India (Marxist), or CPI (M). The CPI (M)-led coalition victory in the 1967 West Bengal state elections spurred dissension within the party because a Maoist faction headed a peasant rebellion in the Naxalbari area of the state, just south of Darjiling (Darjeeling). The suppression of the Naxalbari uprising under the direction of the CPI (M)-controlled Home Ministry of the state government led to denunciations by Maoist revolutionary factions across the country. These groups—commonly referred to as Naxalites—sparked new uprisings in the Srikakulam region of Andhra Pradesh, Bihar, and other parts of West Bengal. In 1969 several Naxalite factions joined together to form a new party—the Communist Party of India (Marxist-Leninist)—CPI (M-L). However, pursuit of insurrectionary tactics in the face of harsh repression by the government along with an array of ideological disputes kept Naxalite factions isolated in their local bases.

In the 1990s, the CPI (M) enjoys the most political strength of any communist group. Nationally, its share of the vote has gradually increased from 4.2 percent in 1967 to 6.7 percent in 1991, but it has largely remained confined to Kerala, Tripura, and West Bengal. In Kerala the CPI (M) in coalition with other parties wrested control from the Congress and its allies (frequently including the CPI) in 1967, in 1980, and in 1987. Support for the CPI (M) in Kerala in general elections has ranged from 19 percent to 26 percent, but the party has never won more than nine of Kerala's twenty seats in Parliament. From 1977 to 1989, the CPI (M) dominated Tripura's state government. It won two parliamentary seats in 1971, 1980, and

1984, but it lost all of its seats in 1977, 1989, and 1991. In West Bengal, the CPI (M) has ruled the state government with a coalition of other leftist parties since 1977, and, since that time, the party has also dominated West Bengal's parliamentary delegation.

Support for the CPI is more evenly spread nationwide, but it is weak and in decline. The CPI share of the parliamentary vote has more than halved from 5.2 percent in 1967 to 2.5 percent in 1991.

In 1982 a CPI (M-L) faction entered the parliamentary arena by forming the Indian People's Front. In the 1989 general elections, the front won a parliamentary seat in western Bihar, and in 1990 it won seven seats in the Bihar legislative assembly. However, the Indian People's Front lost its parliamentary seat in the 1991 parliamentary elections when its vote in Bihar declined by some 20 percent.

REGIONAL PARTIES

Given India's social, cultural, and historical diversity, it is only natural that regional parties play an important role in the country's political life. Because of India's federal system, state assembly votes are held in an electoral arena that often enables regional parties to obtain power by espousing issues of regional concern. Simultaneously, the single-member district, first-past-the-post electoral system has given the advantage to national parties, such as the Congress, which possess a realistic chance of gaining or retaining power at the national level and the opportunity to use central government resources to reward their supporters.

Although regional parties have exercised authority at the state level, collectively they receive only from 5 to 10 percent of the national vote in parliamentary elections. Only during the governments of the Janata Party (1977-79) and the National Front (1989-90) have they participated in forming the central government. However, as India's party system becomes more fragmented with the decline of the Congress (I), the regional parties are likely to play an important role at the national level.

Regional political parties have been strongest in Tamil Nadu, where they have dominated state politics since 1967. Regional parties in the state trace their roots to the establishment of the Justice Party by non-Brahman social elites in 1916 and the development of the non-Bhraman Self-Respect Movement, founded in 1925 by E.V. Ramaswamy Naicker. As leader of the Justice Party, in 1944 Ramaswamy renamed the party the Dravida Kazhagam (DK—Dravidian Federation) and demanded the establishment of an independent state called Dravidasthan. In 1949, charismatic film script writer C.N. Annadurai, who was chafing under Ramaswamy's authoritarian leadership, split from the DK to found the DMK in an attempt to achieve the goals of Tamil nationalism through the electoral process. The DMK dropped its demand for Dravidasthan in 1963 but played a prominent role in the agitations that successfully defeated attempts to impose the northern Indian language of Hindi as the official national language in the mid-1960s. The DMK routed the Congress in the 1967 elections in Tamil Nadu and took control of the state government. With the deterioration of Annadurai's health, another screen writer, M. Karunanidhi, became chief minster in 1968 and took control of the party after Annadurai's death in 1969.

Karunanidhi's control over the party was soon challenged by M.G. Ramachandran (best known by his initials, M.G.R.), one of South India's most popular film stars. In 1972 M.G.R. split from the DMK to form the All-India Anna Dravida Munnetra Kazhagam (AIADMK). Under his leadership, the AIADMK dominated Tamil politics at the state level from 1977 through 1989. The importance of personal charisma in Tamil politics was dramatized by the struggle for control over the AIADMK after M.G.R's death in 1988. His widow, Janaki, herself a former film star, vied for control with Jayalalitha, an actress who had played M.G.R.'s leading lady in several films. The rivalry allowed the DMK to gain control over the state government in 1989. The AIADMK, securely under the control of Jayalalitha, who was cast as a "revolutionary leader," recaptured the state government in 1991. However, since 1980, the Congress (I), usually in alliance with the AIADMK, has won a majority of Tamil Nadu's seats in Parliament.

After three decades of Congress rule, the politics of Andhra Pradesh during the 1980s also became dominated by a charismatic film star who stressed regional issues. In 1982 N.T. Rama Rao (popularly known as N.T.R.), an actor who frequently played Hindu deities in Telugu-language films, formed the Te-lugu Desam. The party ruled the state from 1983 to 1989. It also won thirty of Andhra Pradesh's forty-two parliamentary seats in 1984. With the objective of enhancing Andhra Pradesh's regional autonomy, N.T.R. played a key role in the formation of the National Front coalition government in 1989. However, in the 1989 elections, the Telugu Desam won only two parliamentary seats and lost control over the state government to the Congress (I). It was able to improve its showing to thirteen seats in Parliament in the 1991 elections. The Telugu Desam returned to power in Andhra Pradesh after winning the state legislative assembly elections in November 1994.

The Akali Dal (Eternal Party) claims to represent India's Sikhs, who are concentrated primarily in Punjab. It was first formed in the early 1920s to return control of *gurdwaras* (Sikh places of worship) to the orthodox Sikh religious community. During the 1960s, the Akali Dal played an important role in the struggle for the creation of Punjab as a separate state with a Sikh majority. Even with the majority Sikh population, the Akali Dal's political success has been limited by the Congress's ability to win votes from the Sikh community. The Akali Dal won nine of Punjab's thirteen parliamentary seats in the general elections of 1977 and seven in 1984 but only one in the 1971 and 1980 elections. Similarly, the Akali Dal headed coalition state governments in 1967 and 1977 and formed the state government in 1985, but it lost state government elections to the Congress (R) in 1972, and to Congress (I) in 1980 and in 1992. As the 1980s progressed, the Akali Dal became increasingly factionalized. In 1989 three Akali Dal factions ran in the elections, winning a total of seven seats. The Akali Dal factions boycotted parliamentary and state legislative elections that were held in February 1992. As a result, voter turnout dropped to 21.6 percent, and the Congress (I) won twelve of Punjab's thirteen seats in Parliament and a majority of seats in the legislative assembly.

The National Conference, based in Jammu and Kashmir, is a regional party, which, despite its overwhelmingly Muslim following, refused to support the All-India Muslim League (Muslim League) during the independence movement; instead it allied itself with the Indian National Congress. The National Conference was closely identified with its leader, Sheikh Mohammed Abdullah, a personal friend of Nehru, and, after Abdullah's death in 1982, with his son, Farooq Abdullah. Friendship, however, did not prevent Nehru from imprisoning Sheikh Abdullah when he became concerned that the "Lion of Kashmir" was disposed to demand independence for his state. Ultimately, Sheikh Abdullah struck a deal with Indira Gandhi, and in 1975 he became chief minister of Jammu and Kashmir. The National Conference remained Jammu and Kashmir's dominant party through the 1980s and maintained control over the state government for most of the period. In parliamentary elections, it won one of Kashmir's six parliamentary seats in 1967, none in 1971, two in 1977, and three in 1980, 1984, and 1989. However, popular support for the National Conference was badly eroded by allegations of electoral fraud in the 1987 state elections—which were won by the National Conference in alliance with the Congress (I)—and the widespread corruption of the subsequent state government under the leadership of Farooq Abdullah. There was little popular sympathy for Farooq Abdullah and the National Conference even after the government was dissolved and President's Rule declared in 1990. Jammu and Kashmir remained under President's Rule through 1995, and the absence of elections makes it difficult to ascertain the extent of the National Conference's popular support. Nevertheless, it appears that Farooq and the National Conference remain discredited.

During the late 1980s, the AGP rose to power in Assam on the crest of Assamese nationalism. Immigration to Assam—primarily by Muslim Bengalis from neighboring Bangladesh—had aroused concern that the Assamese would become a minority in their own state. By 1979 attention was focused on the controversial issue of determining how many immigrants would be allowed on the state's list of eligible voters. The Congress (I), which gained a substantial share of the immigrants' votes, took a more expansive view of who should be included while the Assamese nationalist organizations demanded a more restrictive position. An attempt to hold state elections in February 1983, and in effect to force the Assamese nationalists to accept the status quo, resulted in a breakdown of law and order and the deaths of more than 3,000 people. The subsequent formation of a Congress (I) government led by Hiteshwar Saikia was widely viewed in Assam as illegitimate, and it was dissolved as part of the terms of the Assam Accord that was signed between Rajiv Gandhi and Assamese nationalists on August 15, 1985. The Assam Accord also included a compromise on the voter eligibility issue, settled the issue of the citizenship status of immigrants, and stipulated that new elections were to be held in December. The AGP was formed by Assamese student leaders after the signing of the accord, and the new party won the December 1985 elections with 35 percent of the vote and sixty-four of 108 seats in the state legislature.

The victory of the AGP did not end the controversy over Assamese nationalism. The AGP was unable to implement the accord's provisions for disenfranchising and expelling illegal aliens, in part because Parliament passed legislation making it more difficult to prove illegal alien status. The AGP's failure to implement the accord along with the general ineffectiveness with which it operated the state government undercut its popular support, and in November 1990 it was dismissed and President's Rule declared. As the AGP floundered, other nationalist groups of agitators flourished. The United Liberation Front of Assam (ULFA) became the primary torchbearer of militant Assamese nationalism while the All Bodo Students' Union (ABSU) and Bodo People's Action Committee (BPAC) led an agitation for a separate homeland for the central plain tribal people of Assam (often called Bodos). By 1990 ULFA militants ran virtually a parallel government in the state, extorting huge sums from businesses in Assam, especially the Assamese tea industry. The ULFA was ultimately subdued through a shrewd combination of ruthless military repression and generous terms of surrender for many of its leaders. The ABSU/BPAC-led mass agitation lasted from March 1987 until February 1993 when the ABSU signed an accord with the state government that had been under the Congress (I) control since 1991. The accord provided for the creation of a Bodoland Autonomous Council with jurisdiction over an area of 5,186 square kilometers and 2.1 million people within Assam. Nevertheless, Bodo agitation continued in the mid-1990s as a result of the demands of many Bodo leaders, who insisted that more territory be included under the Bodoland Autonomous Council.

CASTE-BASED PARTIES

One irony of Indian politics is that its modern secular democracy has enhanced rather than reduced the political salience of traditional forms of social identity such as caste. Part of the explanation for this development is that India's political parties have found the caste-based selection of candidates and appeals to the caste-based interests of the Indian electorate to be an effective way to win popular support. More fundamental has been the economic development and social mobility of those groups officially designated as Backward Classes and Scheduled Castes. Accounting for 52 and 15 percent of the population, respectively, the Backward Classes and Scheduled Castes, or Dalits as they prefer to be called, constitute a diverse range of middle, lower, and outcaste groups who have come to wield substantial power in most states. Indeed, one of the dramas of modern Indian politics has been the Backward Classes and Dalits' jettisoning of their political subordination to upper castes and their assertion of their own interests. The Backward Classes are such a substantial constituency that almost all parties vie for their support. For instance, the Congress (I) in Maharashtra has long relied on Backward Classes' backing for its political success. The 1990s have seen a growing number of cases where parties, relying primarily on Backward Classes' support, often in alliance with Dalits and Muslims, catapult to power in India's states. Janata Dal governments in Bihar and Karnataka are excellent examples of this strategy. An especially important development is the success of the Samajwadi Party, which under the leadership of Mulayam Singh Yadav won the 1993 assembly elections in India's most populous state, Uttar Pradesh, relying almost exclusively on Backward Classes and Muslim support in a coalition with the Dalit-supported BSP.

The growing support of the BSP also reflects the importance of caste-based politics and the assertiveness of the Dalits in particular. The BSP was founded by Kanshi Ram on April 13, 1984, the birthday of B.R. Ambedkar. Born as a Dalit in Punjab, Kanshi Ram resigned from his position as a government employee in 1964 and, after working in various political positions, founded the All-India Backward, Scheduled Caste, Scheduled Tribe, Other Backward Classes, and Minority Communities Employees Federation (BAMCEF) in 1978. Although both the BAMCEF and BSP pursue strategies of building support among Backward Classes, Scheduled Tribes, and Muslims as well as Dalits, Kanshi Ram has been most successful in building support among the Dalit Chamar (Leatherworker) caste in North India. In the November 1993 Uttar Pradesh state elections, Ram's BSP achieved the best showing of any Dalit-based party by winning sixty-seven seats. At the same time, the BSP increased its representation in the Madhya Pradesh state legislature from two to twelve seats. On June 1, 1995, the BSP withdrew from the state government of Uttar Pradesh and, with the support of the BJP, formed a new government, making its leader, Mayawati, the first Dalit ever to become a chief minister of Uttar Pradesh. The alliance, however, was seen by observers as doomed because of political differences.

THE MEDIA

The Press: Compared with many other developing countries, the Indian press has flourished since independence and exercises a large degree of independence. British colonialism allowed for the development of a tradition of freedom of the press, and many of India's great English-language newspapers and some of its Indian-language press were begun during the nineteenth century. As India became independent, ownership of India's leading English-language newspapers was transferred from British to Indian business groups, and the fact that most English-language newspapers have the backing of large business houses has contributed to their independence from the government. The press has experienced impressive growth since independence. In 1950 there were 214 daily newspapers, with forty-four in English and the rest in Indian languages. By 1990 the number of daily newspapers had grown to 2,856, with 209 in English and 2,647 in indigenous languages. The expansion of literacy and the spread of consumerism during the 1980s fueled the rapid growth of news weeklies and other periodicals. By 1993 India had 35,595 newspapers—of which 3,805 were dailies—and other periodicals. Although the majority of publications are in indigenous languages, the English-language press, which has widespread appeal to the expanding middle class, has a wide multicity circulation throughout India.

There are four major publishing groups in India, each of which controls national and regional English-language and vernacular publications. They are the Times of India Group, the Indian Express Group, the Hindustan Times Group, and the Anandabazar Patrika Group. The *Times of India* is India's largest English-language daily, with a circulation of 656,000 published in six cities. The *Indian Express*, with a daily circulation of 519,000, is published in seventeen cities. There also are seven other daily newspapers with circulations of between 134,000 and 477,000, all in English and all competitive with one another. Indian-language newspapers also enjoy large circulations but usually on a statewide or citywide basis. For example, the Malayalam-language daily *Malayala Manorama* circulates 673,000 copies in Kerala; the Hindi-language *Dainik Jagran* circulates widely in Uttar Pradesh and New Delhi, with 580,000 copies per day; *Punjab Kesari*, also published in Hindi and available throughout Punjab and New Delhi, has a daily circulation of 562,000; and the *Anandabazar Patrika*, published in Calcutta in Bengali, has a daily circulation of 435,000. There are also numerous smaller publications throughout the nation. The combined circulation of India's newspapers and periodicals is in the order of 60 million, published daily in more than ninety languages. India has more than forty domestic news agencies. The Express News Service, the Press Trust of India, and the United News of India are among the major news agencies. They are headquartered in Delhi, Bombay, and New Delhi, respectively, and employ foreign correspondents. Although freedom of the press in India is the legal norm—it is constitutionally guaranteed—the scope of this freedom has often been contested by the government. Rigid press censorship was imposed during the Emergency starting in 1975 but quickly retracted in 1977. The government has continued, however, to exercise more indirect controls. Government advertising accounts for as much as 50 percent of all advertisements in Indian newspapers, providing a monetary incentive to limit harsh criticism of the administration. Until 1992, when government regulation of access to newsprint was liberalized, controls on the distribution of newsprint could also be used to reward favored publications and threaten those that fell into disfavor. In 1988, at a time when the Indian press was publishing investigative reports about corruption and abuse of power in government, Parliament passed a tough defamation bill that mandated prison sentences for offending journalists. Vociferous protests from journalists and opposition party leaders ultimately forced the government to withdraw the bill. Since the late 1980s, the independence of India's press has been bolstered by the liberalization of government economic policy and the increase of private-sector advertising provided by the growth of India's private sector and the spread of consumerism.

Broadcast Media

The national television (Doordarshan) and radio (All India Radio, or Akashwani) networks are state-owned and managed by the Ministry of Information and Broadcasting. Their news reporting customarily presents the government's point of view. For example, coverage of the 1989 election campaign blatantly favored the government of Rajiv Gandhi, and autonomy of the electronic media became a political issue. V.P. Singh's National Front government sponsored the Prasar Bharati (Indian Broadcasting) Act, which Parliament considered in 1990, to provide greater autonomy to

Doordarshan and All India Radio. The changes that resulted were limited. The bill provided for the establishment of an autonomous corporation to run Doordarshan and All India Radio. The corporation was to operate under a board of governors to be in charge of appointments and policy and a broadcasting council to respond to complaints. However, the legislation required that the corporation prepare and submit its budget within the framework of the central budget and stipulated that the personnel of the new broadcasting corporation be career civil servants to facilitate continued government control. In the early 1990s, increasing competition from television broadcasts transmitted via satellite appeared the most effective manner of limiting the progovernment bias of the government-controlled electronic media.

Since the 1980s, India has experienced a rapid proliferation of television broadcasting that has helped shape popular culture and the course of politics. Although the first television program was broadcast in 1959, the expansion of television did not begin in earnest until the extremely popular telecast of the Ninth Asian Games, which were held in New Delhi in 1982. Realizing the popular appeal and consequent influence of television broadcasting, the government undertook an expansion that by 1990 was planned to provide television access to 90 percent of the population. In 1993, about 169 million people were estimated to have watched Indian television each week, and, by 1994, it was reported that there were some 47 million households with televisions. There also is a growing selection of satellite transmission and cable services available.Television programming was initially kept tightly under the control of the government, which embarked on a self-conscious effort to construct and propagate a cultural idea of the Indian nation. This goal is especially clear in the broadcasts of such megaseries as the Hindu epics *Ramayana* and *Mahabharata*. In addition to the effort at nation-building, the politicians of India's ruling party have not hesitated to use television to build political support. In fact, the political abuse of Indian television led to demands to increase the autonomy of Doordarshan; these demands ultimately resulted in support for the Prasar Bharati Act.

BIBLIOGRAPHY

Adas, Michael. *Machines as the Measure of Men: Science, Technology, and Ideologies of Western Dominance*. Ithaca: Cornell University Press, 1989.

Ali, Tariq. *An Indian Dynasty: The Story of the Nehru-Gandhi Family*. New York: Putnam, 1985.

Ashton, S.R. *British Policy Towards the Indian States, 1905-1939*. London Studies on South Asia, No. 2. London: Curzon, 1982.

Baird, Robert. *Religion in Modern India*. New Delhi: Manohar, 1981.

Cunningham, Joseph Davey. *History of the Sikhs, From the Origins of the Nation to the Battles of the Sutlej*. Delhi: Sultan Chand, 1955.

Damodaran, A.K., and Bajpai, U.S., eds. *Indian Foreign Policy: The Indira Gandhi Years*. New Delhi: Radiant, 1990.

Eldridge, P.J. *The Politics of Foreign Aid in India*. New York: Schocken, 1970.

Fischer, Louis. *The Life of Mahatma Gandhi*. New York: Harper, 1950.

Gandhi, Mahatma. *Essential Writings of Mahatma Gandhi*. Ed., Raghavan Iyer. New Delhi: Oxford University Press, 1991.

Habib, Irfan. *The Agrarian System of Mughal India, 1556-1707*. New York: Asia, 1963.

Ilankovatikal. *The Cilappatikaram of Ilano Atikal: An Epic of South India*. Trans., R. Parthasarathy. Translations from the Asian Classics. New York: Columbia University Press, 1993.

Jain, M.P. *Outlines of Indian Legal History*. 2d ed. Bombay: Tripathi, 1966.

Keay, John. *The Honourable Company: A History of the English East India Company*. London: Harper Collins, 1991.

Lewis, Martin D. *The British in India: Imperialism or Trusteeship.* Lexington, Massachusetts: Heath, 1962.

Mahalingam, T.V. *South Indian Polity.* 2d ed., rev. Madras: University of Madras, 1967.

Nanda, B.R. *Mahatma Gandhi.* Boston: Beacon Press, 1958.

Pandey, B.N. *The Break Up of British India.* London: Macmillan, 1969.

Qureshi, I.H. *The Muslim Community of the Indo-Pakistan Subcontinent, 1610-1947.* The Hague: Mouton, 1962.

Rangarajan, L.N. *Kautilya: The Arthasastra.* New York: Penguin, 1992.

Saksena, N.S. *India: Towards Anarchy, 1967-1992.* New Delhi: Abhinav, 1993.

Talwar, S.N. *Under the Banyan Tree: The Communist Movement in India, 1920-1964.* New Delhi: Allied, 1985.

Venkataramanayya, N. *The Eastern Calukyas of Vengi.* Madras: Vedam Venkataray Sastry, 1950.

Wolpert, Stanley. *Jinnah of Pakistan.* New York: Oxford University Press, 1984.

Woodruff, Philip: *The Men Who Ruled India, 2: The Founders.* London: Cape, 1963.

Zimmer, Heinrich. *The Art of Indian Asia.* New York: Pantheon, 1955.

INDEX

A

Achievements, 8, 10, 11, 28, 56, 186, 189, 247.
Associations, 134, 145, 160, 238.

B

Brahma, 31, 57, 60, 125.
British Empire, 27, 86.
British Raj, 32.
Buddhism, 8, 9, 11, 13, 41, 48, 49, 50, 51, 79, 81, 133.
Bureaucracy, 21, 157, 161, 245, 247.

C

Castes, 50, 54, 63, 82, 83, 88, 89, 90, 91, 92, 93, 94, 95, 99, 100, 101, 104, 112, 115, 116, 121, 124, 125, 126, 127, 128, 129, 130, 131, 132, 133, 134, 135, 136, 141, 142, 143, 144, 146, 157, 204, 227, 228, 229, 239, 250, 254, 258, 272.
Christianity, 28, 31, 42, 79, 81, 82, 83, 133.
Civil war, 33, 39.
Communication, 16, 31, 64, 134, 196.
Constitutions, 224, 226.
Culture, 2, 3, 4, 5, 10, 11, 40, 41, 43, 54, 85, 87, 88, 187, 189, 256, 276.

D

Developments, 1, 12, 149, 157, 159, 183, 186, 187, 188, 189, 223.

E

Economic Development, 39, 40, 148, 153, 155, 159, 166, 199, 272.

F

Freedom, 22, 39, 83, 84, 105, 203, 226, 273, 275.

G

Governments, 132, 134, 147, 151, 160, 163, 165, 175, 185, 193, 203, 205, 219, 225, 226, 237, 246, 247, 248, 256, 261, 262, 267, 269, 272.
Great Mutiny, 32.
Green Revolution, 134, 191, 197, 198, 210, 213, 214.

I

Independence Movement, 222, 252, 270.
Indian Society, 54, 87, 88, 90, 94, 95, 118, 132, 138, 145, 224, 249.

Industry, 30, 84, 151, 153, 154, 155, 160, 162, 164, 167, 168, 172, 173, 174, 175, 176, 177, 178, 179, 182, 185, 186, 191, 193, 194, 195, 197, 212, 218, 219, 240, 272.

Islam, 13, 14, 17, 20, 21, 36, 37, 42, 72, 73, 74, 77, 78, 79.

J

Jainism, 13, 20, 41, 45, 47, 51.

Judaism, 42, 85.

Judiciary, 227, 233, 240, 242.

L

Laws, 25, 29, 30, 64, 105, 106, 113, 114, 117, 118, 122, 129, 170, 203, 204, 206, 228, 233, 235, 237, 240, 241, 245, 248.

M

Marathas, 21, 22, 23.

Market Economy, 15.

Mauryan Empire, 6, 7, 8, 9, 48, 49.

Missions, 8.

Mughals, 17, 20, 21, 22, 25, 188.

O

Operations, 27, 192, 196.

Opportunity, 38, 78, 190, 267.

P

Philosophy, 42, 49, 51, 62, 76, 78.

Pilgrimage, 47, 64, 68, 70, 72, 73, 138, 264.

Political Power, 22, 24, 25, 92, 106, 149, 237, 275.

Politics, 9, 16, 30, 36, 43, 134, 135, 141, 222, 223, 234, 238, 247, 249, 250, 260, 262, 263, 268, 269, 273, 274, 276.

Punishment, 132, 140.

R

Revolution, 134, 191, 197, 198, 210, 213, 214, 254.

S

Security, 27, 69, 97, 108, 120, 130, 194, 197, 204, 207, 227, 229, 231, 232, 237.

Shiva, 13, 16, 45, 54, 57, 58, 59, 60, 63, 71, 138, 139.

T

Technology, 174, 177, 186, 188, 189, 190, 191, 192, 193, 194, 195, 196, 210, 219.

V

Vedas, 3, 43, 44, 45, 46, 54, 66, 67.

Vishnu, 13, 45, 54, 55, 56, 57, 60, 61, 63, 64, 69.

W

Warfare, 9, 92.

Wars, 4, 21, 27, 32, 155.

Weapons, 2, 28, 44, 62, 71.

Worship, 11, 43, 47, 52, 53, 54, 59, 61, 80, 85, 101, 138, 139, 143, 148, 269.

Z

Zoroastrianism, 42, 83.

□□□